# Faulkner and Humor
## FAULKNER AND YOKNAPATAWPHA
### 1984

# Faulkner and Humor

FAULKNER AND YOKNAPATAWPHA, 1984

EDITED BY
DOREEN FOWLER
AND
ANN J. ABADIE

UNIVERSITY PRESS OF MISSISSIPPI
JACKSON AND LONDON

*This book has been sponsored*
*by the University of Mississippi's Center for the Study of*
*Southern Culture*

*Library of Congress Cataloging-in-Publication Data*

Main entry under title:

Faulkner and humor.

Includes index.
1. Faulkner, William, 1897–1962—Humor, satire,
etc.—Congresses.   2. Humorous stories, American—
History and criticism—Congresses.   3. Yoknapatawpha
County (Imaginary place)—Congresses.   I. Fowler,
Doreen.   II. Abadie, Ann J.
PS3511.A86Z7832116   1986        813'.52        85-40518
ISBN 0-87805-281-X
ISBN 0-87805-282-8 (pbk.)

The University Press of Mississippi thanks the following for
permission to reprint material from their publications: Tribune Media Services for the Smilin Jack cartoons; King
Features for the Popeye, Katzenjammer Kids, Barney
Google, Polly and Her Friends, and Bringing up Father
cartoons; and Viking Penguin Inc, for the John Held cartoons from *The Most of John Held, Jr.*, by Margaret Janes
Held. Copyright © 1972 by Margaret Janes Held.

TO
*John Pilkington*
*Distinguished Professor of English* Emeritus

# Contents

# Introduction

The impulse to categorize is a strong one, and among writers of fiction, there appear to be two clear and distinct categories: comic writers and tragic writers. Among the former, Mark Twain, the creator of undying boyhood fantasies, is typically grouped; and often numbered among the latter is William Faulkner, the chronicler of mansions and magnolias in a brooding Southern clime, a modern-day prophet decrying the decay of values in a crass, materialistic, modern world. But such set and exclusive designations can never adequately define or describe writers of the stature of Faulkner or Twain, who explode categories and clichés, and for whom reality is always continuum, a totality in which laughter and tears blend and merge.

While the essays in this volume explore various aspects of Faulkner's rich and inexhaustible comic art, they all hold in common one axiom: that William Faulkner, the recognized genius of tragic art, is a master of comic forms as well and, further, that neither mode, tragic or comic, is ever very far from the other in Faulkner's world. Among the first to recognize this merger of tragic and comic in Faulkner's art was Katherine Anne Porter who, in 1948, wrote: "William Faulkner has the deepest and most serious humor in this country at present." Porter's statement, which at first might appear to be paradoxical, in fact, expresses a fundamental truth about the nature of Faulkner's comic vision: Faulkner is always in touch with the potentiality of humor within tragic situations. Thus, *As I Lay Dying* is both a celebration of community survival and a bitter denunciation of community values; *The Hamlet* is both a comic folk epic and an investigation of mean-spirited materialism; and *Go Down, Moses* is both a twentieth-century comedy of manners and a probing exploration of Southern racial sin and guilt.

Examples of this tension between tragic and comic modes are in evidence throughout all of Faulkner's fiction. A typical instance is Cash Bundren's wagon ride in *As I Lay Dying*. For days, Cash lies, his leg broken, atop the decomposing corpse of his mother, in a wagon without springs. To ease the jolts to his leg, his family members make him a cast of cement. Stretched out beneath the blazing summer sun all day, his leg, encased in cement, cooks. That evening, to free the baked leg, the cement cast is smashed off and torn away, taking with it shredded flesh. Throughout his agony, Cash says only, "It dont bother me none." While the unspeakable outrage to Cash's flesh is unquestionably tragic, the absurd disparity between that outrage and Cash's hyperbolic understatement elicits a smile: we smile in amusement at the preposterousness of the human situation, but we smile also in recognition and celebration of man's limitless ability to endure that preposterousness.

Faulkner's humor, then, a humor which explores the entire range of human possibilities from communal celebration to sharp-edged satire, is the subject of the essays which are contained in this volume and which were presented originally in late July 1984 at the Faulkner and Yoknapatawpha Conference held on the Oxford campus of the University of Mississippi. At this six-day convocation, the eleventh in a series sponsored by Ole Miss, the conference directors tried something new—a new method for selecting conference papers was tested. In the past, recognized Faulkner scholars with a demonstrated interest in the conference theme were invited to lecture. For the 1984 conference, for the first time, a call for papers was issued and, from a large number of essays submitted, six were chosen for presentation. The winners of this competition, whose essays are included in this collection, are (in alphabetical order) William Bedford Clark, William N. Claxon, Jr., Virginia V. Hlavsa, Thomas L. McHaney, Nancy B. Sederberg, and Patricia R. Schroeder. In addition to the essays of these authors, a number of other papers are contained in this volume and were heard at the 1984 conference—these papers were delivered by invited speakers. By choosing some papers for conference presentation from an open-to-all competition, the conference directors hope to encourage greater diversity and originality and to expand conference participation to a wider population. Encouraged by the results of this experiment, the University of Mississippi plans to continue the practice initiated at the 1984 Faulkner and Yoknapatawpha conference: at future conferences, papers will be presented by invited lecturers joined by speakers whose essays were selected in a competition.

As arranged in this volume, the essays fall into two groups. In the first group, the essays take for their subject a single Faulkner novel and attempt to show how humor operates in that novel; these papers are arranged in chronological order according to the novel discussed. In the latter half of the collection, the essays start with an area of inquiry—for example, what uses Faulkner made of the tall tale or the funnies—and work backward to Faulkner's novels, making references to a number of different works.

The first two essays in the anthology explore the relationship between humor and humanity in Faulkner's tragic masterpiece, *The Sound and the Fury.* In "Humor as Vision in Faulkner," James M. Cox uses *The Sound and the Fury* to illustrate what he calls "the brilliant achievement of Faulkner's humor." According to Cox, humor and analytical interpretation are incompatible human responses, which in fiction ordinarily repel one another. But in Faulkner's fiction, remarkably, these two antithetical responses are somehow suspended in equipoise, side by side, countering and completing one another. The Jason section of *The Sound and the Fury* is a case in point. Jason, who is clearly ruthless, greedy, and vicious, necessarily evokes our harsh judgment; at the same time, however, Jason, who beats his breast, tears his hair, and loudly bewails his fate in extravagantly exaggerated language, is also comical. While this humor cannot exonerate Jason or reverse our judgment, it does serve to remind us constantly that Jason, like us, is human.

Picking up where Cox leaves off, William N. Claxon, Jr., also discusses Jason's humanizing humor and claims that Jason's witty quips subliminally seduce us into sharing his view of the Compson family. But Claxon goes on to identify two instances in the monologue that are narrated entirely without humor: when Jason dupes Caddy who has paid him for a chance to see her daughter and when Jason destroys the circus ticket before Luster's anguished and incredulous eyes. According to Claxon, "the absence of humor here is as significant as its presence elsewhere." Previously Jason's humor had mitigated his culpability; stripped of this humor, Jason is exposed as a man who deliberately inflicts pain on the helpless.

Comic strains in two early works are taken up in the next two essays, "The Comic World of *As I Lay Dying*" and "The Levity of *Light in August*." In the first of these essays, Patricia R. Schroeder identifies two comic patterns in the saga of Addie Bundren's funeral journey: at one level *As I Lay Dying* conforms to a classical model of comedy which celebrates social conventions, rituals, and forms contrived to impose order on nature; juxtaposed with this framework of classical comedy is another type of humor—black comedy or the comedy of the absurd—which enters the novel through the voices of Addie and Darl, two antisocial characters, who perceive the futility and absurdity of the social effort to erect systems of order. While Schroeder finds classical comedy and black comedy in *As I Lay Dying*, Virginia V. Hlavsa looks closely at *Light in August* and unearths buried references to St. John's Gospel and James Frazer's *The Golden Bough*. According to Hlavsa, Faulkner, like Chaucer, Shakespeare, and Joyce, often uses literary classics as the organizing structure for his novels. What, then, asks Hlavsa, is so funny about *Light in August?*—the fact that Faulkner's Mississippi folk have immortal forms.

*Go Down, Moses*, Faulkner's tragicomic novel about race relations in the South, is the subject of essays by three speakers, Daniel Hoffman, Nancy B. Sederberg, and William Bedford Clark. In the first of these essays, "Faulkner's 'Was' and Uncle Adam's Cow," Daniel Hoffman examines the hilarious opening story-chapter of *Go Down, Moses* and shows how Faulkner borrows a plot from a rather crude, sexist Ozark folk tale and then "reverses, turns inside out, stands on its head whatever conventions he borrows or steals" to produce a tale which is both a comic masterpiece and a fitting prelude to a novel of tragic meaning. In " 'A Momentary Anesthesia of the Heart': A Study of the Comic Elements in Faulkner's *Go Down, Moses*," Nancy B. Sederberg analyzes the mood, tone, and type of comedy that informs each of the story-chapters in *Go Down, Moses* and notes a change, a swing in the underlying comic sense. While in the early stories, the comic tone is light, merry, and anecdotal, in the later stories, comedy fuses with tragedy and comic elements function to temper emotionalism and to provide a more balanced perspective from which to view tragic events. In the last of the essays on *Go Down, Moses*, William Bedford Clark contrasts the comic impulse in Faulkner's novel about race and miscegenation with the comic stance of Mark Twain's comparable novel, *Pudd'nhead Wilson*, and finds that, in terms of their comic spirit, the two novels differ significantly. According to Clark, the humor in Twain's work derives from a narrative voice which is wry, ironic, and, at times, even condescending, while Faulkner's humor in *Go Down, Moses* springs from an acceptance and an affirmation of the human condition born of a recognition of man's indestructibility at the bottom of the tragic abyss.

The remaining essays in the volume focus primarily on topics related to humor, rather than on specific Faulkner novels. Thomas L. McHaney, for example, takes for his subject the lie that tells the truth—the tall tale—which, McHaney asserts, in Faulkner's hands, becomes "a fine-edged tool in the modernist artist's battle against the regimentation, dull empiricism, and everydayness of modern times"; Hans Bungert, in a wide-ranging essay, touches on a number of issues including the German response to Faulkner and his humor, the methodological problems inherent in studies of comedy, and a typology of the various comic styles and methods found in Faulkner's fiction; M. Thomas Inge examines Faulkner's novels for comic strip references and finds that Faulkner took from the funnies but used the material in his own way, working in a vein that was distinctly his own; and comic novelist Barry Hannah suggests a possible source for the small man in Faulkner's fiction—the little tramp, Charlie Chaplin.

The collection closes with two essays which deal with the building blocks of humor: jokes. In an essay that brings together Freud, Saussure, Lacan, and Faulkner, James M. Mellard analyzes the structure of Faulkner's jokes in terms of Freudian and Lacanian principles and concludes that all humor, like all art, exists because of the primal debarring of the signifier from the signified, consciousness from unconsciousness, desire from attainment. While Mellard focuses on the structure of Faulkner's jokes, George Garrett observes the placement of jokes in Faulkner's texts and finds humor where we might least expect it. In "'Fix My Hair, Jack': The Dark Side of Faulkner's Jokes," Garrett uses the executioner's famous one-liner in *Sanctuary* to illustrate his thesis that Faulkner's jests are never more than "a paper-thin partition away from the most tragic or poignant or pathetic or horrifying scenes." According to Garrett, jokes are almost always present, even in Faulkner's most serious works, because laughter is essential to caring, and Faulkner's aim, always, is to make us care. Faulkner, the brilliant humorist, then, is simultaneously Faulkner, the passionate humanist, "a great man whose vision was so open and inclusive that if he always felt the tears of things, he likewise could hear, as some hear voices, the sourceless laughter which is at least half the music of this world."

In addition to the lectures contained in this volume, the 1984 Faulkner and Yoknapatawpha Conference also featured a number of special events. On the first day of the conference the University Museums opened an exhibition of photographs depicting people and scenes of Faulkner country; The Friends of the Library hosted a reception honoring Mr. and Mrs. Douglas C. Wynn, who donated forty-eight manuscript pages of early Faulkner poetry to the University; the Theatre Arts Department presented *Voices from Yoknapatawpha II*, dramatic readings of humorous passages from Faulkner's works; The Friends of the Performing Arts of Oxford joined the University in hosting a buffet supper at the home of Dr. and Mrs. Beckett Howorth, Jr.; architectural historian Thomas S. Hines presented a slide lecture at the Lafayette County Courthouse; and Square Books hosted an autograph party. Other special events during the week included a slide presentation narrated by J. M. Faulkner and Jo Marshall; a workshop for teachers conducted by Sister Thea Bowman; "Faulkner in Oxford," moderated by M. C. "Chooky" Falkner, and other small-group discussion sessions; a picnic served on the grounds of Rowan Oak, Faulkner's antebellum home; and tours of North Mississippi led by Evans Harrington, Beckett Howorth III, Howard L. Bahr, James Seay, and Frank Childrey. The John Davis Williams Library exhibited books, manuscripts, photographs, and memorabilia from the University of Mississippi Faulkner Collection and from the Louis Daniel Brodsky Faulkner Collection. Also, the University Press of Mississippi sponsored an exhibit of Faulkner books submitted by various university presses throughout the United States.

In conclusion, the editors of this volume wish to express their deep appreciation to all those who, each year, generously support the University of Mississippi Faulkner and Yoknapatawpha Conference.

Doreen Fowler
The University of Mississippi
Oxford, Mississippi

# Faulkner and Humor
## FAULKNER AND YOKNAPATAWPHA
### 1984

# Humor as Vision in Faulkner

## James M. Cox

Everyone knows that William Faulkner is a humorous writer, which is far from saying that he is a humorist. Because he is so much more than a humorous writer, it is not surprising that the trainload of commentary on his works has little to say about his humor.[1] It is so much easier in writing about him to struggle for the meaning, the answers to his riddles and confusions, and the philosophy informing his novels than it is to remember the incredible laughter at the heart of his world. Indeed, the very search for meaning, solutions to riddles, and informing philosophy is a way of forgetting the humor in his genius. Yet surely I am not alone in having laughed at his very greatest work. And here I am not speaking of having chuckled, or been amused, or having enjoyed immensely (as we are likely to say) Faulkner's humor. I am acknowledging having been broken up, torn to pieces, and brought to the floor in helpless laughter. I am thinking specifically of the Jason section in *The Sound and the Fury*, of almost the whole funeral journey in *As I Lay Dying*, the entire conception of *The Hamlet*, and the sequel adventures of the Snopeses.

The point to be made about this humor is that it is not a separate, subordinate aspect of Faulkner's world. It is, as I said, and as I shall contend, at the very heart of his world. Thus we are not talking about scenes of comic relief that provide relaxation to some tragic intensity. If we took the great episode in *The Hamlet* in which Ike Snopes is portrayed in love with the cow, we would have a text that might put us in touch with the humor. In that episode, Faulkner devotes an extended passage of such rich lyric intensity to the description of an interior relationship between lovers that many a reader *on first reading* is likely to be well into the passage before discovering that the lovers are a man and a cow. Almost simultaneously showing the scene from the outside, Faulkner discloses the enterprising Snopeses charging admission for their neighboring countrymen to get a peek at the show. Faced with such an extreme example of Snopes venality, V. K. Ratliff, the central narrative consciousness, is reduced to helpless indignation at their depravity. Despite his attempt to claim for himself a degree of moral superiority over the Snopeses, Ratliff finds himself at the end of the novel falling for that oldest trick in the world of speculation: the salted gold mine. That ending shows just how much Ratliff is vulnerable to the greed he deplores in the Snopeses. To discover him digging feverishly in the front yard of the Old Frenchman's place is to see his presumptive moral judgments and his determination to best Flem Snopes collapse into the very earth in which he descends for money.

It is of course possible—even inevitable—to get the *meaning* out of such a sequence. To get meaning is almost inevitably to set up a moral paradigm in which the Snopeses "represent" the greed principle in the universe—the effort to convert nature into land, land into money, and money into the matter which the depraved human spirit attempts to grasp. If Snopeses *are* the essence of that depravity, the attempt to judge them leads Ratliff—the novelistic agent for observing them as well as the dramatic actor who attempts to beat them—into spiritual descent and defeat. Thomas Greet, in a fine essay on the book, points out that as Ratliff more and more turns toward conventional judgment—as when he deplores the Snopes raree show exhibiting a peek at Ike and the cow—he turns from humor to sardonic wit.[2] It is precisely in that turn that his determination to best or beat Flem Snopes takes its rise.

If we hold to the moral paradigm and see the Snopeses as evil—some ruthless, predatory principle at the heart of human life viciously expressing itself through the capitalistic system—

we get at once a typological vision of the perennial fall of man coupled with a secular historical vision of the descent of man into the degeneration of time. To get so much is to get meaning out of Faulkner. But meaning, as I have said in another connection, is *mean;* it is an acquisitive act of the mind bent on extracting significance by a process of abstraction.[3] As such, it is a mental process as loaded with calculation and manipulation as the horse trade between Pat Stamper and Ab Snopes that initiates us into the world of *The Hamlet.* Even so, there is no way to avoid the quest for meaning in the world of William Faulkner, for Faulkner's work requires such a response. Readers are as helpless before that requirement as I would like to believe they are before Faulkner's humor. In the face of Faulkner's style and structure we *have* to interpret, and the interpretation of the Snopeses as illustrative of the greed principle in human society, though by no means the only interpretation advanced about them, is just as clearly a means of seeing them. Interpretation is, after all, hardly confined to the world of literary critics. Many of Faulkner's own characters—Quentin, Ike McCaslin, Mr. Compson, V. K. Ratliff, Gavin Stevens, to name a few—spend themselves in the attempt to see the meaning of events. And those who don't interpret—figures such as Benjy Compson or Cash Bundren—provoke interpretation in us as readers.

I am willing—even delighted—to acknowledge that the need for meaning is greater in Faulkner's world than the need for humor. Precisely because it is so great, the humor that is so irrepressibly present in Yoknapatawpha County is inordinately neglected. Meaning is, after all, antithetical to humor. Getting meaning involves the collaboration of the reason and the will—to resort to terms from the old psychology of the faculties of mind. The will joins the reason in an act of aggression upon the object of interpretation. Humor, on the other hand, is a response which suspends both will and reason. What is remarkable about Faulkner is his determination to keep these antithetical activities of experience in juxtaposition. In that respect he is a vastly different writer from the Mark Twain of *Huckleberry Finn.* In that book, although a serious sentiment provides the current on which the humor rides, Huck's vernacular works steadily against metaphysics and meaning as if to ward them off by perpetually dodging them. Faulkner's style, leaning so visibly toward tragedy and loss, just as clearly seeks them out. Small wonder that *Absalom, Absalom!*, the very essence and act of this inclination toward interpretation and meaning, is often critically acclaimed as Faulkner's greatest book. Perhaps I should at this point admit to feeling that Faulkner, having exhausted himself with the overdriven rhetorical intensity of *Absalom, Absalom!*, sought recovery in *The Hamlet*. Indeed, the Snopeses, whom he had foreseen early in his career, constituted the comic world that would provide him with his last great creative opportunity. No matter how "evil" they are in terms of theme, in terms of form they afforded Faulkner a vast field of exuberant fecundity. They literally multiplied in response to his imaginative attention to them, a multiplication that is nowhere more evident than in *The Hamlet*. Having held Frenchman's Bend in abeyance as an isolate poor corner of his postage stamp of a world, Faulkner's imagination was free to find, at the end of the artist's life, some of its richest possibilities.

Much as *The Hamlet* and the Snopeses might provide us with the contradictory paradigm between meaning and humor, that book is not the one I want to use in order to display just how the principle of humor works in Faulkner. I want to take instead *The Sound and the Fury*, which, along with *As I Lay Dying*, at once constitutes Faulkner's breakthrough to both his form and theme and his breakout from all the conventions which, after supporting him in his apprenticeship, had suddenly become constricting. That book, every reader will helplessly remember, ends with an idiot's wild and dismaying cry of pain at being taken out of the iron principles of his own order, whereas *As I Lay Dying* concludes with a madman's insane laughter as he is taken toward the iron confines of an asylum because he can no longer live in the absurd logic of society. Because *As I Lay Dying* ends with a mad laugh and because it is so incontrovertibly filled with grotesque comedy, I might well choose it to display the workings of Faulkner's humor; but because *The Sound and the Fury*, with its dominant emphasis on pain, loss, suicide, death, and decline, puts humor in a subordinate position, I think it will disclose both the essence and meaning of Faulkner's humor.

In discussing *The Sound and the Fury*, I want first to posit what I hope will be a fair description of a first reading of the book. In a real sense I shall be pursuing something akin to what is called affectivist criticism and thus encountering the risks attendant on such an enterprise. My description is admittedly not an accurate account of my own first reading. I well remember completing the book late at night, almost forty years ago, after a long afternoon's reading—and then beginning it over again in the early morning hours until, having read the Benjy section a second time, I had come to have a growing hold on the time dislocations. If the paradigmatic first reading I shall project is a "better" reading than I then gave the book, drawing as it does upon my experience of teaching the book, it is nonetheless related to my clear memory of first encountering the book.

To encounter *The Sound and the Fury* is, first of all, to be lost. That loss is, for me, fully equal in importance to all the loss that the book is about. You will remember that, in what we inaccurately but inevitably call the Benjy section, Benjy and Luster are by the golf course looking for a quarter—or rather Luster is looking for it. We are ultimately to learn that the golf course itself is part of the land the Compsons have lost; and we learn that Benjy has lost his sister, that Luster is about to lose his chance to go to the show, that the golfers lose their balls. And we are to learn that Caddy has lost her virginity, that Quentin has lost his life, that Jason has lost his money, that the Compsons have been in a long descent of loss in a world that has lost its war and that still suffers one long continuity of loss. All those losses are what we are going to discover—but we discover them only because *we* have first been lost ourselves. If Faulkner hadn't, by means of his great form, made us experience *being lost,* we would only have been reading about loss instead of discovering it.

We are, of course, in that first section, lost in *time,* even though the sections are temporally denominated, as if Faulkner were determined to set the time only to emphasize how lost in time we were to be. We are lost because the idiot narrator, in relation to us, seems free in time, shifting abruptly from one spot of time to another. Actually, Benjy is ruthlessly held, not in time but in an iron principle of association that constantly transcends progressional time. What the book makes us do from the outset is to begin a long process of reconstruction of the so-called rational sequence of "real" time that has so rudely been taken away. There are of course abundant associations present in Benjy's account that enable us to reconstruct our rational version of time—a version possessing all the iron principles as well as the irony that Benjy's helpless submission to association has. Obsessed by Caddy and the loss of Caddy, Benjy is helpless but no more helpless than we are to our own obsession with "logical" sequence.

Much more is of course going on in our first reading than this effort to recover rational time. Faulkner's form remarkably enables us to hear the voices that Benjy hears—particularly the black voices. Those voices—as they come through Luster and Versh and T. P.—carry the familiar black vernacular, almost stereotypically minstrel in its structure, home to us. At the same time, our lost rational structure of time is primarily recovered through our discovery that Versh, T. P., and Luster are the successive servants who, in that order, have taken care of Benjy through his thirty-three years. They are, in short, the figures who mark the time for us, a fact that is as thematically important for us as anything we can ever learn about them.

Lost in Benjy's consciousness, we hear the voices of his world, and, if we are not too obsessed with regaining our lost temporal sequence, we feel the poetry of that world. When we enter Quentin's section, though associational obsession continues to fracture sequence, we gain an even richer dimension of feeling. What was bewilderment in the Benjy section beautifully and steadily grows into a sense of sympathy. Quentin is as obsessed as Benjy, but his obsession is different. Knowing what time it is, he is nonetheless helpless before the intrusions of his past, and we now feel them as we could not—because we did not know how to—in the first section. Possessing both will and deliberation, Quentin can plan his suicide—though few readers on a first reading would know exactly what he is planning. Because time and will and choice occupy the foreground of Quentin's interior consciousness, all the loss in Quentin's past is perpetually at the threshold of inrushing upon his mind. Whereas all time is present to Benjy, Quentin holds on to present time, allocating it through the day as well as marking its advancing shadow on the dial of his life as he determines to stop it forever in order to ward off all the past and all the loss that preys upon him as powerfully as it preys on Benjy. For Quentin's father, *was* is the saddest of all words, but for Quentin it is *again*. Anguished in relation to what he knows is past and helpless to prevent its intrusions, Quentin can see only repetition—but the point is that he can see it, and see in it the hopelessness that it will bring.

With Jason we seem to come out of the pain and poetry and loss—our own, as readers, as well as that of the characters. To be sure, we are still in the consciousness of a character, but it is consciousness in the form of voice rather than of mind. Because Jason's vernacular objectifies his character, we hear his own voice in a way we never heard Benjy's or Quentin's. Moreover, we are brought toward the realm of the common sense that had been withheld in the first two sections of the book. Returning us to the familiar categories of temporal sequence, Jason's consciousness represents a decisive clearing of the confusion. Yet precisely in that clearing, where we at last are able to see, we are also enabled to judge. Judgment is one of the necessary and habitual acts that has been largely suspended in the first two sections, having been displaced first by the effort to reconstruct, by means of puzzling out, the temporal sequence that has been taken away from us—and displaced also by poetic feelings of sympathy that cling to the pathos of Benjy's plight and the anguish of Quentin's obsession. Because Jason's selfishness and evil are fully objectified (even on a first reading we can see, without benefit of handbooks and commentaries, Jason's full evil when he burns the extra ticket to the show that he might have given to poor Luster), we gain the arrogant high ground where the clear moral categories of good and evil assume prominence in the clearing landscape of temporal sequence.

It is just here in the third section that we once again face the problem I outlined concerning humor. For anyone who has read *The Sound and the Fury* enough to reflect upon it knows that Jason's section is one of the most humorous pieces in all of Faulkner. In a profound way it is hilarious from beginning to end. Yet because Jason releases us into the commonsense world and because he is recognizably selfish and cruel to the point of sadism, the fullness of his humor—which is to say the meaning of it—is slighted. The pleasure of judging him, coupled with the pleasurable illusion of getting control of what has been a confusing form, leads readers to repress their laughter and critics to displace their recognition of the humor with lamentations about Jason's depravity. The reader who represses the humor never allows it to qualify the judgment of Jason; the critic who displaces it, though invariably conscious of it, fixes it in a decisively subordinate place in the hierarchy of values in order to deal with it cursorily. I am not saying that every critic has done this,[4] nor am I saying that to proceed in this direction leads to a barren vision. There has been much fine criticism of Faulkner emerging precisely from such pursuits. Who has not been helped by Cleanth Brooks's meticulous probing of the novel, or by Olga Vickery's fine comprehension of the novel's structure, or by André Bleikasten's patient pursuit of textual implications. Yet all these critics and many others hardly touch the humor, and those who concentrate on it are likely to abstract it as a subject, specializing it into an isolated trait of Faulkner's art or relating it to Mark Twain and his Southwest precursors.

If we pursue the two aspects of Jason's character—his ruthless greed and meanness on the one hand, and his humor on the other—we may achieve an integration of Jason's character that will cast light backward as well as forward through the book. The vivid presence of Jason's selfish and all but sadistic character is, after all, what releases us into our moral judgment of him. And it is Jason's inimitable vernacular that makes that whole character *present* to us, as present as Huckleberry Finn is to us in his narrative. Significantly enough, Jason—unlike Benjy, for whom all time is one, and unlike Quentin, who pushes present action into the past tense only to feel the pressure of the prior past abruptly intruding through his helpless efforts to keep it from being *again*—speaks in a particular vernacular that pushes his past conversations into the present tense, concluding the stream of his recorded conversations with "I says," "she says," and "he says." That vernacular use of the present tense is his means of converting past dramatic dialogue into present monologue, keeping his active voice ever in the foreground of his narrative. Because his voice is active, we feel for the first time that we are being told a story in the sense of hearing it rather than overhearing it—though in formal fact Benjy and Quentin are telling their stories as much as Jason is. It is just this voice that gives us Jason's character, and it is just this character that at once provokes our moral judgment and accelerates our hold on the world of the novel. If such a hold, animated by our recognition of Jason's depravity, facilitates our grasp of the action, it nonetheless may leave us blind to a comprehensive understanding of Jason.

The humor of Jason's section is for me the means of fully understanding him, and to understand Jason is to enlarge our understanding of the novel. A part of the humor in Jason's section arises from his unconscious contradictions as when, after he picks up the check for Lorraine's beer, he is moved to moralize:

> After all, like I say money has no value; it's just the way you spend it. It dont belong to anybody, so why try to hoard it.[5]

This from a man who is stealing money from his mother, his sister, and his niece and hoarding it in a strong box. Another part comes from his instinctive impulse to denigrate others. He says that Quentin's face, before she paints it, "looked like she had polished it with a gun rag" (228); and, surveying his and his family's lot, he complains:

> Well, Jason likes to work. I says no I never had university advantages because at Harvard they teach you to go for a swim at night without knowing how to swim and at Sewanee they dont even teach you what water is. I says you might send me to the state University; maybe I'll learn how to stop my clock with a nose spray and then you can send Ben to the Navy I says or to the cavalry anyway, they use geldings in the cavalry. (243)

All this is said to his simpering mother—or he is reporting having said it to her—at the time he grudgingly offered to take on Caddy's baby. He suggests to her that, by way of shoring up the failing finances, she rent Ben out to a side show for people to pay a dime to see him. And at his father's funeral, he says of Uncle Maury,

> Then I knew what I had been smelling. Clove stems. I reckon he thought that the least he could do at Father's funeral or maybe the sideboard thought it was still Father and tripped him up when he passed. Like I say, if he had to sell something to send Quentin to Harvard we'd all been a damn sight better off if he'd sold that sideboard and bought himself a one-armed strait jacket with part of the money. (245)

After the funeral he helps his Uncle Maury and his mother into the carriage while he waits in the rain, saying, "Little they cared how wet I got, because then Mother could have a whale of a time being afraid I was taking pneumonia" (250-51).

I touch on the high points (which are by no means all the points) of this particular sequence because it leads directly to Jason's account of how he revenged himself on Caddy by taking her money and, keeping to the terms of his promise to Caddy by the narrowest technicality, showing her one fleeting glimpse of her daughter Quentin as he dashes by in the hack. All of Jason's humor intricately exposes his ruthless, vengeful, vicious character, and yet just as surely it remains humor. If we don't laugh, I don't know what to make of us. And if we do laugh, we are not laughing at Jason, because Jason as character is by no means funny, nor are we laughing with him, because he is by no means laughing. Rather we are laughing at his performance, since his consciousness alone of the three brothers' expresses itself in dramatic performance.

His long lamentation, though a monologue, is not spoken to himself; rather it is his self-dramatization of his plight in a language devoted to reckless and exaggerated criticism of all the ills his flesh is heir to. Moreover, he somehow knows that his continuous cry, coming from all his spleen and all his pain, is funny. Though he has no consciousness of what his brothers have said—he is as locked as they are in the prison of his ego—he knows his situation and is taking whatever pleasure he can from it by his shrewd vernacular reduction of everyone around him. At the same time, his account of trying to thwart what he claims to be their conspiracies to victimize him inevitably discloses that all his efforts are fruitless failures. Thus his whole long monologue is a performance dramatizing his hapless, hopeless, and helpless effort to stay afloat in, to adopt his vernacular, this damned world. At the same time, his versions of all the characters he has had to live with may be distortions, but they are nonetheless caricatures that tellingly expose many characters about whom we have formed negative opinions—and here I am thinking of Mrs. Compson, Uncle Maury, even Mr. Compson. However we may deplore his portrait of those characters toward whom we readily, and perhaps too readily, extend our sympathy (and here I am thinking of Benjy, Quentin, Luster, and Dilsey), we do not reject all his judgments as lies. Certainly no reader of the novel concludes that Earl, the storekeeper, is other than a pious, prying, self-satisfied ass. We *believe* Jason about such a man because we instinctively trust his capacity to record Earl's speech. That capacity may not make Jason a good man, but it does not prove him a complete liar.

The high point of Jason's humor comes when, after having to dig up a blank check on a St. Louis bank to fake for his mother so that she can go through the monthly ritual of burning it to keep her sense of pride and Southern honor, after trying to get out from under Earl's watchful and pious eye, after finding that his stock market investments are in a radically falling market, he sees his niece and the man in the red tie helling it through town in a Ford and determines to give chase in the car he has borrowed a thousand dollars to get, thereby losing his partnership in Earl's store. His account of his pursuit embraces all these woes and builds on many more—on his sentimental and hypochondriac mother, on his shameless niece, on the Jews he feels are doing him in on the stock market, on the wretched roads he has to drive over, on the ill-farmed land he has to walk over, and on his headache, pounding like a hammer inside his head. Listen to his lamentation as he tells of his effort to save his family's honor:

> I parked and got out. And now I'd have to go way around and cross a plowed field, the only one I had seen since I left town, with every step like somebody was walking along behind me, hitting me on the head with a club. I kept thinking that when I got across the field at least I'd have something level to walk on, that wouldn't jolt me every step, but when I got into the woods it was full of underbrush and I had to twist around through it, and then I came to a ditch full of briers. I went along it for awhile, but it got thicker and thicker, and all the time Earl probably telephoning home about where I was and getting Mother all upset again.
>
> When I finally got through I had had to wind around so much that I had to stop and figure out just where the car would be. I knew they wouldn't be far from it, just under the closest bush, so I turned and worked back toward the road. Then I couldn't tell just how far I was, so I'd have to stop and listen, and then with my legs not using so much blood, it all would go into my head like it would explode any minute, and the sun getting down just to where it could shine straight into my eyes and my ears ringing so I couldn't hear anything. I went on, trying to move quiet, then I heard a dog or something and I knew that when he scented me he'd have to come helling up, then it would be all off.

I had gotten beggar lice and twigs and stuff all over me, inside my clothes and shoes and all, and then I happened to look around and I had my hand right on a bunch of poison oak. The only thing I couldn't understand was why it was just poison oak and not a snake or something. So I didn't even bother to move it. I just stood there until the dog went away. Then I went on.

I didn't have any idea where the car was now. I couldn't think about anything except my head, and I'd just stand in one place and sort of wonder if I had really seen a ford even, and I didn't even care much whether I had or not. Like I say, let her lay out all day and all night with everything in town that wears pants, what do I care. I dont owe anything to anybody that has no more consideration for me, that wouldn't be a damn bit above planting that ford there and making me spend a whole afternoon and Earl taking her back there and showing her the books just because he's too damn virtuous for this world. I says you'll have one hell of a time in heaven, without anybody's business to meddle in only dont you ever let me catch you at it I says, I close my eyes to it because of your grandmother, but just you let me catch you doing it one time on this place, where my mother lives. These damn little slick haired squirts, thinking they are raising so much hell, I'll show them something about hell I says, and you too. I'll make him think that damn red tie is the latch string to hell, if he thinks he can run the woods with my niece. (299–301)

This remarkable passage gives so much because Jason clearly has as much going on in his mind as any of his brothers do. Moreover, we can see it all crowding and pushing him all but into the earth that he hates. Yet for all his pain and dismay, we are utterly spared sympathizing with him. His miraculous ability to imagine a worse world for himself than that which is already undoing him gives his account hyperbolically bizarre twists, as when he cannot understand why he had put his hand merely on poison oak and not a snake. At such a moment, his habitual indulgence in lamentation about the crosses he has to bear is all but disappointed because the situation fails to be as bad as his narrative requires it to be. Yet if his deep desire to tell a story in which things are worse than they are suggests his hunger for disaster, his genius for discovering the maximum grief and griev- ance in every situation and his capacity to pour forth this sea of troubles in a tide of associational linkage give his narrative not only a fullness of sardonic complaint but also an exuberance for distortion and exaggeration.

The undeniable and irrepressible humor of this passage does not contradict so much as it attends Jason's meanness. After all, once he comes back from his fruitless quest, he avenges his failure, first in tormenting Luster by burning the tickets to the show and then in relentlessly taunting Quentin at the dinner table until he has reduced her to impotent and inarticulate rage. Jason's day ends with Quentin silent in her room while he, counting his money in his own room to the music of "the Great American Gelding snoring away like a planing mill" (329), wishes that the knife that castrated Benjy had started cutting sooner than it did and stopped cutting later.

Faulkner's brilliant achievement of keeping the humor and the meanness in attendance upon each other in Jason's monologue gives this section of the novel great emotional complexity expressed through relative clarity—relative, that is, to the preceding sections of the novel. More important, the contradictory emotions of humor and moral judgment are held in miraculous suspension. Thus although Jason's vicious character comes into incredibly sharp relief, there is nonetheless the complicating presence of the humor. For Jason, as much as Iago, is a performer. But whereas Iago has wit, Jason is funny. Iago feels put upon and passed over, but we can never be sure that the wrongs he feels are not invented. Jason, however, may be as evil as Iago, but he *is* put on. He *has* headaches; he has been denied the love of his father; he has been passed over, and not in the form of a Passover. It is not too much to say that he has been wronged. To acknowledge so much is neither to justify nor to forgive his behavior. His viciousness spares us the need to forgive him, thereby economizing our sympathy—sympathy which we have been so easily willing to extend to Benjy and Quentin and which, faced with Jason, we even more readily grant them.

Spared from sympathizing, we laugh—or at least we ought to. The laughter which Jason's great vernacular performance provokes and evokes is itself the form our recognition of Jason's suffering humanity takes. Indeed, Jason's own humor—his creative force in language—at once arises from and is a recognition of his plight. He sees himself as the butt of a monstrous joke on him—a conspiracy of family history that concentrates all the ills of the universe into one vast excremental discharge on the top of his already throbbing cranium. For all his fury and malice, his very linguistic performance is to make his wretchedly wronged life into a joke. In this sense, though he never laughs or quite sees the fun he is creating, he is nonetheless insistently and desperately *making* a joke both on and of himself. Take, for example, the moment late in his account, when he starts for home:

> There was a ford in front of the drugstore, but I didn't even look at it. I know when I've had enough of anything. I dont mind trying to help her, but I know when I've had enough. I guess I could teach Luster to drive it, then they could chase her all day long if they wanted to, and I could stay home and play with Ben. (314)

There is first of all the humor of his noticing the Ford yet insisting that he didn't look at it. And then his contending that he knows when he has had enough of anything when clearly he can't get enough of anything, let alone ever knowing when he's had enough. Then his empty claim of not minding helping his mother, when he minds everything but his own business. All this we can attribute to Jason's claims about himself—claims which are utterly contradictory to what we know him to be. But the climax of the humor is in the last lines of the passage, when, looking back to the Ford he saw and didn't look at because he was still rankled about the other Ford he had hunted and so can't quit thinking about, he frees his mind momentarily to imagine teaching Luster to drive his mother in the car in perpetual pursuit of Quentin while he stays home to play with Ben. At such a moment, we have to acknowledge that Jason himself is, in a kind of contorted mental agony, wrenching his vision of a hopeless future into a grotesquely comical image. Racked with

anger and smoldering resentment, he literally imagines a possibility at once so improbable and so futile that, whether he can
quite laugh at it or not, in *making* its extravagance, he is twisting
his vision into the visage of a monstrous joke.

Seeing this visage is to begin to see the supreme generosity of
Faulkner's creative force. Faulkner had, after all, given Benjy a
language that no naturalistic or realistic mode of representation
would have allowed; and so, lost in the time of that language, we
gained the very presence of poetry. He had given to Quentin the
poetic resonance that sounded down the corridors of memory
and tradition. To Jason he gives the remarkable vernacular that
clears the confusion sufficiently to free our judgment and at the
same time embodies the humor that reduces us to laughter.

The clarity and the judgment unencumbered by the humor
readies us for the fourth section of the book in which we enter an
omniscient perspective. There we will, or should, see that our
judgment of Jason is going to be superseded as much as his own
judgment is by the events that overtake him. For what neither
we nor Jason knows at the end of his section is that Quentin is
going to rob him of his money and that his first futile effort to
catch her in the act of love is but a prelude to an even more futile
pursuit of his lost money—a pursuit which takes him to Mottson
and a confrontation with the little man, not with a red tie but a
hatchet, who comes within an ace of delivering a final, fatal blow
upon his throbbing head. In that section, from the point of view
of eyes that look down and over the action we see not only the
large drooling idiot Benjy from the "outside," but also Jason, his
hair parted in the middle, presenting a face like that of a stereotypical bartender. And we see Dilsey and Luster and the
landscape and the weather, and the society too, in the form of
the church service, the Compson breakfast table, the sheriff, and
the town square with its monument. We have heard the voices
and we have felt all these presences throughout the narrative,
but always from the inside. Indeed Jason's section is the perfect
transition to the omniscient fourth section, since the relative
clarity and objectivity of his vernacular have released us to the

moral judgment held in abeyance during the first two sections by our intellectual struggle to penetrate the lost temporal sequence.

In the fourth section we see Jason get all the justice that our worst opinion of him could require. That fact alone should tell us that whatever indignation we may have felt at his conduct is finally superfluous in terms of the literal action of the novel. It should tell us, but usually doesn't, and for a very particular reason: the presence of Dilsey, the figure who comes into central focus under the omniscient eye of consciousness. Dilsey, in the terms of emotional exchange that Faulkner so masterfully exploits, at once attracts and commands all the sympathy that was suspended in Jason's section. For that reason, the vivid contrast between her seeming self-sacrifice and Jason's selfish vengefulness is likely to leave the moral judgment upon him unabated, despite the actual judgment he suffers in the book.

The humor of Jason's section and the laughter it provokes are surely the displacement of the suspension of sympathy we experience in reading his vernacular. They are in fact the *active* displacement of that sympathy, and as such they put us, if we truly reflect upon them, in touch with a much more profound moral and intellectual relation to the world of the novel. Such reflection should, for example—or can, at least—add a dimension to the opening scene of the novel in which Luster is leading Benjy to look for golf balls. Surely it is not amiss, in the light of humor, to see the joke of this opening passage in which Luster is leading the castrated Benjy in quest of lost balls. We don't have to give a horselaugh at the scene, but if we don't get to the point of at least suppressing one, we have sounded neither our own depths nor those of Faulkner's perspectivist world. To see, or rather to feel, the irrepressible potentiality of humor in the opening passage of the book is to be fully in touch with the humanity of the large loss Faulkner is at once envisioning and enacting.

Humor is, after all, intricately related to loss—is really dependent on it. To see the joke in that scene is to be immediately in touch with Benjy's perspective, which has its own great humor. His description of a golf putt as hitting little is at once hilariously accurate in both its physical and metaphysical possibilities. The golfers trudging on that ground we are ultimately fated to understand are indeed hitting little, which is to say missing much. And when Benjy, describing the wedding scene at which he and T.P. get drunk, tells of the ground repeatedly hitting him, we ought to get, from the reflection of our laughter, the difference between hitting little and hitting much.

I merely suggest the ways in which, once the humor is fully experienced in Jason's section, the experience can in turn radiate light into the other sections. But the title of my paper is humor as vision in Faulkner, and I want to conclude this discussion with a sense of what the sense of humor can contribute to an understanding of this book. If, by virtue of having come to understand Jason through the humor of his vernacular, we begin to look at the other sections, then sharp questions begin to emerge. To understand Jason fully is, as I have tried to show, to experience the humor his vernacular provokes. That humor does not make us sympathize with him. Rather it is the very form that displaces sympathy. Thus, to see Jason's humor is to see how related he is to his brothers. He too is in pain; he too is a victim of life itself; he too is helpless before the repetitions that assault him in his selfishness; he too has been robbed of love and been given in return the selfish sentimentality of his mother's cant.[6] There is no way that we can ever feel that he is "good" or even sensitive in the way we feel Benjy and Quentin are sensitive. Yet in the humor that he makes possible, or rather out of that humor, we can perhaps see that his brothers are as selfish as he is.

Beyond this relationship between the three—a relationship defined in terms of selfishness and pain and helplessness—some exquisite moral problems begin to emerge if we are but willing to see them. How often, for example, have we read interpretations of the book that dwell on Jason's sadistic treatment of Luster on the matter of the show tickets. We don't even have to read the interpretations; we have *felt* that sadism and judged it

without benefit of interpretation. Yet who has read of or felt
Luster's comparable sadism in relation to Benjy? What of his
trickery of Benjy before the fire? What of his shouting Caddy's
name in Benjy's ear? I am not trying to say that Luster's trickery
is as bad as, or worse than, Jason's. Yet surely we wouldn't want
to come again and again out of Faulkner's great world without
having seen that Jason is by no means solitary in his sadism. To
be blind to Luster's capacity for cruelty is to sentimentalize him,
to deny him his full humanity. To engage in an emotional exchange that sentimentally exonerates Luster and pleasurably
judges Jason is to practice a narrow moral capitalism that takes its
profit both greedily and complacently. We can of course always
justify Luster on the grounds that he and all the blacks in the
novel are victimized by selfish whites, but living forever in that
realm keeps us from realizing how helpless and cruel and selfish
and pathetic and powerful everyone is in Faulkner's world of loss.
It is just this kind of deluded moral generosity that has enabled
us as a nation to create two rednecks for every black we pride
ourselves on freeing. Faulkner's generosity and judgment in this
novel are of a far higher order.

The merest glimpse of this higher order places us in a strong
relation with the ending of *The Sound and the Fury*—that ending
surely none of us can ever forget. There, where dear Luster,
driving the carriage to the cemetery for the first time, turns to
the left at the Confederate monument, he suddenly confronts, in
the sound of Benjy's roaring fury, a chaos beyond anything he has
ever been able—out of boredom or exasperation—to tease or
trick out of him. Here, in other words, out of no conscious
intention, he touches off a sound that no childish meanness
could ever sound. Yet just here it is Jason—he whom we have, in
all likelihood, morally discounted throughout the book and he
who has experienced the worst day of a hopeless life—yes, Jason,
who not only *knows* the order of procession, but who, thank
heavens, not out of self-sacrificing goodness but in violent outrage, achieves the order by violently turning the carriage to the
right. Here, in the glaring presence of Jason's violent act at the

end of Easter Sunday, April 8, 1928, in Mississippi, we experience nothing less than a blessed rage for order—raging in its fury, but blessed in its serenity, as "cornice and facade [flow] smoothly once more from left to right; post and tree, window and doorway, and signboard, each in its ordered place" (401).

## NOTES

1. There are critics who have given attention to Faulkner's humor. Both Warren Beck *(Man in Motion)* and Walter Slatoff *(Quest for Failure)* are sensitively in touch with Faulkner's comedy. Beck is particularly good in discussing the grotesquerie that animates the Snopes trilogy. Michael Millgate's *The Achievement of William Faulkner,* though it does not specifically concentrate on Faulkner's humor, unfailingly remains alert to its presence. Walter Brylowski *(Faulkner's Olympian Laugh)* seeks to relate Faulkner's comedy to mythic patterns. Lyall Powers *(Faulkner's Yoknapatawpha Comedy)* pursues Faulkner's comic vision in relation to Dantean patterns. For a fine brief discussion of the presence of humor in Faulkner's work, see Robert D. Jacobs, "Faulkner's Humor," in *The Comic Imagination in American Literature,* ed. Louis Rubin (New Brunswick: Rutgers University Press, 1983), 305–18.

2. Thomas Y. Greet, "The Theme and Structure of Faulkner's *The Hamlet,*" in *William Faulkner: Four Decades of Criticism,* ed. Linda W. Wagner (Lansing: Michigan State University Press, 1973), 302–17.

3. See my "Humor and America: The Southwestern Bear Hunt, Mrs. Stowe, and Mark Twain," *Sewanee Review,* 83 (Fall 1975), 573–601.

4. A particular exception is Donald M. Kartiganer, *The Fragile Thread: The Meaning of Form in Faulkner's Novels* (Amherst: The University of Massachusetts Press, 1979), 15–17.

5. William Faulkner, *The Sound and the Fury* (New York: Random House, Vintage Books, n.d.), 241. I use this paperback edition of the novel because it is readily available and because it was reproduced photographically from a copy of the first printing of the book. All subsequent quotations from *The Sound and the Fury* are from this edition and will be cited parenthetically following each quotation. Of all the editions of *The Sound and the Fury,* I actually prefer the Modern Library Edition of 1946, which also included *As I Lay Dying*. Not only was that volume one of the best buys ever published, it also was the first edition to include Faulkner's appendix. Best of all, it had the appendix in the right place: *before* the novel rather than after it.

6. Even Mrs. Compson deserves some understanding. The Compsons clearly *do* lord it over her in the matter of family. Faulkner's treatment of her should be compared with Harriet Beecher Stowe's treatment of Marie St. Clare, the character Faulkner must have remembered as he imagined Mrs. Compson. Both characters are embodiments of neurotic self-pity; both are contemptibly selfish and self-indulgent; both feel that they are robbed of love; and both *are* robbed of it; finally both live in books whose readers rob them again in order to lavish sympathy on other characters—on Dilsey, let us say, or on little Eva and Uncle Tom.

# Jason Compson: A Demoralized Wit

## WILLIAM N. CLAXON, JR.

Like William Shakespeare's King Richard III, Jason Compson, malevolent monarch of the third section of William Faulkner's *The Sound and the Fury,* elicits widely divergent reactions from readers. While most concur with Stephen M. Ross's view that "Jason evinces a moral depravity frightening in its implications for the American 'folk' character," a few would side with Linda Wagner's view that Jason is really a victim of circumstances whose efforts to meet his obligations to his family "took a kind of love, a kind of honor."[1] Like Richard III, Jason's power to evoke admiration, in the darkness of malice, comes from his rhetorical skill. The most influential aspect of his rhetoric is his wit, which enables Jason to create a protective, fantasy world for himself.[2] In his fantasy, Jason sees himself as a martyr in a world determined to destroy him and, as David Aiken notes, a possessor of "a special wisdom which elevates him above the great mass of foolish humanity."[3] Moreover, Jason's wit seduces the reader into believing his delusion, thus intensifying the startling revelation of Jason's true character, stripped of its camouflaging wit, in the final section of the novel.

Jason's wit generally falls into three categories: self-irony, riddles, and what I call scenic descriptions. The clearest example of self-irony occurs in the chase sequence involving Jason and Miss Quentin. Forced to stop and lean against a tree because of a dog, he sees his hand is resting on poison oak and thinks, "The only thing I couldn't understand was why it was just poison oak and not a snake or something."[4] Jason's comment, directed towards himself, emphasizes his feeling of martyrdom—even nature is against him. In this case, however, only a mistake by nature has prevented him from incurring the worst that could happen. Nature, had it been alert, would have provided a snake for Jason to put his hand on—at least this is what Jason thinks. Jason's comment is also a protective one, as James Mellard points out, because envisioning the worst lessens the pain of the actual situation. Mellard suggests that Jason actually "turns the pain into pleasure, saying in essence, as Freud puts it, 'I am too big to have these causes affect me painfully.'"[5]

The humor for us comes from our knowledge of Jason. By this time, almost halfway through the segment, we know that Jason feels the world is against him, and that he expects everything to go wrong. He makes us expect it too, so when he envisions the worst, we laugh because he verbalizes what we think—we too would not have been surprised if it had been a snake. Furthermore, we genuinely sympathize with Jason, with his head pounding, his body covered by burrs, his face dripping with sweat, and Quentin enjoying herself not far away. This sympathy for Jason makes us more willing to accept his view of martyrdom, because we recognize, as Mellard points out, "that Jason *can* be hurt by inner forces, that he may be more sensitive than he usually appears."[6]

Another example of Jason's self-irony occurs in his recollection of a conversation with his mother. To her suggestion that she would be happy for him to have a wife, if he could find one that would be worthy of him, Jason responds: "I says no thank you I have all the women I can take care of now if I married a wife she'd probably turn out to be a hophead or something. That's all we lack in this family, I says" (307–8). The veracity of this statement is one source of humor. With a mother who pretends to relinquish the management of the house to her son, a niece whose promiscuity threatens the family's name, a cook, Dilsey, who openly rejects his authority by showing more respect for others of the household, less deserving of course, and a kept woman, Lorraine, who gets more than she gives, Jason does have as many women in his life as he needs. A second, more important source for the humor is the double irony involved in the statement. First, Jason cannot really take care of the women he has now, although his statement implies that he thinks he can. Second, Jason is incapable of a meaningful relationship with a woman. All he can handle is an affair with a whore in Memphis, and even there he is not successful.

Jason's self-protection here operates on two levels. He protects himself from his own failure to relate to women and he protects himself from his family. By putting off the suggestion of a wife, Jason is reminding himself of his martyrdom, and by attacking his mother and his family with "that's all we lack" he is reminding them that they are a burden to him. His wit is an attempt to beat back that which threatens him from within his own family. As in the first instance of self-irony, we sympathize with Jason's problems and tend to accept his stated position of martyr, because he has made us see the whole situation in humorous terms and because we recognize the veracity of his statement, recalling that the family consists of a hypochondriac mother, a suicidal brother, a sister who gets pregnant by only the critics know whom, an idiot brother, a father who drinks himself to death, a sponging uncle, and a niece who lies in the bed her mother made.

Jason's second verbal technique for creating wit involves a variation of one of the basic forms of humor, the riddle. In the riddle, a question is asked which suggests some ingenuity is necessary for discovering the right answer. An example of this is the age-old riddle of the sphinx: What goes on four legs in the morning, two legs at noon, and three legs in the evening? In a pure riddle, the solution fits in logically and smoothly with the question, as the answer, man at his three stages of life, does here. In the impure riddle, the solution does not fit in smoothly with the question, that is, to understand its logic requires some thought. The answer to the latter kind of riddle shocks the listener because it is not an answer that logical thinking will produce, yet it is an answer that logical thinking can understand. Jason adapts this basic riddle form of question and answer to create his own version of wit. Instead of posing a question, he makes a statement which requires some sort of explanation. The explanation, when given, frequently has the ring of truth.

One of the best examples of this kind of wit is Jason's response to Earl's moralizing on the value of honesty: " 'Well, then,' I says, 'I reckon that conscience of yours is a more valuable clerk than I am; it dont have to go home at noon to eat' " (286). The first half of the statement corresponds to the question of the riddle and the last half to the answer or solution. The personification of the conscience and the preservation of its unpersonified needs result in the logical explanation that it is superior to Jason as a clerk because it does not have to go home to eat. The illogic, of course, is that if the conscience does not function like a man, it cannot function as a clerk. So Jason's explanation is both logical and illogical. In addition, the humor is derived from the irony involved: Earl's conscience is a better clerk than Jason because Jason tends to his own business instead of Earl's.

Furthermore, Jason takes the riddle a step beyond its pure form because he removes the contest element. Albert Rapp points out that the riddle is purely a duel of wits with one person testing his mental skill against another.[7] But Jason has taken away the duel aspect, first by not asking a question and then by not giving Earl the chance to respond. Yet his form of the riddle serves the same function of making the riddler superior to the recipient, and so adds to Jason's own feeling of superiority. He is fulfilling his earlier promise: " 'Yes?' I says, letting him go on. Listening to what he would say before I shut him up" (284). It also shows Jason's need for defense, for the content of the riddle goes back to Earl's opening remark which immediately put Jason on the defensive: " 'You go home to dinner?' " (283). Here Jason is attacking, not himself, but his employer, someone external to his immediate family. His attack is necessary because he feels Earl is a threat to his welfare. Earl can inform Jason's mother of the truth of Jason's business connection, and thus end Jason's quest for financial independence, or the Golden Fleece. This attack upon Earl indicates, again, Jason's feeling of martyrdom, his feeling that the world is against him.

Later Jason shows the same economy of expression when he again attacks Earl: "'You ought to have a dollar watch,' I says. 'It wont cost you so much to believe it's lying each time'" (306). Again, this statement shows Jason's remarkable ability to respond verbally and caustically to a situation and his special wisdom which enables him to recognize the folly of a man who has a watch but cannot believe its accuracy without checking the courthouse clock. We respond positively to Jason's recognition of a characteristic of mankind in general, not just a peculiarity of Earl, and we admire his ability to put down his protagonist in the battle of wits.

Jason also uses his variation of the riddle to attack his family. At one point he says, "I haven't got much pride, I can't afford it with a kitchen full of niggers to feed and robbing the state asylum of its star freshman" (286). Until one realizes that pride has nothing to do with a "kitchen full of niggers to feed" and an idiot brother, this sounds like a logical explanation. Subsequent consideration reveals that this statement, though not universally true, is quite true of Jason. He does equate pride with these elements, or at least he feels they are partly responsible for his lack of pride (his martyrdom again). The humor is partly due to the revealing diction of Jason. Pride becomes something one can or cannot afford, a commodity that can be bought and sold. The humor also comes from Jason's exaggerated description of Benjy. He raises the state asylum to the level of an institution of higher learning, and Benjy to the status of a National Merit Finalist, both of which are incongruous with the actual situation. In attacking his family, Jason is attempting to preserve what pride he has, to show cause for not having more, and, in short, to place the blame upon someone other than himself.

Of the three types of wit involved in Jason's section, his scenic descriptions perhaps merit the highest accolades because of their effectiveness in providing protection and humor. These descriptions can be elaborate or brief, universal or personal. One of the finest examples of this kind of wit is Jason's description of the birds:

> The swallows had begun, and I could hear the sparrows beginning to swarm in the trees in the courthouse yard. Every once in a while a bunch of them would come swirling around in sight above the roof, then go away. They are as big a nuisance as the pigeons, to my notion. You cant even sit in the courthouse yard for them. First thing you know, bing. Right on your hat. (309)

The description of the scene involves a certain technical mastery on the part of Jason (or Faulkner). A word count shows that Jason's sentences move from longer ones of twenty words to increasingly shorter ones, ending with the shortest of all, the four word punch line. Because of Jason's verbal skill, we can visualize the event, and so we laugh for the same reason we laugh when someone slips on a banana peel. At the same time, the scene represents a universal experience and thus draws our sympathy because we have either been in that position or have feared that we might be in it. Although the situation is universal, Jason's description implies that he is the person on the receiving end of the mishap, and emphasizes his feeling of being put upon by the external world, nature in this case. Here we see Jason attempting to stave off even an incidental threat to his person.

Another instance of Jason's skill in creating scenes that protect him and make us laugh occurs near the beginning of the section:

> It's bad enough on Sundays, with that damn field full of people that haven't got a side show and six niggers to feed, knocking a damn oversize mothball around. He's going to keep running up and down that fence and bellowing every time they come in sight until first thing I know they're going to begin charging me golf dues, then Mother and Dilsey'll have to get a couple of china door knobs and a walking stick and work it out, unless I play at night with a lantern. (232)

The exaggeration of the description, the incongruity of the imagined scene with reality, and the knowledge we have of Jason create the humor in this passage. Jason exaggerates when he sees the golfball as an "oversize mothball" and door knobs and a walking stick as possible implements of the game. These exaggerations also establish the incongruity of the situation. Should Mother or Dilsey ever manage to hit one of the door knobs with the walking stick, it would probably shatter. Even more incongruous is the image of the stiff-legged Dilsey and the fragile, whining Mrs. Compson out playing golf. And that incongruity pales beside the subsequent suggestion that Jason might get out and play by the light of the lantern, for when has Jason had the time or the inclination for leisurely activity?

We laugh not only because the scene Jason describes is ludicrous in terms of reality, but also because it is precisely the kind of thing that Jason would try to make his mother and Dilsey do, if he were forced to pay golf dues. In fact, he would get his money's worth, even if it meant playing himself. Here, Jason protects himself by releasing in the form of wit his bitterness at having the family's, and therefore his, property squandered by Quentin. By envisioning the worst way that the sold pasture can come back to haunt him, that is by requiring him to pay for what used to be his family's, Jason is able to keep in clear sight his feeling of martyrdom.

Jason's verbal ability enables him to convey a visual image with only a few words. Recollecting his father's funeral and his discovery at the time that his Uncle Maury was drinking, Jason says: "I reckon he thought that the least he could do at Father's funeral or maybe the sideboard thought it was still Father and tripped him up when he passed" (245). In a few words, Jason has created a Saturday morning cartoonlike image of an animated piece of furniture wantonly tripping up his uncle, and, at the same time, has launched into a witty attack on his father and his father's drinking habits. The scene implies that Jason's father paused at the sideboard for a drink so frequently that it expected any passing man to stop.

Using this opening image as a springboard, Jason continues his assault on his father: "Like I say, if he had to sell something to send Quentin to Harvard we'd all been a damn sight better off if he'd sold that sideboard and bought himself a one-armed strait jacket with part of the money. I reckon the reason all the Compson gave out before it got to me like Mother says, is that he drank it up. At least I never heard of him offering to sell anything to send me to Harvard" (245). The only way Jason can protect himself against his father's actions which continue to haunt him as he tries to be financially and spiritually free of the family, and the only way he can maintain his martyrdom, is to attack verbally the memory of his father. Here we see Jason's ability to turn everything towards himself. What begins as an observation about Maury ends up as a complaint about the way the family has treated him.

The family is the focal point for another of his biting descriptions: "Blood, I says, governors and generals. It's a damn good thing we never had any kings and presidents; we'd all be down there at Jackson chasing butterflies" (286). In two words, "chasing butterflies," Jason summons up an image of a lush pasture filled with butterflies and Compsons. Benjy is in the lead, bellowing and dragging Caddy along; Quentin is staring at a crushed butterfly in his hand; Mrs. Compson is whining, "This is no way for a lady to have to behave"; Miss Quentin is forming a cradle with her skirt for the butterflies, exposing thigh; Mr. Compson is tipping the bottle, thinking, "if only I can get this finished quick enough, I can put butterflies in it"; and Jason is sitting on the ground, clutching his ankle, a butterfly net over his head, thinking, "Damn. Can't even catch a butterfly without hurting myself. Not a hole in the entire field except this one and I got to step in it. Only thing that surprises me is that there wasn't a cowpie beside it for me to sit in." Again there is a technical mastery here as the description concludes a cataloguing of his family's foibles, serving as the punch line to a joke. Furthermore, Jason's scene is appropriate for his view of the Compson family. He sees them all as romantics, impractical and incapable of surviving in the real world. Unwittingly, he includes himself in this view, an irony in light of his belief in pragmatism, yet accurate because Jason chases butterflies as much as anyone else.

From these examples we see that whether Jason is attacking his family, his community, or himself, his wit serves as insulation from what he considers is a world out to get him. It protects him from the tyrannical discipline of Earl's watchful eye; from the degrading of the family pride by his niece's promiscuity; from his mother, who has a hold over him that he wishes to deny and cannot; from the servants who consume his money; from his idiot brother, who threatens his pride; from his dead father, who sold the pasture to send Quentin to school but did nothing to help him, Jason; from his brother Quentin, who committed suicide, thus escaping what Jason cannot; and even from himself. For Jason, the best defense is a good offense.

His delusion of martyrdom and wisdom, achieved through his wit, enables him to survive. Expecting the worst of the world and getting less makes him feel he is coming out ahead. Thinking that all circumstances are not of his own making but the results of others' actions and inactions makes him feel heroic in his fight to get on top—"I'm doing the best I can," he says—and looking down upon the world makes him feel he will get there. At the end of his narrative, Jason states his objective:

> I dont want to make a killing; save that to suck in the smart gamblers with. I just want an even chance to get my money back. And once I've done that they can bring all Beale Street and all bedlam in here and two of them can sleep in my bed and another one can have my place at the table too. (329)

There is something heroic in this goal of not getting ahead so much as getting financially even. And though we know that Beale Street and bedlam are already sleeping in Jason's bed, we sense his ability to believe they are not.

Our own participation in his delusion is a subtle one. As Ross reminds us, Jason is an enthralling storyteller.[8] His furious, witty monologue, filled with digressions and variety, enraptures us partly because of its rhetorical versatility, and partly because of its swiftly refreshing quality in comparison to the preceding sections, which lack Jason's narrative vitality and lucidity. Getting caught up in his narrative, and laughing both at and with him, we become susceptible to and sympathetic with his vision of the world and of himself. The sheer weight of his martyr-dom—scarcely a page is without it—crushes us into accepting it as truth. It is a case of subliminal seduction.

Moreover, we sympathize with Jason's view because in some sense we share it. Though not, perhaps, as paranoid as Jason, there are times when we feel the world is against us, that we are put-upon, and we find ourselves saying "I'm doing the best I can," or exhorting ourselves that our best is all we can do. We sympathize in addition because Jason attacks what we would like to attack: spinsters who tell us how to raise children, ministers who stand in the way of what we want, employers who mistreat us, birds that poop in our hair, and impersonal institutions which protect their interests at the expense of our own—"Only be damned," Jason says, "if it doesn't look like a company as big and rich as the Western Union could get a market report out on time. Half as quick as they'll get a wire to you saying Your account closed out" (282). We admire Jason's wit and envy his skill in putting down others. Finally, Jason's wit enables us to see the members of the Compson family from a different angle, an angle that, in the words of Ross, "exposes a kind of common-sense truth" about them.[9] Providing this perspective increases Jason's credibility. And so we begin to believe his vision.

The cumulative effects of Jason's wit are demonstrated by two scenes, similar in malicious content but dissimilar in the reactions they evoke from us. The first scene occurs early in Jason's monologue when he tricks Caddy by accepting $100 from her in return for the chance to see her daughter. Like his other moments of trickery, this scene has comic potential—Jason promises something, fulfills his promise, and yet his adversary gets nothing—but it is not presented by Faulkner in a comic way and does not have the mitigating element of Jason's wit.[10] In fact, it is the longest segment of the section without humor of any kind. As we watch the scene unfold, we experience a sense of foreboding, because we, like Caddy, distrust Jason. When Jason speeds by in the carriage with Caddy's child held up to the window, our fears are confirmed and our expectations of Jason's character fulfilled.

The second scene occurs near the end of Jason's narrative when he teases Luster about the tickets. Here, we experience hope instead of foreboding. We scoot to the edge of our chairs, and we clench our fists, wishing for one soft spot in Jason, for one sign of compassion which will allow us to stand up and cheer his perseverance, because we feel that Jason is a victim of circumstances and not a product of his own malicious intent. When he drops the tickets in the fire because Luster cannot come up with a single nickel, our hopes are frustrated and our expectations, altered by Jason's wit, are unfulfilled. Had Faulkner permitted Jason to transform our frown into a smile with a witty remark, the impact of this scene would have been lessened. Because he does not and because the hostility is directed towards a child who does not deserve it, the stark reality of Jason's maliciousness dawns upon us. The absence of wit here is as significant as its presence elsewhere.

Jason's delusion and our acceptance of it come crashing down in the last section of the novel when his true self is fully revealed. The destruction of Jason's fantasy, prophesied by Job, the only man who can match wits with Jason, occurs when Quentin steals Jason's hoard.[11] Jason suddenly finds himself confronted with the reality that he needs other people. He needs the sheriff's assistance; he gets the sheriff's cold refusal and his suspicions. He needs information from the man at the carnival; he gets a hatchet instead. He needs someone to drive him back to Jefferson; he has to pay four dollars for the service. Having fooled himself that he could safely hoard his money and exist without other people, Jason now faces the frustration of defeat. As Cleanth Brooks points out: "At the end of the novel he has scarcely made good his boast that he is a free man able to stand on his own feet with no help from anybody. He has indeed finally succeeded, with his brittle rationalism, in outsmarting himself."[12]

More importantly, these encounters show Jason as a demoralized wit. Without his protective armor of verbal assault, Jason is no longer able to cope with his circumstances. He is reduced to empty threats. " 'You'll regret this. I wont be helpless. This is not Russia, where just because he wears a little metal badge, a man is immune to law' " (380), he says, but the sheriff will not budge from his previously stated view: " 'That's not any of my business.' " (380). Jason has lost his ability to show his superiority by wit. Even his ability to envision the worst, his car stalled and himself "slogging through the mud, hunting a team" (381), lacks the protective humor of his earlier visions.

Stripped of his protective wit, Jason pursues Quentin in a demented fury, "thinking of himself, his file of soldiers with the manacled sheriff in the rear, dragging Omnipotence down from His throne, if necessary; of the embattled legions of both hell and heaven through which he tore his way and put his hands at last on his fleeing niece" (382). This pursuit is made all the more demonic by its contrast with the earlier ramble through the woods after Quentin and the man with the red tie. "The latch string to hell" (301) has become Jason's. By the time he confronts the man at the carnival, he has become inarticulate, incapable of explaining his quest, blundering on in the "cluttered obscurity" (386). Reality has replaced delusion.

Reality overtakes us, too, as we side with the sheriff, sharing his view that Jason drove his niece away from home. We empathize with the carnival man affronted with the meaningless question, " 'Where are they?' " (386). This last section makes evident the full effect of Faulkner's decision to camouflage Jason with wit. Of this revelation, David Aiken says: "Jason is more than a bigot, a sexist, a mean-spirited materialist, an anti-Semite, a criminal, and an egoist; beneath his surface lies a depth not plumbed in his own monologue. Only in the last chapter does Faulkner reveal the full truth about his radically egocentric character."[13] At the end of *The Sound and the Fury* the distorting mirrors of Jason's funhouse are gone and we see the true reflection of Jason.

NOTES

1. Stephen M. Ross, "Jason Compson and Sut Lovingood: Southwestern Humor as Stream of Consciousness," *Studies in the Novel*, 8 (Fall 1976), 288; Linda Welshimer Wagner, "Jason Compson: The Demands of Honor," *Sewanee Review*, 79 (1971), 575.

2. See James M. Mellard, "Jason Compson: Humor, Hostility and the Rhetoric of Aggression," *Southern Humanities Review*, 3 (1969), 267; John Lewis Longley, Jr., *The Tragic Mask: A Study of Faulkner's Heroes* (Chapel Hill: University of North Carolina Press, 1957), 145.

3. "The 'Sojer Face' Defiance of Jason Compson," *Thought*, 52 (1977), 191.

4. William Faulkner, *The Sound and the Fury* (1929; rpt. New York: Vintage-Random House, 1954), 300. All further references to this book appear in the text.

5. "Humor, Hostility and the Rhetoric of Agggression," 260.

6. Ibid., 259.

7. *The Origins of Wit and Humor* (New York: E. P. Dutton, 1951), 74.

8. Ross, 279.

9. Ibid., 30.

10. James Mellard disagrees with this view because he sees Jason's success in "forcing Caddy into an excessive expenditure of energy and money" as fulfilling comic conventions, even though Jason's trick comes close to cruelty. "Humor, Hostility and the Rhetoric of Aggression," 263.

11. For a discussion of Job's role in Jason's section, see James M. Mellard's "Type and Archetype: Jason Compson as 'Satirist,'" *Genre*, 4 (1971), 183–86.

12. *William Faulkner: The Yoknapatawpha Country* (New Haven: Yale University Press, 1963), 347–48.

13. Aiken, 192.

# The Comic World of *As I Lay Dying*

## Patricia R. Schroeder

The comic genius of Faulkner's *As I Lay Dying* has been recognized only in bits and pieces. The grotesque humor, the Southwestern humor, and the black humor which inform the novel have been seen primarily as isolated devices, highlighting by contrast the tragedy of Faulkner's fictional world.[1] Readers have persistently failed to see that these different strands of humor are woven onto a comic framework and that the novel dynamically interrelates these various forms of humor to celebrate the indefatigable in man. Despite social pressures, acts of God, their own ineptitude, and simple bad luck, the Bundren family will survive and multiply, and this triumphant continuation of society is the essence of the comic vision.

Faulkner's sophisticated narrative strategy probably accounts for much of the critical blindness to the book's fundamentally comic impulse. Because each character relates his or her own version of the Bundren family saga, many readers are driven to search for a central intelligence, a moral center that will reveal the author's point of view. Indeed, a widespread critical response to the novel has been to choose one character (most often Darl) as the authorial surrogate and then to interpret all other narrations from this limited point of view. This approach, however, does violence both to the multiplicity of viewpoints Faulkner has permitted us to share and to the comic vision which that very multiplicity promulgates. The variety of narrators offers insight into a community perspective as well as detachment from the sometimes painful events—two qualities which are crucial defining elements of comedy.

In its classical form, comedy is the inverse of tragedy: it celebrates community survival, applauds the status quo, and affirms life in the face of death.[2] Probably developed from pagan fertility rituals, classical comedy documents the return of spring, when life and fertility replace hunger and death. The action of classical comedy concerns the incorporation of the comic hero into his society at large. Moving from one social center to another, the hero (who is not necessarily scrupulous or competent) overcomes obstacles to win his heroine and so join the community. Along the way the *pharmakos*, a scapegoat for the forces of dissension within the society, is expelled, and the comedy ends with an unforeseen marriage and a wedding feast. The overt bawdiness which so often characterizes comedy is thus central to its function as a celebration of fertility and social continuation.

*As I Lay Dying* quite obviously—and quite deliberately, I would argue—follows this classical model of comedy. The novel begins with the death of Addie Bundren and ends with Anse's marriage to his popeyed bride. As comic hero, Anse moves from one social center to another—that is, from his rural community to the town of Jefferson—and along the way surmounts the obstacles of fire, flood, and community reproach. Sex is treated with humor: recall the young druggist's "hair of the dog" cure for Dewey Dell's pregnancy, or the specious logic ("if the sack is full when we get to the woods . . . I cannot help it"[3]) that led to her pregnancy in the first place. Finally, the novel depicts the expulsion of antisocial forces in the form of Darl the barnburner, and concludes with a wedding feast of bananas (replete with phallic overtones) and the imminent birth of Dewey Dell's child. By burying Addie and finding a new wife, Anse defeats death and prepares for the continuation of his family. If, as Doc Peabody declares, death is "merely a function . . . of the minds of the ones who suffer the bereavement" (42), the Bundrens end up triumphing over Addie's death and reintegrating themselves into the society of the living.

An American regional variant of this classical pattern is found in many of the humorous tales of the Old Southwest—tales that Faulkner knew and admired. And indeed, it is through his use of a number of the techniques and devices of Southwestern humor that Faulkner most directly reveals the comic impulse of *As I Lay Dying*. In their published form of the mid-nineteenth century, these humorous stories, an outgrowth of backwoods, oral tall tales, center on a rural narrator's creation of a fictional reality in which to control the violence of his frontier environment.[4] In Southwestern tales, bullets can bounce off a charging bear's head and seeds can grow to fruition overnight, but diverting violence and excess into language makes them seem less threatening.

A particularly noteworthy convention of the Southwestern humorists' tales is the framing device. The tall tale is, essentially, a tale-within-a-tale, recounted by a backwoods hero to a sophisticated, urban listener, who in turn relates the circumstances of the telling to us. Using this device, the authors emphasize the backwoods narrator's hyperbolic vernacular by humorous contrast with the gentleman narrator's more formal, educated speech. The gentleman speaker also implies a civilized social norm somewhat removed from that of the backwoods hero and affords the reader a comfortable measure of distance from the violent or grotesque action of the tale itself.

*As I Lay Dying* is not bounded by such a framing device, but Faulkner's inclusion of a number of non-Bundren narrators produces many of the same effects. The country folk and townspeople who witness the Bundrens' passing serve as a sort of Greek chorus—or, perhaps, as a framing narrator—by expounding on their shared social assumptions. Rachel Samson (111) and Lula Armstid (178) echo the prevailing sentiments when they each denounce the protracted Bundren journey as "a outrage," and Moseley, the pharmacist, specifically cites his community credentials—"'Me, a respectable druggist, that's kept store and raised a family and been a church-member for fifty-six years in this town'" (192)—to explain the community basis of morality to the pregnant and bewildered Dewey Dell. These outside commentators also provide us with the distance necessary to see the humor of the story—a distance usually furnished by the framing narrator, and once described explicitly by George Washington Harris's Sut Lovingood, a favorite character of Faulkner's.[5] As Sut, perched high on a cliff, looks down to see his father dive frantically into a creek to escape a swarm of bees, he says:

> Tu look at hit from the top ove the bluff, hit were pow'ful inturestin, an' sorter funny: I were on the bluff myse'f, mine yu.
> Dad cudent see the funny part frum whar he wer, but it seem'd tu be inturestin tu him frum the 'tenshun he wer payin tu the bisniss ove divin an' cussin.[6]

The Bundren narrators allow us to see the "inturestin" aspects of the burial journey, while the outside narrators elevate us to Sut's bluff, from which the adventure appears "sorter funny." It is often at the moments of deepest pain and most profound loss that Faulkner interjects a community narrator and so removes us to a vantage point that diminishes what could very well be individual agony. It is Armstid, not Jewel, who recounts Anse's triumphant swapping of Jewel's beloved horse for a team of mules; it is Peabody, not Cash, who describes the latter's mangled leg. And who can help but share Peabody's outrage at the Bundrens' collective breach of common sense? As he examines Cash's cement-encased, blackened leg, the doctor exclaims:

> "Concrete," I said. "God Almighty, why didn't Anse carry you to the nearest sawmill and stick your leg in the saw? That would have cured it. Then you all could have stuck his head into the saw and cured a whole family. . . . If you had anything you could call luck, you might say it was lucky this is the same leg you broke before," I said.
> "Hit's what paw says," he said. (230)

The framing device typical of the Southwestern tale added further to the humor by providing linguistic contrast between the educated speech of the gentleman and the rich vernacular of the backwoods hero. This linguistic contrast is maintained by a few characters in *As I Lay Dying*: in the dialogue just cited, for example, Peabody's correct speech contrasts with the foolish-sounding rural dialect of Cash's reply. And although many of the outside commentators do share the Bundrens' homely dialect, the humor inherent in that dialect is preserved. The colloquial metaphors, exaggeration, understatement, and attention to detail that characterize the characters' speech elicit our laughter and so run counter to the sympathy we might otherwise feel for them. The pain Cash must have suffered in falling off a barn roof is largely undercut when he tells us that he fell " 'twenty-eight foot, four and a half inches, about' " (85); Tull's comparison of his wife to a quart of milk held securely in the wellmade jar of his hard-worked farm subverts the pride he feels in his handiwork—especially when he himself realizes that the milk can still go sour (132).

The focal point of the Southwestern humor techniques, both in linguistic treatment and character type, is Anse Bundren, the comic hero. Like many frontier heroes, Anse is continually described in animal imagery by everyone who knows him. We are told that "the stubble gives his lower face that appearance that old dogs have" (17); that he stood still "like he was a steer standing knee-deep in a pond and somebody come by and set the pond up on edge and he aint missed it yet" (69); that he "looks like right after the maul hits the steer and it no longer alive and dont know yet that it is dead" (58); that he resembled an "uncurried horse dressed up" (117); and that his eyes were "like two hounds in a strange yard" (163). The effect of this repeated beast imagery is to displace any possible sympathy we might have for the bereaved husband. Anse Bundren is clearly a low form of animal life, worthy of our laughter rather than our compassion.

Anse also reveals his frontier roots through his actions. Despite his apparent ineptitude, Anse is a sharp trader so skilled that he astonishes even his victims. The Southwestern humorists frequently celebrated the pioneer virtues that would enable a hero to survive on the wild frontier, and these are the qualities repeatedly exhibited by Anse Bundren. Anse genially manipulates the members of his family and his rural society, and functions as a rather mild but nonetheless effective scourge of fools. Having concocted the story that "if he ever sweats, he will die" (17) (a story that Darl supposes even Anse believes by now), Anse perennially calls upon his neighbors to help out with the running of his farm. The neighbors resent Anse's manipulation, but they continue to comply with his schemes. Tull explains that "like most folks around here, I done holp him so much already I cant quit now" (32), and Armstid goes so far as to attribute super-natural powers to his lazy neighbor: "Be durn if there aint something about a durn fellow like Anse that seems to make a man have to help him, even when he knows he'll be wanting to kick himself next minute. . . . I be durn if Anse dont conjure a man, some way" (183–84).

It is clear from watching Anse in action that most of his "conjuring" comes from his abilities as a sharp talker, despite the veneer of humility he takes care to preserve. During the burial journey to Jefferson Anse manages to talk Cash out of his "graph-ophone" money, Jewel out of his cherished horse, and Dewey Dell out of her abortion money. In each case he succeeds by playing upon the emotional weaknesses of his dupes. Witness his speech to the distraught Dewey Dell, who has already been tricked into her "hair of the dog" cure, and who has not yet come to terms with her own pregnancy or her mother's death:

> "I have fed you and sheltered you. I give you love and care, yet my own daughter, the daughter of my dead wife, calls me a thief over her mother's grave. . . . My own born daughter that has et my food for seventeen years, begrudges me the loan of ten dollars. . . . Addie. It is lucky for you you died, Addie." (245–46)

This self-deprecating method of fast talking is typical of a stock frontier hero, one like Sut Lovingood, a self-proclaimed "nat'ral born durn'd fool." In fact, Anse echoes Sut's oft-repeated claim that he "kin git intu more durn'd misfornit skeery scrapes, then enybody"[7] with his own perennial complaints about being "a luckless man" (18) or a "misfortunate man" (150). In the light of Anse's animal-like qualities and his skills as a manipulator, we can see that his cunning response to Addie's death sets him squarely in the tradition of a comic hero. As he tries unsuccessfully to smooth the covers over his wife's body, Anse mutters, "'God's will be done. . . . Now I can get them teeth'" (51). His selfish reason for undertaking the burial journey to town is thus revealed, but despite the personal motive, the journey also insures the well-being of his family by providing a new wife and some new tools. Anse's world, like the world of classical comedy, is clearly far from ideal; it is, however, the best world he knows, and with the help of his machinations, it endures.

It is not merely the language or the character of Anse that places *As I Lay Dying* in the tradition of Southwestern humor, however. The entire plot line belongs to a type of Southwestern story often called "the frustrated funeral."[8] These tales, which use humor to reduce the familiar frontier spectre of death to comic proportions, are characterized by grotesquerie (a corpse was often used as a comic prop) and shockingly realistic detail. In Henry Clay Lewis's "The Curious Widow," for example, a medical student conceals the head of a corpse in his closet to discourage his nosy landlady from snooping. In Harris's "Frustrating a Funeral" Sut dresses a corpse in devil's garb to shock some self-righteous neighbors. And in the opening line of Harris's "Mrs. Yardley's Quilting" Sut explains his whereabouts by claiming to have been "Helpin tu salt ole Missis Yardley down. . . . Fixen her fur rotten cumfurtably, kiverin her up wif sile, tu keep the buzzards from cheatin the wurms."[9] The Bundrens, too, are engaged in just such an activity, and Addie's body functions as a comic device from the moment she dies. We see Vardaman drill auger holes into the corpse's face to keep his mother from suffocating in the coffin; we witness Cash's outrage when the womenfolk place Addie's body backwards in his perfectly balanced coffin so as not to crush her skirt. And many of the Bundrens' troubles during the latter part of their journey stem from their inability—despite Vardaman's frantic scarecrow routine—to "keep the buzzards frum cheatin the wurms." What we should remember through all these grisly events is that the conventional response to a "frustrated funeral" story is laughter, not revulsion; its purpose is to reduce death to manageable proportions. Faulkner's novel follows the pattern of comedy by ending happily after Addie's burial, as the Bundrens finally put her death behind them.

As the gruesome details of the Bundrens' journey remind us, though, comedy has a dark side as well as a humorous one. After all, the comic hero must be faced with obstacles; the threat to social continuation must be a real one; and life needs its defining opposite, death, in order to triumph at the end. It is a tribute to the richness of Faulkner's vision—and perhaps a reason for the critical misunderstanding of the humor in *As I Lay Dying*—that he used yet another form of comedy to portray this dark side of life within the overall comic framework of the novel. I refer, of course, to what might be termed the black humor or the comedy of the absurd that informs the narratives of Addie (representing death) and Darl (the *pharmakos*).

Faulkner openly acknowledged his debt to the thinking of Henri Bergson, and Bergson's essay *Laughter* can help illuminate the grim comedy beneath the surface of *As I Lay Dying*.[10] For Bergson and Faulkner, life consists of movement, of flux, of inescapable change through time, and any effort to arrest this movement—with rituals, with unchanging truths, with imposed forms of any kind—produces comedy. Any sort of rigidity, postulates Bergson, elicits our laughter—which is, of course, the conventional response to the humorous. *As I Lay Dying* is full of this comedy of the rigid. We see it in Jewel's impassive physical actions, as he strides woodenly "with the rigid gravity of a cigar store Indian . . . endued with life from the hips down" (4). We see it in the mechanical list Cash makes in an attempt to impose order on the chaos he feels when his mother dies, a list in which words like "animal magnetism" and "except" are given equal emphasis with befuddled notions of physics and with justifications for his own decisions. We see it in the unthinking linguistic repetitions that abound, such as Anse's frequent mention of his teeth, or Vardaman's continued assertions that his mother is a fish.

Despite the fun he pokes at his beleaguered characters' attempts to order, somehow, the turmoil of their lives, Faulkner himself recognized the inevitability of forms, rituals, and conventions, and their importance to social commerce. On one level of its comedy, *As I Lay Dying* celebrates the shaping of forms despite their absurdity. As Fred Miller Robinson has brilliantly demonstrated, forms of all kinds dissolve throughout the novel; Faulkner glories in his characters' ability to keep creating new forms, new rituals, even as he reveals these forms to be pointless and obsessive. Dewey Dell's makeshift logic as she and Lafe "pick on down the row" to their trysting place evaporates in the emotional reality of her sexual urges; Cora's mind-boggling calculations about the number of eggs her hens must lay before she can bake a free cake disintegrate even before the unforeseeable (in the shape of the lady who decides not to order the cakes after all) destroys her plans. In every case, the permanence of flux and change overwhelms the temporary forms the characters nevertheless continue to erect.

Most of the characters survive quite contentedly in the world of *As I Lay Dying* because they are simply unaware of the futility of their own conventions. Two characters, however, recognize the arbitrary nature of human systems of order, and through these two characters—Addie and Darl—Faulkner's grimmest comedy emerges. For Addie, the distinction between nature and convention boils down to the difference between actions and words, since language is the instrument that enables us to shape the false world of forms. Addie recognizes the barriers that words can set up between man and life's fundamental impulses; claiming that words simply provide "a shape to fill a lack," she says that "sin and love and fear are just sounds that people who have never sinned nor loved nor feared have for what they never had and cannot have until they forget the words. Like Cora, who could never even cook" (165–66). It is fitting, therefore, that

Addie's posthumous revenge on Anse is to make him keep a promise—"keep his word," colloquially; she forces him to shape his actions to a word that she knows is meaningless. It is also fitting—in the light of Faulkner's overall comic purpose—that Addie's revenge is subverted by Anse's own selfish motives for the journey he wanted to take anyway.

Darl shares his mother's awareness of the absurdity of forms, and even extends her vision of man's inability to arrest life's movement. He explores how "our lives ravel out into the no-wind, no-sound, the weary gestures wearily recapitulant: echoes of old compulsions with no-hand on no-strings: in sunset we fall into furious attitudes, dead gestures of dolls. . . . It would be nice if you could just ravel out into time" (196–98). Like Bergson, Darl sees mutability as the truest reality; his resulting failure to see both the inevitability of forms and the social necessity of adhering to them is what eventually drives him to madness. We know early in the novel that the community sees Darl as different from itself; he is "the one folks talk about," "the one folks say is queer." Darl himself exhibits an emotional distance from himself in the very first chapter, when he says:

> Jewel and I come up from the field, following the path in single file. Although I am fifteen feet ahead of him, anyone watching us from the cottonhouse can see Jewel's frayed and broken straw hat a full head above my own. (3)

Here, Darl reveals his tendency to see himself from two different perspectives simultaneously: from the elevated bluff of Sut Lovingood, as it were, where the absurdities of life (the "sorter funny" parts) appear, and from the stream of life itself, where the need to preserve oneself (from swarming bees and other dangers) is of the utmost importance. Later, as the Bundrens attempt to cross the flooded river, Darl speaks of himself in the third person, and on several occasions—as the funeral procession begins, and again as he is being led away to a madhouse—his distance from himself causes him to collapse in mirthless laughter.

In the context of the novel as comedy, Darl's words and actions must be seen as detrimental to him and disruptive of the accepted norms by which his society functions. No matter how much we appreciate his ironic detachment, or how much we sympathize with his attempt to cremate his mother's putrefying corpse, we must also accept his isolation from his community as a fundamental weakness within the world he inhabits. Even the genial Tull perceives Darl's alienation as unhealthy; he says, "that's ever living thing the matter with Darl: he just thinks by himself too much" (68). His crime, too, is an antisocial one: to burn a man's barn is to destroy his livelihood, to render him dependent on society and so to weaken it. Society rather than any one character is the authorial spokesman in *As I Lay Dying;* the world of the novel is circumscribed by social definitions of love, of death, and finally of insanity. Despite the attractiveness of the clairvoyant Darl, in the context of his world we must finally accept the conventional wisdom of Cash's famous description of madness:

> Sometimes I think it aint none of us pure crazy and aint none of us pure sane until the balance of us talks him that-a-way. It's like it aint so much what a fellow does, but it's the way the majority of folks is looking at him when he does it. . . . That's how I reckon a man is crazy. That's how he cant see eye to eye with other folks. And I reckon they aint nothin else to do with him but what the most folks says is right. (223)

The plot ends with the expulsion of the *pharmakos* (a scoundrel in society's eyes, if not by nature) who cannot adapt to the world of social norms. Unlike Dewey Dell and Vardaman, who never even recognize the absurdity of forms, and unlike Cash and Jewel, who each sacrifice something precious (a leg, a horse) to reinvest the old form of a funeral procession with a new and personal significance, Darl cannot adjust. "This world," Cash tells us, "is not his world" (250).

Many readers of *As I Lay Dying,* attracted to the intensity of Addie's emotions or to the perceptiveness of Darl, see these characters' visions as reflecting Faulkner's own—which, indeed, they may. It is important to note, however, that neither Addie nor Darl gets the final word in *As I Lay Dying;* they both cast suspicion on the value of conventions, but their views are undercut by their placement in the novel—that is, by their position relative to the community they inhabit.[11] Addie's narration about the futility of words is sandwiched between a speech by the myopic Cora and a narration by the hypocritical Whitfield—both of whom supply evidence that in the world of *As I Lay Dying* words can and often do replace actions. Darl's madness, too, and the brutality of his incarceration lose something of their pathos by contrast with the chapters that surround them. Darl's final, incoherent speech is followed immediately by Anse's hilarious "borrowing" of Dewey Dell's ten dollars and then by Cash's ruminations on madness and the need to conform.

In weaving together elements of Southwestern humor, a more modern black humor, and the general pattern of classical comedy, Faulkner has created one of the richest modern examples of the comic vision—a vision capable of presenting the necessary darkness of human travail and then celebrating man's ability to overcome it. The world that is not Darl's world is severely indicted in *As I Lay Dying*, but it endures, and its inhabitants prosper and multiply. The bungling Bundrens return home with all the implements necessary for their survival: a new span of mules, new teeth for eating "God's appointed food," a new wife to cook that food, Cash's newly baptized tools, and Dewey Dell's as yet unborn child. What Faulkner demonstrates, finally, is the fundamental principle of comedy: that even when confronted with the death of an individual, life will prevail.

NOTES

1. Barbara Cross ("Apocalypse and Comedy in *As I Lay Dying*," *Texas Studies in Literature*, 3 [Summer 1961], 251–58) and Walter Brylowski (*Faulkner's Olympian Laugh: Myth in the Novels* [Detroit: Wayne State University Press, 1968]), for example, have recognized the structure of ritual comedy in *As I Lay Dying*. M. Thomas Inge ("William Faulkner and George Washington Harris: In the Tradition of Southwestern Humor," *Tennessee Studies in Literature*, 7 [1962, 47–57]) and Otis B. Wheeler ("Some Uses of Folk Humor by Faulkner," *Mississippi Quarterly*, 17 [Spring 1964], 107–22) have found

elements of tall tales. John K. Simon ("What Are You Laughing at, Darl? Madness and Humor in *As I Lay Dying*," *College English*, 25 [1963], 104–10) has commented on the black humor in Darl's laughter. Fred Miller Robinson (*The Comedy of Language* [Amherst: University of Massachusetts Press, 1980]) has demonstrated the comedy of the language. None of these critics, however, has argued for the fundamental comedy of the work as a whole, as evidenced by the dynamic interplay of these various forms of humor.

2. For helpful discussions of the patterns of classical comedy, see Albert Cook, *The Dark Voyage and the Golden Mean: A Philosophy of Comedy* (New York: Norton, 1949); Francis MacDonald Cornford, *The Origin of Attic Comedy* (Cambridge: Cambridge University Press, 1934); and Northrop Frye, *Anatomy of Criticism: Four Essays* (Princeton: Princeton University Press, 1957).

3. *As I Lay Dying* (New York: Random House, Vintage Books, 1964), 26. Hereafter cited in the text.

4. For helpful discussions of the violent and grotesque elements of Southwestern humor, see Alan B. Howard, "Huck Finn in the House of Usher: The Comic and Grotesque Worlds of *The Hamlet*," *Southern Review*, 5 (January 1972), 125–46, and Hennig Cohen and William B. Dillingham, eds., *Humor of the Old Southwest* (Boston: Riverside Press, 1964).

5. Cited in Kenneth S. Lynn, *Mark Twain and Southwestern Humor* (Boston: Little, Brown, 1959), 137.

6. George Washington Harris, *Sut Lovingood's Yarns*, ed. M. Thomas Inge (New Haven: Yale University Press, 1966), 37.

7. Ibid., 138.

8. See Cohen and Dillingham, xxiv–xxv, for a more detailed description of the frustrated funeral tradition.

9. Harris, 114.

10. See Joseph Blotner, *Faulkner: A Biography* (New York: Random House, 1974), 1302, 1441. Also see Henri Bergson, *Laughter: An Essay on the Meaning of the Comic*, trans. Cloudesley Brereton and Fred Rothwell (New York: Macmillan, 1912).

11. For a more detailed examination of this point, see Robinson, whose analysis of the black humor and of the relationship between the characters and their community is indispensable.

# The Levity of *Light in August*

## Virginia V. Hlavsa

What's so funny about *Light in August?* It gives one pause to read an article on this subject in which eight out of the ten examples seem more poignant than funny. Many involve Joe: his stealing "toothpaste which he knows no more about than to make himself sick by eating"; his "mental translation of the dietitian's proffered dollar into 'ranked tubes of toothpaste, like corded wood'"; and the dietitian's image of him at the Negro orphanage as *"a pea in a pan full of coffee beans."* This same article also calls Joe's throwing Joanna's dishes against the wall "almost slapstick" and describes "Grimm's madly methodical pursuit" of him as "hilarious."[1] Of course, when we consider these episodes from Joe's perspective as victim, they are drained of humor. But stepping back, we can smile at the irony of miscommunication or even at Joe as victim, an exaggeration of our own fears of help-lessness, like laughing at Charlie Brown.

But there is another level of humor. Suppose I tell you the story of a great big fellow named King who finds and adopts a valuable little animal and is killed trying to protect it. Not very funny on the surface, although we note the irony and the exag-geration. But what if I add that this fellow was shot holding onto the ledge of a tall Manhattan skyscraper. If you are not a moviegoer, you still might miss the humor. In fact, the story can now be a private joke for movie buffs who guess that King represents King Kong and the valuable animal is Faye Wraye. Thus, I suggest that the real humor in those episodes comes from Faulkner's pleasure in creating hidden parallels, privately out-Joyceing Joyce, for all of them represent patterns Faulkner

47

imposed on himself, using religious, mythic, and primitive traditions. In fact, once we know the underlying patterns, these episodes must be comic or Faulkner will seem ghoulish. Let me review his game plan[2] and then reconsider some of those examples of his humor.

The first rule for Faulkner's game plan was to parallel the twenty-one chapters of *Light in August* with the twenty-one chapters of the St. John Gospel. Consider some of the prominent stories. Echoing John's famous statement, "In the beginning was the Word, and the Word was with God," is Lena's insistent faith in the "word" of Lucas, who is, after all, the father:

> "I said for him to . . . just send me word. . . . Like as not, he already sent me the word and it got lost. . . . I told him . . . 'You just send me your mouthword.' . . . But me and Lucas dont need no word promises between us. . . . he [must have] sent the word and it got lost."[3]

The healing of the lame man by immersion occurs in chapter 5 where, in Faulkner, Joe is repeatedly immersed in liquids, real and imagined:

> In the less than halflight he appeared to be watching his body . . . turning slow and lascivious in a whispering of gutter filth like a drowned corpse in a thick still black pool of more than water. . . . The dark air breathed upon him, . . . he could feel the dark air like water; . . . He watched his body grow white out of the darkness like a kodak print emerging from the liquid. (99–100)

The teaching in the temple—learning the Father's will—occurs in chapter 7, the chapter in which McEachern is trying to teach Joe his catechism, while Joe is actually learning his father's will: "the two backs in their rigid abnegation of all compromise more alike than actual blood could have made them" (139). In John 14 the end of the Last Supper is signaled by the words "Arise, let us go hence," just as in Faulkner's 14 Joe "rises" (317) and goes to turn himself in, at peace because he " 'dont have to bother about having to eat anymore' " (320). Most important, the crucifixion occurs in chapter 19, the chapter in which Joe, slain and castrated, soars into memory like a "rising rocket" on the "black blast" of his breath.

The second rule of Faulkner's game plan was that he know and respond to biblical commentary on John.[4] Consider just the outlines of the two books. Following John's prologue, the chapters through 12 are called the Book of Signs; chapters 13 through 20, the final days, are the Book of Glory; and chapter 21 was written by someone other than John. In *Light in August*, after the coming and history of Lena, the chapters through 12 depict events leading up to the explanation of the murder; chapters 13 through 20 depict Joe's final days; while chapter 21, beyond Jefferson, introduces a new narrator.

The third rule was that John be read in the light of James Frazer's complete work, *The Golden Bough*, not in any casual way, but using particular sections to develop particular themes in John. For example, the Good Shepherd discourse in John's chapter 10 opens, "He that entereth not by the door into the sheepfold, but climbeth up some other way, the same is a thief and a robber." In Faulkner's chapter 10, Joe's first action is to guide himself out the door, saying, about his own body, "It never would have opened a window and climbed through it." And his last action is to climb into Joanna's window, feeling (as he later thinks) "like a thief, a robber." But a fuller explanation of his odd behavior in this chapter may be found in Frazer's discussions of St. George's Day, when animals, first driven out to spring pasture, are exposed to the hazards of wolves and witches. The shepherd ceremonies involve doors and gates, begging processions, giving "tail money," and coupling animals.[5] Thus Joe herds his body, "flagged and spurred," along a "thousand streets," taking "begged and stolen rides," sitting "with his still, hard face" beside a driver who does not know "who or what" the passenger is, and pausing "beneath the dark and equivocal and symbolic archways of midnight [where] he bedded with the women and paid them when he had the money, and when he did not have it he bedded anyway" (210–11).

Without considering the other rules—for example, the reli-

gious and mythic character parallels such as Christmas as Christ
and his precursor, Dionysus—we might ask, how important is it
to know Faulkner's game plan? Certainly, it can settle some
critical questions. For example, in chapter 20, when Hightower
is seen as the Doubting Thomas who must be shown everything
before he believes, we are less likely to glorify his one dim
moment of insight. But a more important reason involves
Faulkner's humor, his enjoyment in creating many levels of
understanding. Back in chapter 10, we ought finally to respond
to his pleasure in depicting a driver not knowing "who or what"
his passenger was, when the "still, hard face" might be the face
of a sheep. Or that Joe's "bedding" with the prostitutes could
represent the coupling of animals, including the "tail money."
Moreover, like Joyce, burying flower references in his *Ulysses*
chapter on the Lotus Eaters, Faulkner must have enjoyed burying animal references in the stream of Joe's just barely conscious
hearing: *here bobbie, here kid, chicken feed, keep, leave it lay,*
and *hey kid*. It might even include in*stall*ment; certainly the
poet in Faulkner would have wanted us to pause over every
word.

Let us return to the first three examples of Faulkner's humor,
since all of them happen to occur in chapter 6, John's multiplication of the loaves. Now a less brilliant parallel for this story might
present a picnic, to which more and more come and find themselves satisfied, the "miracle" arising from the sharing. But
Faulkner understood that when John said the five barley loaves
multiplied, he meant there were twelve baskets of leftovers. The
same tough insistence arises in the accompanying discourse on
the Bread of Life, which John alone calls flesh: "for my flesh is
meat indeed." To parallel these themes of food replication and
the Eucharist,[6] Faulkner followed the discussion in Frazer on
homeopathic magic and eating the god's flesh.

Consider first the homeopathic magic. After all, the principle
behind the multiplication of the loaves is of like producing like.
Presumably, Jesus could have made food out of thin air, but

instead, he makes bread out of bread. So when the primitive wishes to multiply something, he will make a likeness of the desired object or act out its behavior. Frazer reports that the Cora Indians create a wax or clay model of food which they bury in a mountain cave. The Todas of India make an offering of a silver buffalo. The Arunta mimic the appearance of the emu, wearing long-necked headdresses and peering in all directions. Or to multiply the witchetty grub, they squat in a long narrow structure and then shuffle out, pantomiming and singing of its emergence from the chrysalis. In fact, Frazer notes that animal representations in prehistoric caves and Egyptian hieroglyphics have been edible prey rather than dangerous carnivores, suggesting a strong belief in the efficacy of artistic representation.[7] We must take care what monsters we create.

The ceremony of the Eucharist is related to this homeopathic principle of like producing like. Bread, made of grain, symbolizes (as does wine) the primitive hopes for next year's crop. Grain is used to reproduce grain. Moreover, the mouth is anciently a dual symbol of both destruction and creativity. You take in the power of what you eat; you give power to what you say. Thus, the primitive, wishing to ensure next year's crop, will mark this year's with first-fruit ceremonies. Beginning with purgatives, the Creek Indians drink "a bitter decoction of button-snake root in order to vomit and purge their sinful bodies" or the Seminoles drink a nauseous "Black Drink." Frazer suggests that these purgatives have their parallel in the Eucharistic fasting, both honoring the sacredness of the new food. But then even confession, given before communion, can be seen as a cleansing of the soul by the mouth.

Once purified, the people take the first of the harvest, make a dough man, and break it into pieces so that all may eat of it. In France, a man made of dough was hung on a tree and carried to the mayor's house, kept there until the vintage was over, then broken in pieces and handed out for the people to eat. The Aztecs made images of their god, fashioned out of seeds and kneaded into a dough with the blood of children. Even when the first fruits were of war, the dough men might be made of a "paste," using the ashes of the victims.[8]

How does this become the stuff of Faulkner's comedy? Chapter 6 describes Joe's beginnings at the orphanage. That Joe is "bred" in this chapter on bread is one example of Faulkner's humor. Actually, appropriate to Joe Christmas as J.C., Bethlehem means House of Bread. Also appropriate to the Eucharist is that Joe, descendant of Ham, is fed "bread, with ham between" on the way out of the orphanage, and "bread, with ham between" on the way back.[9] Moreover, Joe goes from the bleakness of the "cinderstrewnpacked compound" with its fence like "a parade of starved soldiers," to what McEachern promises and delivers: food and shelter under the care of Christian people, even as he ironically dispatches the "heathenish name" of Christmas under the banner of "he will eat my bread" (136).

As we know, however, man does not live by bread alone. The real multiplication going on in this chapter is both less physical and more sustaining. Echoing the ceremonies of the Arunta, squatting in and shuffling out of long, narrow structures, singing of the witchetty grub, Faulkner shows the process of Joe's birth as a "grub." Born "out of the mouths" as the "little nigger bastard," Joe is both the disgusting pink worm at the heart of the South's rose, and he is the Eucharistic food, the little dough man, to be broken and fed to more and more communicants. The humor is pretty grim.

Central to the process is the dietitian, the one who determines how much and what kind of food she will then feed to everyone. Joe thinks of her as "a mechanical adjunct to eating, food, the diningroom, the ceremony of eating at the wooden forms." He finds and eats the toothpaste because of her. In fact, while he thinks of her as "young, a little fullbodied, smooth, pink-and-white . . . making his mouth think of something sweet and sticky to eat, and also pinkcolored and surreptitious" (112), she also thinks of him in terms of food—the *"pea in a pan full of coffee beans"* (122). Now when we consider these hints of cannibalism in the context of John's "for my flesh is meat indeed" and Frazer's little dough men, fashioned from a paste with the blood of children or the ashes of victims, we had better start laughing before we begin to squirm.

The replicating birth process involves many long, narrow structures, including tubes, passageways, and especially corridors. Of course, corridors are found elsewhere in Faulkner, but the insistence here (occurring fourteen times versus three other times in the book),[10] illustrates that, in establishing his parallels, Faulkner felt free to use favorite images.

In any case, following the corridor to the dietitian's room, Joe finds the tube of toothpaste, watches "the pink worm" coil onto his finger until he hears voices, whereupon he slips behind the curtain and, "squatting," feels the "once cylindrical tube" and tastes "the cool invisible worm as it coiled onto his finger." It is this worm which produces the first creation, a kind of test-tube concoction:

> Motionless now, utterly contemplative, he seemed to stoop above himself like a chemist in his laboratory, waiting. He didn't have to wait long. At once the paste which he had already swallowed lifted inside him, trying to get back out. . . . In the rife, pinkwomansmelling obscurity behind the curtain he squatted, pinkfoamed, listening to his insides, waiting with astonished fatalism for what was about to happen to him. Then it happened. He said to himself with complete and passive surrender: "Well, here I am." (114)

"Here I am," he says, as if he had not been there before. That I-am, the *ego eimi*, as in "I am the bread of life," has great significance in John. It reflects the solemn I-am of the Old Testament (I AM THAT I AM, or "I am Yahweh"), a formula important to pagan religions as well.

Joe's I-am has come from his vomiting, a reaction to his fearful ingesting of the dietitian's "pink worm" (what a marvelous metaphor for illicit sex!). When the dietitian promptly sings out the name of this grub, this transubstantiated pink worm, as "little nigger bastard," she exemplifies and fosters the multiplication process. It is a process which involves taking something in—

usually with the eyes—something which, reacting with an inner guilt or fear, multiplies within, and produces a monster through the mouth. In the next few days, because Joe is "always against her eyelids or upon her retinae," the dietitian finally seeks him in the "empty corridor," and offers him money to buy "'some to eat every day for a week.'" What poor Joe envisions is a boundless multiplication of the toothpaste—"the ranked tubes . . . like corded wood, endless and terrifying"—which causes "his whole being" to coil "in a rich and passionate revulsion." And that response produces in the dietitian a "long shuddering breath," with this doubled monster: "'You little nigger bastard! You nigger bastard'" (115–17).

The chapter is rife with such strange engendering, one of the funniest being when the janitor's eyes repeatedly "envelop" the dietitian, they "contract upon her shape and being," until she produces the mouth monster (Yes, Joe will be sent to the "nigger orphanage"), whereupon "the eyes released her and enveloped her again" before the janitor at last departs, pronouncing his final "womanfilth" (123–24).

If we might agree that Joe as "little nigger bastard" is the child of the dietitian and the janitor—who made evil "'get up and walk God's world. . . . Out of the mouths of little children'"—we might ask how this unwanted conception came about. In keeping with the chapter's many eyes, the watching and the divination of the psychic dietitian and the mad janitor, "mad eyes looking into mad eyes" (119), the most Faulknerian explanation may be that they are like the "seers," the sacred men and women of the temple. According to Frazer, the "sacredness" of these ancient divines was used to explain both their madness and their begats, even their dirtiness. The Syrian "holy men" often wore "filthy garments," yet none would shrink from them because they were thought to be acting in God's name and speaking with his voice. Among the Semites, sanctuaries were "the seats of profligate rites," and the offspring of the sacred men and women were believed to be the emanations of "uncouth but worshipful idols." In both Asia and Africa, sacred prostitutes attached to the temples were regarded as the wives of the god.[11] Now Faulkner would have found these ideas funny—there is evidence that Frazer did—and enjoyed creating his parallel of the janitor, a "small, dirty man," who says, " 'Don't lie to me, to the Lord God,' " and produces his little monster with the temple prostitute, herself exemplifying " 'womanfilth. . . . Before the face of God' " (123–24).

Certainly I have been guided by the echoes of Faulkner's laughter—raunchy, sexist, or cute as it often is—throughout *Light in August*. Let me give one last example. Although I knew that Hightower represented Hippolytus (with his many associations to horses), I must have read Frazer's extended description of this figure many times before I noticed this singular formulation: "Diana, for the love she bore Hippolytus, persuaded the leech Aesculapius to bring her fair hunter back to life by his simples."[12] Simples? What are simples? Checking with the OED, I decided this referred not to Hippolytus's elementary parts but to Aesculapius's herbs. But the word had made me laugh. Had it made Faulkner laugh? Sure enough, when I looked up the word "simple" in the concordance, it led me to a passage in chapter 16, in which Hightower is responding to the lowly Byron (who is trying to bring him back to life), by saying: " 'That's all. That's simple. Simple. Simple.' Apparently he cannot stop saying it. 'Simple. Simple.' " (368).

It is interesting that the towering geniuses have frequently turned to organizing frameworks for their writing. Chaucer used Boccaccio and Boethius; Shakespeare used Plutarch and Holinshed; Milton used the Bible and the Talmud. With the rise of nineteenth-century Romanticism, which glorified the individual imagination, the practice of telling tales based on the classics came into disfavor. Although Coleridge evidently used ships' logs for his descriptions in "The Rime of the Ancient Mariner," he kept it quiet. Writers of the twentieth century such as Eliot, Pound, and especially Joyce and Faulkner returned to the practice, but Faulkner was Romantic enough not to admit it. So it will take the patient work of scholars to reveal what we might have guessed all along: that Faulkner was writing on the highest levels of literary expression, where it may be that the brain so teems with ideas and images that the writer needs only the container to hold and shape the ripeness of it all. Still, the fact that Faulkner's Mississippi folk have immortal forms beneath their not-so-simple adventures, that's what's so funny about *Light in August*.

NOTES

1. Audrey Bledsoe, "Faulkner's Chiaroscuro: Comedy in *Light in August*," *Notes on Mississippi Writers*, 9 (Winter 1979), 55–63.

2. Described in my article, "St. John and Frazer in *Light in August*: Biblical Form and Mythic Function," *Bulletin of Research in the Humanities*, 83 (Spring 1980), 9–26.

3. William Faulkner, *Light in August* (New York: Random House, 1968), 16–17. All subsequent references are to this edition.

4. We have evidence that Faulkner read such commentary. Laurence Stallings wrote from Hollywood: "Unlike practically everyone else, he has remained cold sober. He bought one book to read over his lonely nights. It is a second-hand twelve volume . . . Cambridge edition of the Holy Bible." Joseph Blotner, *Faulkner: A Biography* (New York: Random House, 1974), 1:777.

5. James Frazer, "St. George and the Parilia," *The Golden Bough: A Study in Magic and Religion*, 3d ed. (New York: St. Martin's Press, 1911–15), 2:342–48.

6. Another feature of John 6 is Jesus' walking on the water. John emphasizes Jesus' miraculous departure in the middle of the night, the people wondering how he came to the other shore. In Faulkner we have two mid-night departures: when Joe is carried off, "riding high in the invisible arms," he thinks of another orphanage child, Alice, "grown heroic at the instant of vanishment beyond the clashedto gates, fading without diminution of size into something nameless and splendid, like a sunset" (128). This demonstrates Faulkner's ability to fold even disparate themes in on each other.

7. Frazer, "Sympathetic Magic," *The Golden Bough*, 1:52–219.

8. Frazer, "Eating the God," *The Golden Bough*, 8:48–108.

9. The precedent is in Joyce's Laestrygonian chapter of *Ulysses:* "Sandwich? Ham and his descendants mustered and bred there."

10. Carl Ficken notes corridors are the dominant image in chapter 6. See "A Critical and Textual Study of William Faulkner's *Light in August*" (Ph.D. diss., University of South Carolina, 1973), 125–26.

11. Frazer, "Sacred Men and Women," *The Golden Bough*, 5:57–109.

12. Frazer, "Diana and Virbius," *The Golden Bough*, 1:20.

# Faulkner's "Was" and Uncle Adam's Cow

## Daniel Hoffman

*"There is no such thing as* was—*only* is. *If* was *existed, there would be no grief or sorrow."*
—WILLIAM FAULKNER

### 1

Faulkner's "Was" is either his most successful comic story, or one of the most objectionable. Assuming for the moment the comic view, there is no denying that the characters in this knockabout farce are by Restoration comedy out of Li'l Abner: the woman-shy old bachelor, the huntin'-gamblin' country squire, the mincing overaged coquette; add for good measure to this seamless patchwork of stereotypes the scheming servant familiar in *commedia dell'arte*. But the venue is Dogpatch, or somewhere like it. Faulkner himself has mentioned "a certain sociological importance" in defining the backcountry setting of "Was"; he wished, he says, "to show my country as it really was in those days. The elegance of the colonial plantation didn't exist in my country. My country was still frontier. . . . People lived from day to day, with a bluff and crude hardiness, but with a certain simplicity."[1] Every reader responds to the contrast, in "Was," between the "certain simplicity" of this near-frontier life and the complexity of plot of which it is the setting. Is it only the country setting that makes us think, as Lewis Dabney says, that in this tale "through the folklore he cherishes Faulkner reaches back to the Southern frontier, subverting the official legend of the old South"?[2]

The opinion that Faulkner is using, or writing, folk humor remains for the most part a general statement, unsubstantiated by demonstration of specific allegiances to folk traditions. One reason for the paucity of documentation on this head is probably

the paucity of documentation available. We know from the testi-
mony of those who knew him, those who grew up with Faulkner
in Oxford, that

> there was still a strong tradition of oral story-telling in the South of
> Faulkner's boyhood, and traces of it survive even yet. . . . Faulkner
> himself knew this oral tradition well, both as listener and as nar-
> rator. . . . From my own boyhood days in Oxford, Mississippi, I can
> well remember the aging veterans (known locally, with affectionate
> indulgence, as 'The Sons of Rest'), sitting under the trees around the
> courthouse and swapping stories about the war. But Faulkner seems
> to have learned even more about it from the women at home.[3]

Calvin S. Brown includes, as folktales, both the tall tale and the
family reminiscence, including "Was" in the latter. But this is a
grouping too loosely conceived to show that Faulkner's "Was" is
indeed, as Dabney terms it, a "classic comedy of the frontier."

When we seek evidence of the folktales Faulkner knew, they
prove hard to pin down. We know he heard such things, and told
them, among those loiterers on the courthouse steps as well as to
children at his daughter's parties, to drinking companions, and
especially to friends on the annual pilgrimage to General Stone's
camp in the wilderness. One such fellow-hunter reports, "Sometimes at night he'd tell stories. He'd tell some tall tales like the
rest of us would around there—yarns and things. I don't remember too many of them. There were so many tales told I
didn't try to keep up with them. He could tell some big ones all
right. Some of them he kind of made up as he went along."[4]
Nobody took down what Faulkner said on any of these hunting
trips; in fact he was not recorded at all until he was a visiting
writer at the University of Virginia, at Nagano, and at West
Point, where they taped and transcribed every word he said in
classrooms and seminars. But that is not where folktales are told,
so the best evidence we have of Faulkner's participation in the
old tradition of Southern storytelling remains the pages of his
fiction—as in "Was." Let us examine the text of "Was," and by a
dissection which will not be a murder, since the tale is indestruc-
tible, we can look at its constituent parts to determine which are

derived from folklore, and perhaps even discover from what folklore "Was," however circuitously, is descended.

This is but one of the problems with the tale, however. Having determined whether or not "Was" is in the American folk humor tradition, we must then consider whether it is simply a short story based on comic stereotypes, or is it, in some way, an appropriate opening chapter in a novel of tragic meaning? And then there is the manner of its telling: The three opening paragraphs present the rest of the tale as the total recall of an old man, Isaac McCaslin, remembering the total recall of his elder cousin McCaslin Edmonds, as Cass Edmonds had told the tale to him many years after its occurrence. Is this device, which gives the story simultaneous closeness and distance, one of Faulkner's idiosyncratic affectations, or is it a functionally effective means of presenting what *"was"* as what *"is,"* of controlling the point of view? If the latter, then why does "Was" have as its actual narrator a nine-year-old boy who tells none of the succeeding chapters of *Go Down, Moses?* And finally, what is the meaning of "Was"? Is it, as some readers have maintained, a sentimental recreation of old times on the plantation, or, as others have done, a black comedy in which the toying with slavery, the avoidance of adult responsibility, and the demeaning treatment of women convey the real meaning of the tale, grotesquely embedded in a seeming farandole of frontier folk humor? To answer these queries will require a definition of the kind of a book *Go Down, Moses* is, whether a short story collection, a novel, or something else.

2

A student at Virginia, during one of those sessions in which every word was taped, asked Faulkner if he remembered the germ of his story "Was." The author replied,

> The germ of the story was one of the three oldest ideas that man can write about, which is love, sex. And to me it was comic, of the man that had got himself involved in an engagement, and he himself

couldn't extricate himself and . . . he had to call on his brother, and his brother used the only tools he had, which was his ability to play poker. Which to me was funny.[5]

So "Was" is a love story, a comic love story. In fact it is also the story of a hunt, a quest, and a wager. Let me capitalize these, for they are the archetypal shapes which gird the structure of Faulkner's comic fable: The Hunt, The Courtships (these subsume The Quest), and The Wager, which provides a solution for the predicament of "the man that had got himself involved in an engagement, and he couldn't extricate himself."

The tale begins with Uncle Buck and Uncle Buddy McCaslin chasing a fox through their house; when caught, he will be kept in a cage until released on a day when they feel like hunting him. But now Uncle Buck, with nine-year-old Cass, must set out on a longer hunt, for his Negro, Tomey's Turl, has run off to visit his girl friend Tennie who is a slave on the Beauchamp place miles away. Why does Buck go after Turl, since Mr. Hubert Beauchamp would surely return him? Because Hubert would bring with him his maiden sister Sophonsiba, and would stay for a week's visit while Sophonsiba tries to entrap Buck in matrimony. In the event, that is what happens at Beauchamp's, for Tomey's Turl, in collusion with Sophonsiba, eludes capture so Buck and Cass must spend the night, and Miss Sophonsiba awaits Buck in the very bed he is likeliest to enter when he climbs the dark stairs. Along the way, Buck and Hubert had made a bet, which Hubert, on a technicality, has lost. So when Hubert presses his claim that to redeem the Beauchamp honor Buck must marry the woman whose bed he had violated, the two obligations offset one another. And Buck used "the only tools he had, which was his ability to play poker." His freedom is wagered against the five hundred dollar bet. Or, we might say, Sophonsiba is wagered against the five hundred dollars.

This is a bare skeleton of the tale—more details will follow—but it puts one in mind of an old story:

One time there was two old men that lived up Magnetic Holler, right close to a little branch they call Mystic Spring nowadays. One of these fellows was Uncle Adam, and he had a wife. The other one was knowed as Uncle Dick, and he didn't have no wife, but he had two cows. They got to trading jackknives and shotguns, and finally Uncle Adam swapped his wife for one of Uncle Dick's cows. Folks used to trade wives pretty free in them days, and nobody said much about it. Lots of them wasn't really married anyhow, so there wasn't no great harm done.

But it wasn't long till word got around that Uncle Adam's woman had up and left him, and moved all her stuff over to Uncle Dick's cabin. The next time Uncle Adam come into town, somebody asked him if Uncle Dick had stole his wife. "Hell no," says Uncle Adam, "it was a fair swap, all open and above board. Dick gave me his best cow for the old woman, and two dollars boot."

Folks got to laughing about it, and one day the sheriff stopped Uncle Adam on the street. "This here trading wives is against the law nowadays," says he. "And everybody knows a woman is worth more than a cow, anyhow." Uncle Adam laughed right in the sheriff's face. "Don't you believe it, Sheriff," he says, "don't you believe it. Why, that cow of mine is three-fourths Jersey!"

That's folklore, the way it's told by Vance Randolph, the collector of folktales from the Ozarks.[6] I could find no text closer to the Oxford courthouse steps than this, from over the state line in Arkansas. Randolph tells the tale as it was told to him by a neighbor in Eureka Springs back in 1950. The story is supposed to have really happened there around 1880, but by then the yarn was already frayed from many tellings. Annotations by the folklore scholar Herbert Halpert show that it was in print in 1800; far from being uniquely "true" in Eureka Springs, this is a tale widespread in American folklore. Since Faulkner wrote "Was" in 1940, twelve years before Vance Randolph published the yarn in *Who Blowed Up the Church House?*, we cannot say that the Arkansas story is the source of "Was." But it seems very likely Faulkner heard it, or something very like it, told as true, years before, in the environs of Oxford, Mississippi. A great writer is not so poor in invention that he cannot make up the plot of a joke, if need be; should he instead prefer to use a hand-me-down from the circle on the courthouse steps, there must be reasons for his doing so, and differences between what he heard told to him and what he tells to us. Faulkner has indeed transformed what he borrowed.

Before considering his transformations, however, let it be said that Vance Randolph is a skilled folk raconteur. Reviewing his books, I pointed out long ago that he is an adept in the art—of which Mark Twain was our principal master—of seeming to speak in the vernacular.[7] Randolph lived in a community of backcountry Homers, like Lafayette County, Mississippi, and his art is an emulation of, or perhaps improvement upon, theirs. In pacing, detail, order of events, and sentence length, Randolph is almost always right. He tells the tale as it should be told:

> One time there was two men that lived up Magnetic Holler, right close to a little branch they call Mystic Spring nowadays.

Already he has told us who, where, and when, the "when" being a good deal earlier than "nowadays." The aura of place names is introduced, and the phrase "lived . . . right close to a little branch" surely suggests that these two men lived on a mountain, far from town: up because close to Mystic Spring; far from town because the stream was still just a little branch.

Faulkner, too, has modelled his language, his syntax, the rhythms of his sentences, on the speech of country people. His purposes are more complex than Randolph's, yet his style has no more elegancies of expression than the plantations in his story have columns or porticos. His tone is that of Southern vernacular speech. But let us see what he makes of the plot he shares with Vance Randolph's joke. Randolph, repeating the tale as it was told to him by a fellow who told it as it was told to him, makes nothing of it. He tells it for its own sake, and that's that. We may remember that Yeats, in *The Celtic Twilight*, defined folktales as "stories that have no moral."

Therefore it doesn't bother the teller that his tale is really rather cruel, and crude, and sexist, and otherwise filled with socially undesirable opinions. In fact his attention may well not be fixed on the "uncompliment" the story pays to Uncle Adam's wife and by extension to anyone else's wife or to any other woman within hearing. But of course who would tell a joke like this with a woman within hearing? The teller's attention is probably fixed on Uncle Dick and Uncle Adam, on their masculine devotion to swapping, to see who gets the better end of the swap, and on their not unattractive attitude to the law, which enables Uncle Adam to tell off the sheriff with a jest.

Nonetheless, no hearer can escape making the equation which is the point of the story: Wife = Cow. This is of course a judgment of value. Surely the weight of the equation is repellent to our moral sensibilities: a woman is equated to a beast, whether of burden, of the dairy, or of pleasure. There is in the Ozark tale the suggested connection of sex with bestiality, though to be sure this remains veiled, implicit. The equation appears as a perfectly natural, taken-for-granted aspect, indeed, an expression of the male ethos which is the basis of the story.

In the folktale, plot is all; the characters are abstractions, mere types. They exist for the sake of the action, and our interest is in what happened. For Faulkner, however, character is all, and plot is a means of revealing it. Our interest is in what happened to whom, and why did he do what he did. Still, his opening sentence, true to the formula of oral telling, like Randolph's, sets the scene, the place, and names the characters:

> When he and Uncle Buck ran back to the house from discovering that Tomey's Turl had run again, they heard Uncle Buddy cursing and bellowing in the kitchen, then the fox and the dogs came out of the kitchen and crossed the hall into the dogs' room. . . .

That's not a sentence yet, it goes on for half a page, but it's enough to start with.[8] One's first question well might be, what in the hell is happening? A pack of dogs chasing a fox from the kitchen into the dogs' own room? And who are "he" and "Uncle Buck" and "Uncle Buddy" and "Tomey's Turl"?

If we have read *The Unvanquished* we know about Uncle Buck

and Uncle Buddy, and since Isaac McCaslin is retelling Cass Edmonds's remembrance of what happened, "he" in this story is Cass. But what about Tomey's Turl? What a strange way to name a child, and keep calling him that as he grows into manhood. But of course Tomey's Turl, in 1859, is a slave. So it's all right to call him by an eponym otherwise appropriate to a racehorse.

Or, to be more accurate, it never occurs to anyone in the story *not* to call him that way. Probably didn't occur to him either. It's just the way it is. But Faulkner doesn't merely accept everything that his tale accepts, or his characters accept. Not that he ever says he doesn't, but if we are attentive to the incidental detail we can sense what Faulkner's attitude is, because he evokes an attitude in us.

This is often done by juxtaposition, as in "Tomey's Turl had run again . . . then the fox and the dogs came out of the kitchen," subliminally establishing a relationship between the running of Tomey's Turl and of the fox. And indeed, later, when Uncle Buck and Cass have pursued Tomey's Turl to the Hubert Beauchamp plantation, several hours' ride away, and still not found him, Mr. Hubert unleashes his pack of hounds to track down Turl, who, like a fox, leads the hounds a merry chase. By nightfall, "they found that Tomey's Turl had doubled and was making a long swing back toward the house. 'I godfrey, we've got him,' Uncle Buck said. 'He's going to earth. We'll cut back to the house and head him before he can den'" (17–18).

As Lewis Dabney has observed of this hunt-and-chase, "There are rules: it is a ritual dance, appropriate to the introduction of the old regime; not, however, the predictable and decorous minuet, or even a gavotte, but a *courante,* a run." This ritual dance Dabney shows to be a comic inversion of a much-collected Negro folk narrative, which tells of the pursuit of runaway slaves by "paterollers" whose runs were in earnest, not in fun.[9]

It is typical of Faulkner to reverse, turn inside out, or stand on its head whichever conventions he borrows or steals. The whole tale is a reversal of our expectations about plantation life, so rough and ready do we find it. And Faulkner has turned inside out for his own purposes yet another strain of Negro folklore. In

Joel Chandler Harris's familiar retellings, Bre'r Rabbit cleverly escapes from Bre'r Fox. But Faulkner makes Bre'r Fox not the pursuer but the pursued, and Tomey's Turl's knowledge of Uncle Buck, of dogs, of his mule, and of the countryside makes possible his foxlike evasion of the pursuit by the white squires and their pack of hounds and their fyce.

The grotesqueries of the fox-hunting imagery serves a further purpose in "Was," for the way foxes were then hunted in back-country Mississippi is a parody of the formal English model, which Faulkner himself so enjoyed, scarlet jacket and all, both in Oxford and in the fox-hunting country of Virginia. In "Was" the fox-hunting vocabulary establishes an executive metaphor for the story, and by the inevitably satirical comparison to hunts which this one parodies, lays the groundwork for the social pretensions of Miss Sophonsiba Beauchamp. Further, the hunting of Tomey's Turl brings into *Go Down, Moses* the theme of the hunt itself; what is here parodic and comic will become sacramental in "The Old People" and epical in "The Bear."

If hunting the runaway slave is a game, Uncles Buck and Buddy, superannuated boys, turn all of life into games. In "Was" they are comic characters, without a hint of Buck's wartime bloodymindedness in *The Unvanquished*, which, though written earlier, takes place a few years later. Even the McCaslin twins' manumission of their slaves is a game, a ritual; these bachelor antebellum abolitionists have moved out of their father's mansion, letting free those slaves who would leave, letting live in the unfinished house the rest whom they lock up each evening in full knowledge that the Negroes are escaping out the back way. It is a point of honor on both sides that the escapes be made not in the brothers' sight, so as not to embarrass them. Tomey's Turl has overstepped the rules by taking off for the Beauchamp place, so, according to those rules, he is pursued. It's all part of the game.

As Uncle Buck and Cass arrive near the Beauchamps'

> they could already hear Mr Hubert's dinner horn a mile away. . . .
> The boy was still sitting on the gatepost, blowing the horn—there
> was no gate there; just two posts and a nigger boy about his size
> sitting on one of them, blowing a fox-horn; this was what Miss

Sophonsiba was still reminding people was named Warwick even
when they had already known for a long time that's what she aimed
to have it called, until when they wouldn't call it Warwick she
wouldn't even seem to know what they were talking about and it
would sound as if she and Mr Hubert owned two separate plantations covering the same area of ground, one on top of the other. (9)

This is our first intimation of Miss Sophonsiba, who in backwoods Mississippi, inhabiting a bare farmhouse, clings to the
romantic fiction that her brother, if he got his deserts, is the Earl
of Warwick. This is by no means the only romantic fiction to
which she clings, but let's not omit to notice that the presumed
Earl is discovered dipping his bare feet in the springhouse,
drinking a toddy. There is in Faulkner's story a clash between
their conceptions of reality: Miss Sophonsiba's genteel feminine
version of reality as romance *versus* the male version of her
romance as reality. Hubert, Uncle Buck, Uncle Buddy, these are
the males in the story, and their world is one of the hunt, the
chase, and, as we soon see, the gaming table.

One can't but feel for Miss Sophonsiba, placed by fate in so
unpropitious a place for the nurture of her fantasies of romance.
She's getting on a bit, has a roan tooth, is still unmarried, and
would seem to have no real prospects. But she has pluck. She
has the rallying coquettry of the true Southern belle who never
passes up an opportunity to be charming to a man in the hope,
however insubstantial, that he may, somehow, succumb to her
charms.

Entering the hall in a jangle of earrings and a cloud of perfume, she greets Uncle Buck with "Welcome to Warwick."

"I just come to get my nigger," Uncle Buck said. "Then we got to get
on back home."
Then Miss Sophonsiba said something about a bumblebee, but he
couldn't remember that. It was too fast and there was too much of it,
the earrings and beads clashing and jingling like little trace chains on
a toy mule trotting and the perfume stronger too, . . . something
about Uncle Buck was a bee sipping from flower to flower and not
staying long anywhere and all that stored sweetness to be wasted on
Uncle Buddy's desert air, . . . or maybe the honey was being stored

up against the advent of a queen and who was the lucky queen and when? "Ma'am?" Uncle Buck said. Then Mr Hubert said:

"Hah. A buck bee. I reckon that nigger's going to think he's a buck hornet, once he lays hands on him. But I reckon what Buck's thinking about sipping right now is some meat gravy and biscuit and a cup of coffee. And so am I." (11)

What is notable here is that Miss Sophonsiba's sexuality has indeed reached a male observer—nine-year-old Cass, who is made dizzy by her perfume and the tingling of her earrings. But as for Uncle Buck, he takes no notice of her at all.

Miss Sophonsiba said Uncle Buck was just a confirmed roving bachelor from the cradle born and this time Uncle Buck even quit chewing and looked and said, Yes, ma'am, he sure was, and born too late at it ever to change now. . . . (11–12)

Miss Sophonsiba will not be discouraged, as she continues her efforts at raillery with no visible success. In this company of fox hunters and nigger hunters she too is a hunter—as Hubert says, a Buck hunter.

The hunting of Tomey's Turl is a complicated, nightlong rigamarole. Especially since he has been in the kitchen during most of the foregoing, and, when Buck and Hubert go upstairs to take a nap before resuming the chase, little Cass finds Tomey's Turl in the back yard. Cass warns Turl, " 'They're going to put the dogs on you when they get up,' " but that doesn't faze him. " 'I got protection now. All I needs to do is to keep Old Buck from ketching me unto I gets the word' " (13).

"What word?" he said. . . . "Is Mr Hubert going to buy you from Uncle Buck?"

"Huh," Tomey's Turl said again. "I got more protection than whut Mr Hubert got even. . . . I gonter tell you something to remember: anytime you wants to git something done, from hoeing out a crop to getting married, just get the womenfolks to working at it. Then all you needs to do is set down and wait. You member that." (13)

With this sibylline prophecy Tomey's Turl disappears, to be pursued later in the afternoon. Cass, of course, doesn't understand Tomey's Turl's advice, and neither do we, unless, after having finished the tale, we happen to remember it. Resuming the hunt, Uncle Buck and Mr. Hubert have their troubles finding Tomey's Turl. After thrashing around on various blind leads, Mr. Hubert expostulates, "'I'll bet you five hundred dollars that all you got to do to catch that nigger is to walk up to Tennie's cabin after dark and call him'" (15). Before the words are out of his mouth, Uncle Buck has taken him up on it: "'Done!'"

Tracked at last to Tennie's cabin near the house, Tomey's Turl bursts out of it, knocking the wind out of Uncle Buck, and gets away once more. By now Mr. Hubert is asleep, snoring, upstairs in Warwick. The house is pitch dark when Uncle Buck and Cass return to it. They grope their way to the stairs.

> "Likely hers will be at the back," Uncle Buck said. "Where she can holler down to the kitchen without having to get up. Besides, an unmarried lady will sholy have her door locked with strangers in the house." (20)

Coming to a door in the darkness, Uncle Buck tries the knob, and it opens. They can barely make out a bedstead with a mosquito bar. Uncle Buck unbuttons his trousers and slips them off. "Uncle Buck lifted the mosquito-bar and raised his feet and rolled into the bed. That was when Miss Sophonsiba sat up on the other side of Uncle Buck and gave the first scream" (20–21).

Hubert comes in with his candle and says to Buck, "'Well, 'Filus, . . . She's got you at last'" (21). How quickly do fortunes turn in the hunts within these hunts! Buck, a moment ago the fox hunter of Tomey's Turl, has suddenly become the fox trapped by Miss Sophonsiba. As Hubert puts it,

> "You come into bear-country of your own free will and accord. . . . You had to crawl into the den and lay down by the bear. . . . After all, I'd like a little peace and quiet and freedom myself, now I got a chance for it. Yes, sir. She's got you, 'Filus, and you know it. You run a hard race and you run a good one, but you skun the hen-house one time too many." (22–23)

But just then, at the moment when it looks as though Uncle Buck has been outfoxed by the heiress of Warwick and her brother, who is as eager for a bachelorhood unencumbered by his sister's presence as is Uncle Buck himself—just then Uncle Buck turns foxy yet again. He recalls to Hubert that bet, made earlier in the evening, five hundred dollars that Uncle Buck would catch Tomey's Turl in Tennie's cabin. True, that's where Turl was *found*, but he wasn't *caught:* "'So you aim to hold me to that fool bet,'" Mr. Hubert asks. Uncle Buck replies, "'You took your chance too.'"

Chance is what it will hinge on, for Hubert fetches a deck of cards.

> "One hand," he said. "Draw. You shuffle, I cut, this boy deals. Five hundred dollars against Sibbey. And we'll settle this nigger business once and for all too. If you win, you buy Tennie; if I win, I buy that boy of yours. The price will be the same for each one: three hundred dollars."
> "Win?" Uncle Buck said. "The one that wins buys the niggers?"
> "Wins Sibbey, damn it!" Mr Hubert said. "Wins Sibbey! What the hell else are we setting up till midnight arguing about? The lowest hand wins Sibbey and buys the niggers." (24)

Uncle Buck seems a bit confused, but what about Mr. Hubert? Isn't he putting a dollar value on his own sister, the same as he has done for Tennie and Tomey's Turl? It's five hundred dollars instead of three, but what an undercutting of Sophonsiba's pretensions, to be laid out on the table, as it were, alongside the niggers. Here is the first phase of Faulkner's appropriation of the folktale plot told in "Uncle Adam and His Cow." But where in Vance Randolph's story each of the men involved felt that what he would get by swapping was more desirable than what he would give, in the wager of exchange which the poker game will settle, Faulkner has reversed the bettors' desires. Now each one wants to *lose* the woman, for these bettors are both bachelors from the cradle born, nor will they ever swap for a wife.

Without changing his impassive comic tone an iota, Faulkner has shown up the chauvinism of the Code of the Southern Gentleman. For it is the gentleman's code which is the basis of this action: a gentleman's word is his bond, hence Hubert is bound to honor his silly bet. And Uncle Buck is bound to marry Sophonsiba, unless, by a gentleman's agreement such as the game of poker, he should manage to win his freedom by losing the game.

But it is Hubert who loses the game, winning freedom from living with his sister. The last card, however, is yet to be played. Uncle Buddy, Buck's brother, with whom he lives in perfect bachelorhood, is not one to let Hubert outmanoeuvre him just because his brother was outfoxed. Foreseeing some such crisis, he had instructed Cass to return home in case of trouble. Now, while Uncle Buck hides out in the woods as Tomey's Turl had done earlier, Cass and Buddy ride to Warwick where Buddy will intervene with Hubert. "The only tools he had," as Faulkner said, "was his ability to play poker." We know, from *The Unvanquished*, that Buddy is a master at cards, better than Buck, for Buddy had won the game between them to determine which one should serve a hitch in the war. This time, the stakes are these:

> "Buck McCaslin against the land and niggers you have heard me promise as Sophonsiba's dowry on the day she marries. If I beat you, 'Filus marries Sibbey without any dowry. If you beat me, you get 'Filus. But I still get the three hundred dollars 'Filus owes me for Tennie. Is that correct?" (26)

This reverses the stakes in the first game between Hubert and Buck in which the winner won Sibbey. So Hubert tells Cass to "'Go to the back door and holler. Bring the first creature that answers, animal, mule or human, that can deal ten cards'" (27). Only Cass doesn't need to holler, for Tomey's Turl is squatting outside the door.

What follows is the second great portrayal in "Was" of playing stud-poker, the tension mounting as the cards, shuffled by Buddy, are dealt by Turl, the first card face down, the four successive cards face up. By the dealing of the fifth cards we know that Hubert has received a king, two threes, an ace, and another three; Buddy, six, two, four, and five. Uncle Buddy takes a look at his face-down card, then proposes new stakes: "'I'll bet you them two niggers. . . . Against the three hundred dollars Theophilus owes you for Tennie and the three hundred you and

Theophilus agreed on for Tomey's Turl.'" Hubert, not un-
naturally, restates the new stakes for clarification: "'If I win, you
take Sibbey without dowry and the two niggers, and I dont owe
'Filus anything. If you win——'" and Buddy interjects, "'Theophilus is free. And you owe him the three hundred dollars for
Tomey's Turl'" (28).

We know how Faulkner relished these dizzying complications,
the labyrinthine deals that match one set of values, one
character's wits, against another's, as witness Ratliff's purchase of
Ike Snopes's promissory note from Flem, and his scheme to buy
a herd of goats, in *The Hamlet*. Here, in the shifting stakes of the
two games of one-hand stud, there may well be Faulkner's
fictional replication of the intricate negotiations he himself was
involved in at the time he wrote the first draft of "Was." Harold
Guinzburg of Viking Press was negotiating to lure Faulkner away
from his regular publisher, Random House; Bennett Cerf, of
Random, made a counterproposal:

> If Guinzburg was willing only to match the offer of a $5,000 advance
> on the novel and book of stories, he should withdraw. If Random
> House was expected to cancel the contract for the next novel, the
> new publisher would be expected to buy the plates for *The Hamlet* at
> a reasonable price and the existing stock of copies; together these
> would come to just over $2,900.[10]

This is but one in a long series of contractual snarls with publishers, agents, and movie studios in which Faulkner was continually involved; in life he seldom showed the acumen in
getting out of such tight corners that he delighted in bestowing
upon Ratliff or Amodeus McCaslin.

If Uncle Buddy has the reputation of being unbeatable at
cards, Hubert is no slouch either; at the least, he's not one to
plunge forward without having carefully considered consequences. Listening to Buddy's restatement of the new stakes,
Hubert says,

> "That's just if I call you. . . . If I dont call you, 'Filus wont owe me
> nothing and I wont owe 'Filus nothing, unless I take that nigger
> which I have been trying to explain to you and him both for years

that I wont have on my place. . . . So what it comes down to is, I
either got to give a nigger away, or risk buying one that you done
already admitted you cant keep at home." (28)

His sister's fate doesn't even enter into this calculation of his
chances. Then, after a long silence, he turns up his face-down
card: another three.

"H'm," he said. "And you need a trey and there aint but four of them
and I already got three. And you just shuffled. And I cut afterward.
And if I call you, I will have to buy that nigger. Who dealt these
cards, Amodeus?" Only he didn't wait to be answered. He reached
out and tilted the lamp-shade, the light moving up Tomey's Turl's
arms that were supposed to be black but were not quite white. . . .
"I pass, Amodeus." (29)

And the comedy ends, as all comedies should, with a marriage in
prospect as, returning homeward, Cass "and Uncle Buddy and
Tennie all three rode in the wagon, while Tomey's Turl led the
pony"(29). The result of the many chases is that Uncle Buck has,
momentarily, escaped Sophonsiba's designs, he and Uncle
Buddy have reclaimed Tomey's Turl, and Tomey's Turl returns
with Tennie, his desire for whom had set the entire circus in
motion.

# 3

This has been rather a complicated story, what Faulkner
makes of the old folktale formula. He has surrounded the bare
motif with a created society, he has imbedded the trade-offs in a
fully realized sense of a whole way of life.

There are, it is true, a few points at which even the most
attentive reader must suspend his disbelief. We will no doubt
readily accept that Tomey's Turl has conspired with Sophonsiba
to delay Uncle Buck until after nightfall so that he will have to
spend the night at Warwick. We are further compelled to believe, or not to disbelieve, that Tomey's Turl is a step or two
ahead of both Uncle Buddy and Mr. Hubert in anticipating the
stakes and fixing the hands of cards he dealt them in their game

of stud. The stakes were complicated enough for the gamblers to have to keep redefining them; to anticipate what Hubert would do if he called and won requires a really intuitive knowledge of gamesman's psychology. Perhaps Uncle Buddy's prowess at the table is hereditary—is it possible that old Carothers McCaslin, his father and founder of the McCaslin estate and line, passed along this kind of hunch-playing among his other bequests of honor and ruthlessness? If so, we may better understand why Tomey's Turl can outfigure the two cardplayers, for he has more of Carothers McCaslin's blood in his veins than does either Uncle Buck or Uncle Buddy. No wonder he has "arms that were supposed to be black but were not quite white," no wonder Hubert had said "he wouldn't have that damn half-white Mc-Caslin on his place even as a free gift." (Hubert is the only one who calls Turl a McCaslin.) There is nothing in "Was" to indicate why Turl is a "half-white McCaslin," but when, in "The Bear," we, with Isaac McCaslin, pore over the half-illiterate ledgers kept by his father, Buck, and his uncle, Buddy, long before Isaac's birth, we learn of *"Turl Son of Thucydus @ Eunice Tomy born Jun 1833 yr stars fell Fathers will."* This statement exemplifies Faulkner's technique of withholding information while giving it, so that the very texture of his tale is a continuing cipher to be decoded as the reader becomes aware later of clues not clear or not available when he met the puzzle in the text. The ledgers tell of the mysterious suicide of Eunice, who drowned herself on Christmas Day, 1832. But we learn also that *"Tomasina called Tomy Daughter of Thucydus @ Eunice Born 1810 dide in Child bed June 1833. . . . Yr stars fell"* (269). And *"Fathers will,"* mentioned along with Turl's birth, bequeaths a thousand dollars to this light-skinned Negro described as the son of two slaves. Isaac laboriously works his way toward the revelation half-hidden in the ledgers: Carothers McCaslin had committed incest with his own half-black daughter, and so was both Turl's father and his grandfather. When Eunice realized that Carothers McCaslin, "her first lover," had made their daughter Tomasina pregnant, she drowned herself. Tomey's Turl, the clever fox, the amiable fugitive in the game of hunt-and-chase, who, on exiting from Tennie's cabin, catches his half-brother Buck as he runs into him so that Buck won't be hurt in a fall, this Turl is the fruit of Carothers McCaslin's original sin. Behind the farce and horseplay, behind the folk comedy in the bachelors' paradise of "Was" is the shadow of this double sin, for McCaslin's incestuous miscegenation is a consequence of his owning human beings as though they were livestock and his treating them not as persons but as the convenient instruments of his vice.

In the comic action of "Was" there is, at a distance, a faint replication of this original offense, since the gaming squires, too, casually deal in human beings; but the vice they would use Turl and Tennie as stakes to indulge is just the opposite of Carothers McCaslin's lust. For Hubert and Uncle Buddy are each determined to avoid women, not to seduce them. Theirs is the dream of perpetual boyhood in which a man never need assume the responsibilities of maturity, a way of life in which women and their dreams and demands are totally irrelevant to the men's work of the world. And that work isn't real work—they have slaves to do that—their occupation is play: either gaming or the hunt. So deep is their fear of women that Sophonsiba too, as we have seen, is treated as a token, a stake, in the card game on which each wagers his freedom from having to live in her presence. Although, thanks to Buddy's intervention and to Tomey's Turl's quick hand at dealing the cards, Buck gets off free this time, in the end he succumbs—as Faulkner explained to a student at the University of Virginia, "Uncle Buck finally just gave up. That was his fate and he might as well quit struggling."[11] He accepts his fate, and becomes Isaac McCaslin's father. Tomey's Turl in time—as we learn in the second story in *Go Down, Moses*, "The Fire and the Hearth"—becomes the father of Lucas Beauchamp, the old man who in the pride of his McCaslin blood has faced down Zack Edmonds, the son of Cass who narrated "Was," when Zack tried to take Lucas's wife.

These interconnections among the characters, their forebears and their descendants, indicate not only how intricate is genealogy down on the McCaslin plantation but how complex are the interwoven experiences among the members of both races of the family. Although *Go Down, Moses* is certainly episodic, spanning several generations, its actions ranging in time from 1859 ("Was") to 1940 for the concluding title story, I join those who maintain that this work is a unified novel, however syncretic its structure. "Was" is designed as prologue, "Go Down, Moses" as epilogue, to the main body of the work. As Faulkner explained the book at Virginia,

> It covered a great deal of time. The central character . . . was a man named Isaac McCaslin who was old at the time of the book. But this background which produced Isaac McCaslin had to be told by somebody, and so this is Isaac McCaslin's uncle, this Cass here is not old Ike, this is Ike's uncle. And "Was" simply because Ike is saying to the reader, I'm not telling this, this was my uncle, my great-uncle that told it. That's the only reason for "Was"—that this was the old time. But it's part of him too.[12]

As sometimes happened when Faulkner was speaking impromptu, he got a detail or two mixed up—Cass is actually Ike's elder cousin, not his uncle. Faulkner's point is that the portrait of Isaac, his principal character, required the depiction of the world into which he had been born; hence we get Cass's reminiscence, told to Ike, of the way it was.

But Faulkner has told us, "There is no such thing as *was*—only *is*. If *was* existed, there would be no grief or sorrow."[13] Therefore, Faulkner can give us the seemingly prelapsarian world into which Isaac will be born, as seen by a nine-year-old boy. The use of this juvenile point of view keeps all of the dark underside of the way it was from coming into consciousness while the unknowing deadpan telling of the naif narrator produces much of the comedy. Evidently the tale of the hunt and the poker games first presented itself to Faulkner in this mode, even before he had conceived of Isaac McCaslin as its auditor-redactor, hence of the need for the psychic distancing from the action that Isaac's later experiences would make necessary in *Go Down, Moses*. The first version of "Was," entitled "Almost," differs from the first chapter of *Go Down, Moses* not in plot but in the identity of some characters. Faulkner had the young narrator as Bayard Sartoris, who, with Uncles Buck and Buddy, makes that version seem a continuation, or rather a prelude, to *The Unvanquished*, written earlier.

What Faulkner started from was a plot of folk comedy, seen through the eyes of a youthful naif, which would at once summon nostalgia for the boys' life (however superannuated the boys) of a frontier plantation in antebellum Mississippi, and would introduce a family saga filled with the revelations of sin and its consequences. Since the tale was a courtship story as well as a hunting yarn, it led immitigably to the further—and prior— history of a family. But which family? By the time Faulkner had written "Delta Autumn," which appears as the sixth, penultimate chapter in *Go Down, Moses* (the chapters were not written in their order in the book), he had made Isaac McCaslin a principal character. Now Isaac seized Faulkner's imagination, as he rewrote another story, "The Old People," in which Isaac McCaslin replaces Quentin Compson as the youth initiated into the hunt by shooting his first deer.[14] And it is not the Compson or the Sartoris family but the McCaslins whose saga Faulkner finds he is writing this time.

"Was" opens *Go Down, Moses* before Isaac's birth, and the title story, from which he is also absent, closes the saga. That tale concerns the execution of Tomey's Turl's great-grandson, Samuel Worsham Beauchamp. Butch Beauchamp had been a bad egg in Jefferson, a numbers runner and finally a murderer in Chicago. The gist of the tale has to do with his grandmother Mollie Beauchamp's wish that he be brought home for his funeral, and the designs by which the lawyer Gavin Stevens, a character newly introduced in this last chapter, arranges for that to happen. If "Was" gives a naif view of antebellum life as carefree comedy, with an easy fraternal feeling between the McCaslin twins and their blacks, "Go Down, Moses," closes the parentheses around Isaac's life by showing a McCaslin Negro as an alienated criminal executed in a distant Northern city. A vestige of the communal feeling of Southern life remains as Stevens inveigles the local editor and merchants on the square to join him and the aged white lady whose grandfather had owned Mollie's parents, in raising money to ship the body home and hire a hearse and flowers.

Like "Was," this tale is jarringly out of key with the story-chapters intervening between them, the first with its farcical comedy, the last with its bleak view of modern life. What such disjunction among its parts suggests is that *Go Down, Moses* is a chronicle, bearing a relation to the novel observant of the unities like that of Shakespeare's *Antony and Cleopatra* to *Hamlet* or *Lear.* We are shown the South into which Isaac McCaslin is born, the timeless wilderness and then the family history into which he is initiated, and the society that lives on after him. Each of Faulkner's novels differs in its form, each is an experiment, an enlargement of what the novel can do. Faulkner has never limited himself to following the dimensions, structure, or shape of what the novel *was*, for his interest in each book is to make the experience of fiction represent what the novel *is*. And while what *is* includes "grief or sorrow," it includes also the admixture, as in the chapter "Was," of comic literary stereotypes with folklore, inverting its sources, analogues, and influences to produce a tale at once a comic masterpiece and a fitting prelude to the darker themes in *Go Down, Moses.*

NOTES

1. *Faulkner in the University: Class Conferences at the University of Virginia, 1957–1958,* ed. Frederick L. Gwynn and Joseph L. Blotner (Charlottesville: University of Virginia Press, 1959), 131.

2. "'Was': Faulkner's Classic Comedy of the Frontier," *Southern Review,* n.s. 8 (1972), 736.

3. Calvin S. Brown, "Faulkner's Use of the Oral Tradition," *Georgia Review* (1968), 160–61.

4. Jerrold Brite, in *William Faulkner of Oxford,* ed. James W. Webb and A. Wigfall Green (Baton Rouge: Louisiana State University Press, 1965), 186.

5. *Faulkner in the University,* 131.

6. *Who Blowed Up the Church House? and Other Ozark Folktales* (New York: Columbia University Press, 1952), 42–43.

7. Reviews of Randolph, *We Always Lie to Strangers: Tall Tales from the Ozarks* and

*Who Blowed Up the Church House?* in *Midwest Folklore*, 2 (1952), 191–94, and ibid., 3 (1953), 251–54.

8. William Faulkner, *Go Down, Moses* (New York: Random House, 1942), 4. Page references to this edition will be shown in parentheses in the text.

9. "'Was': Faulkner's Classic Comedy of the Frontier," 739.

10. Joseph Blotner, *Faulkner: A Biography* (New York: Random House, 1974), 1051. In fact, the letter stating these terms reached Oxford after Faulkner had arrived in New York to negotiate in person. Surely Bennett Cerf put these proposals before him.

11. *Faulkner in the University*, 46.

12. Ibid., 38.

13. "Interview with Jean Stein vanden Heuvel" (1955), in *Lion in the Garden: Interviews with William Faulkner, 1926–1962*, ed. James B. Meriwether and Michael Millgate (New York: Random House, 1968), 255.

14. James Early, *The Making of "Go Down, Moses"* (Dallas: Southern Methodist University Press, 1972), 16–19.

# "A Momentary Anesthesia of the Heart": A Study of the Comic Elements in Faulkner's *Go Down, Moses*

## NANCY B. SEDERBERG

Although there are many funny episodes in Faulkner's work, he is not basically a comic writer.[1] He seldom exploits comedy for its own sake or as "relief" from tragic doings[2] but rather integrates it within "the experiential context of the narration."[3] The result is a fusion of comedy with the deeper sense of tragedy and pathos which dominates his work. Faulkner himself alluded to this very close enmeshing of the humorous and the serious in a 1957 interview at the University of Virginia: "there's not too fine a distinction between humor and tragedy, that even tragedy is in a way walking a tightrope between the ridiculous—between the bizarre and the terrible."[4] Because *Go Down, Moses* is a novel in which the tragic and the comic are inextricably bound, an interpretation of its comic elements can give us an important insight into his art.

The basic component of comedy is incongruity, which Henri Bergson views as the contradiction between an individual's actions and the accepted social norms or, more specifically, between "mechanical inelasticity" and "the wideawake adaptability and the living pliableness of a human being."[5] Whether an inappropriate action elicits a comic response depends on a complex of unconscious and learned behavior patterns. Psychologists believe that laughter derives from two contradictory sources: Men laugh because of self-satisfaction—a feeling of superiority combined with a sensation of pleasure; or they laugh because there is no other way to face the sadness and gloom which surround them.[6]

This duality is reflected in the two basic categories of comedy which permeate *Go Down, Moses*. The first includes the light, anecdotal comedy of "Was," "The Fire and the Hearth," and some portions of "The Old People" and "The Bear," which may be loosely termed "comedy of manners" or "humor of belittlement" because individuals are treated as caricatures.[7] Even this type of comedy, though, in a larger context, humanizes and counterpoints more serious characterization and themes. A second type of comedy, found in the last section of "Pantaloon in Black," part 4 of "The Bear," "Delta Autumn," and "Go Down, Moses," functions primarily to produce a "delayed reaction" by tempering open emotionalism in a tragic situation so as to heighten its thematic significance.[8] Bergson calls this effect of comedy "something like a momentary anesthesia of the heart."[9] In both cases, the comic elements function "to give perspective to the various events, to present a total view in which the values of the story—using the term *values* in something of the painter's sense—can be established and defined."[10]

## "WAS"

The story "Was" presents a good illustration of the first category of comedy. The basic comic situation involves three hunt motifs—all of which are unified through a single metaphor of a fox hunt which, in fact, frames the tale. A second hunt involves the biyearly slave hunt for the love-sick Tomey's Turl, who has slipped off again to visit Tennie on the neighboring Beauchamp plantation. The hilarious hide-and-seek chase which ensues has many levels of comedy. On the first, it is merely an amusing anecdote. The rituals of Uncle Buck's necktie and Tomey Turl's semiclean white shirt, along with the paraphernalia of the fox-horns and baying dogs, provide an element of light social satire against the ceremony which has degenerated into a ludicrous game.[11] A deeper sort of ironic comedy of situation results from the reversal of accepted Negro-white roles in which the pursued

Tomey's Turl is the picaresque hero as he calmly saunters off into the woods with the pack of hunting dogs licking his face and later runs right over Uncle Buck, who becomes the butt of the humor, pathetically feeling his backside to see if there is any blood—or only the contents of his whisky bottle.

A third hunt motif involves Uncle Buck's antic attempts to evade the courting strategems of Hubert Beauchamp's old maid sister, Sophonsiba. Faulkner gains a gentler, more sophisticated social comedy here by merging the theme of empty status assertion with tension between the sexes. The humorous treatment of aristocratic pretension can be seen, for example, in Sophonsiba's insistence that everyone call their run-down plantation Warwick. The discrepancy between romantic illusion and reality is only too clear as she descends the stairs like a faded coquette—amidst jangling and swishing and a smell of perfume—with a little slave girl carrying her fan. The added touches of the ribbon which she gives Uncle Buck for "success" in the hunt, the ritual of sipping his toddy to sweeten it, and his chivalric gesture of dragging his foot parody medieval and antebellum romances. The situation takes on more serious dimensions, though, in the scenes in which Uncle Buck innocently strays into the "bear's den" of Sophonsiba's bedroom and the almost farcical denouement in which his salvation from marriage depends on the turn of a card in a poker game ironically dealt by Tomey's Turl.[12] In both cases, roles are again reversed: The hunter becomes the hunted, and the winner loses—although not immediately.

The treatment of Uncle Buck and Uncle Buddy in "Was" as almost "humors" characters functions on one level to dispel the stereotype of the tyrannical white slaveholder and thus to give both human and historical perspectives from which to judge the complex motives behind Ike's relinquishment of his "tainted" inheritance.[13] Uncle Buck's imminent capitulation to marriage and its concomitant responsibilites at the end of "Was" likewise has far-reaching implications for Ike. As Melvin Bradford suggests, if Ike had better understood the meaning of "Was," he might have had the son he desired—or at least realized why he could not expect it after his behavior.[14] It is ironic that "Was" is narrated to Ike, whose life is a denial of its significance. Finally, the comic treatment of the hunts in "Was" also functions as a counterpoint to the more serious hunts in the rest of the novel.

## "THE FIRE AND THE HEARTH"

The chapter "The Fire and the Hearth" also exemplifies the first category of light, anecdotal comedy in Lucas Beauchamp's dogged search for buried treasure. On the first level is social satire of the sixty-seven-year-old Negro who spends all of his nights digging for gold in a muddy orchard. The tale also has comic ritualistic aspects in the divining machine which he carries "as if it were some object symbolical and sanctified for a ceremony, a ritual."[15] Lucas also comically inverts expected black-white roles when he first runs off with Roth Edmonds's mule as collateral for the divining machine because he won't risk his own money and then turns the tables on the city-slicker salesman who unwittingly sells Lucas the machine and then must pay him twenty-five dollars a day for the use of it.

The characterization of Lucas in "The Fire and the Hearth," however, is deceptive. He does slip into what one critic calls "the mask of the curmudgeon" when attempting to "con" whites.[16] Yet he is not merely a Negro buffoon. As Jane Millgate perceptively argues, Faulkner made numerous minor revisions between the short story "Gold Is Not Always" and the novel version which increase Lucas's dignity, including modifying his pronounced Negro dialect to that of a country man and transferring many of his simpleminded, comic characteristics to his son-in-law, George Wilkins.[17] Lucas also shows both increased scorn for the stupid salesman and stubbornness toward Roth in the novel version, resulting in his evolution into a complex comic hero along the lines which John Longley delineates in *The Tragic Mask:* "being neither saint nor holy idiot, he is merely human, with human limitations and abilities."[18]

The overall tone of "The Fire and the Hearth" is difficult to evaluate.[19] The constant, often ambiguous adumbration of com-

edy into tragedy is evident, for example, in the scene in which
Lucas's wife, Molly, tells Roth she has decided to sue for a
divorce after forty-five years of marriage because " 'Ever since he
got that machine, he's done went crazy' " (101). A type of comedy
which might be termed "comedy of impotence"[20] results when
Roth later can only stand there babbling:

> "Listen to me, Lucas. You are an older man than me; I admit that.
> You may have more money than I've got, which I think you have, and
> you may have more sense than I've got, as you think you have. But
> you cant do this." (120)

Lucas's stubbornness in letting the proceedings go through until
the last moment when he blurts out in court, " 'We dont want no
voce,' " and his appeasement of Molly with a nickel bag of candy
which she can only "gum" because she " 'aint got no teeth left' "
also have comic aspects (128, 130).[21] Yet the situation takes on
overtones of both poignancy and closely averted tragedy in the
final scene in which Lucas solemnly hands the divining machine
over to Roth.

The comedy trenches even more closely on tragedy in the
flashback which tells how Lucas, years ago, swam the flooded
creek to get a doctor for Zack Edmonds's wife who was dying in
childbirth and returned to find her dead and his own black wife
installed in the white man's house. Lucas's attempt six months
later to kill Roth to reinstate his honor culminates in a tragicomic
tussle in which Zack is saved solely by a misfiring gun.[22] The
scene, however, carries bitter knowledge for both because of the
blood and friendship ties between them, and Lucas can only
stand pathetically questioning, " 'How to God . . . can a black
man ask a white man to please not lay down with his black
wife?' " (59).[23]

The comic elements in "The Fire and the Hearth," therefore,
have a dual effect: The humorous treatment of Lucas in the gold-
digging scenes functions to give the reader sympathy for the
black man who embodies the virtues of patience and endurance
which are central to the book; yet this very humanizing makes

Lucas's belief that he has been cuckolded seem all the more "terrible and anguishing."[24] The humor also provides a perspective from which to judge the antithetical figures of the realistic, active, go-getting Lucas and the idealistic, retiring, and ascetic Ike.[25]

## "PANTALOON IN BLACK"

As the novel proceeds, the comedy becomes more infused with tragedy and pathos. This complex amalgamation is illustrated in "Pantaloon in Black" in which the main portion of the story is told in a serious tone. There exist elements of grotesque comedy in Rider's ordering of the ghost of his dead wife to sit down and eat the supper of gelid peas with him and his chugging of the gallon of white mule-whisky; however, the scenes take on deeply tragic overtones in conjunction with his pathetic request of Mannie's fading ghost: "'Den lemme go wid you, honey'" (141).

The comedy here is of the second type which functions not as "relief" from tragic events but rather as a counterpoint to underplay the emotional intensity of the situation, thus reemphasizing its thematic significance. This technique becomes most apparent in the last section of the story in which the imprisonment and lynching of Rider are described by the white deputy sheriff, who misunderstands and totally lacks sympathy with the Negro:

> "Them damn niggers. I swear to godfrey, it's a wonder we have as little trouble with them as we do. Because why? Because they aint human. They look like a man and they walk on their hind legs like a man, and they can talk and you can understand them and you think they are understanding you, at least now and then. But when it comes to the normal human feelings and sentiments of human beings, they might as well be a damned herd of wild buffaloes." (154)[26]

The sheriff's description of Rider "'snatching up ten-foot cypress logs by himself and throwing them around like matches'" and later "'standing in the middle of the cell, holding the cot over his head like it was a baby's cradle'" turns the events into an incredible tall tale and Rider into a sort of superhuman black Paul Bunyan (156, 158).[27] Terrifying irony results from the inversion of expected roles: the white, who is supposed to have acute sensitivity, has almost none, whereas the Negro is overwhelmed by his inexpressible grief. In this light, the sheriff, not Rider, becomes the pantaloon or buffoon of the title. Finally, his philistine wife's callous statement that "'I'm going to clear this table then and I'm going to the picture show'" functions to divert our attention momentarily, only to refocus it more strongly on the tragic tableau of Rider

> "laying there under the pile of them ["niggers"], laughing, with tears big as glass marbles running across his face and down past his ears and making a kind of popping sound on the floor like somebody dropping bird eggs, laughing and laughing and saying, 'Hit look lack Ah just cant quit thinking. Look lack Ah just cant quit.'" (159)[28]

The comedy here is a perfect example of Bergson's dictum that *"the attitudes, gestures and movements of the human body are laughable in exact proportion as that body reminds us of a mere machine."*[29] From the sheriff's viewpoint, Rider does not cry real tears but "glass marbles" which drop like "bird eggs" because, for him, Rider can not really grieve.

On one level, then, the comic elements in "Pantaloon in Black" function to humanize Rider, to make palpable to the reader both his personal tragedy and his virtues of strength and supreme endurance. In the total context of the novel, the tragicomic treatment of Rider also adds yet another perspective from which to view Ike's character. Both have lost a glorious past: Rider his idyllic married days; Ike the wilderness, "his mistress and his wife" (326). Both are also involved in quests which they themselves do not fully comprehend: Rider for a purpose so that "he could stop needing to invent to himself reasons for breathing"; Ike "to preserve a status quo or to establish a better future one to endure for his children" (145, 290). Ironically, Rider gains his goal only through passively committing suicide, and Ike through not engendering any children.

## "The Old People" and "The Bear"

The characterization of Boon in "The Old People" and "The Bear" contains elements of both comic caricature and tragedy and pathos. One source of comedy derives from Boon's grotesque ugliness, often described in mechanical terms: He has "little hard shoe-button eyes without depth or meanness or generosity or viciousness or gentleness or anything else, in the ugliest face the boy had ever seen. It looked like somebody had found a walnut a little larger than a football and with a machinist's hammer had shaped features into it and then painted it, mostly red" (227).[30] A second source of comedy is Boon's childish simplemindedness. He is described, for example, as having "the mind of a child, the heart of a horse" and being "ten all his life" (227, 232). The major humor surrounding Boon, though, derives from his chronic inability to shoot "anything larger than a squirrel and that sitting" (176). In this respect, he is a complete foil to Walter Ewell, whose rifle "never missed" (181). Boon is an anomaly; he fits neither into the woods, which he loves, nor into civilization, which his mechanical features parody.

Boon, however, is not totally a comic caricature. Like Lucas in "The Fire and the Hearth," Boon's dignity is enhanced by a number of revisions Faulkner made between the short story and novel versions, most pronounced in the areas of his relationships with blacks, Lion, and the wilderness. A shift in the nature of Boon's interactions with blacks can be noted in the different treatments of the comic scene in which he shoots five times at a Negro, breaks a plate-glass window, and finally hits a black woman bystander in the leg by default. In the short story "Lion," he manages to hit the "nigger" in the face at six feet with the last shot. References to Boon's overt racism are deleted in the novel.[31] Also, an addition in the novel version functions to deflect some of the comedy onto Major de Spain and McCaslin who cut cards to decide who will pay for the plate-glass window and the woman's leg.

A second type of change concerns the love relationship between Boon and Lion.[32] In the short story, both Boon and Ad vie comically to get Lion to sleep with them, whereas Boon alone does so in the novel. Similar comic references to Boon's odor occur in both versions; however, in the novel some of the humor again is directed at de Spain, who can do nothing about the situation and thus asks not to be informed about whether he is obeyed. A scene also is added to the novel in which after Boon misses hitting Old Ben five times at twenty-five feet, he leaves Lion with Sam Fathers, lamenting, "'I aint fit to sleep with him'" (226). Although the scene is a comic parody of the courtly love tradition, Boon's childlike sense of guilt and inadequacy also evokes pathos.

Finally, the two treatments of the Gum Tree scene show a subtle difference in Boon's relationship to the wilderness.[33] In both versions Boon is greedy in his desire to have all the squirrels to himself. In the short story, though, the narrator explicitly denies Boon a memory—and thus a motive—for his actions, which is omitted from "The Bear" version. There is also a phrasing change which seems significant. Whereas the "Lion" text describes "his walnut face wild and urgent and streaming with sweat,"[34] the novel reads "his scarlet and streaming walnut face" (331). In his own frustrated and simpleminded manner, Boon is grieving for the loss of the wilderness—unlike Ike who accepts the finality of it.

## "THE BEAR," PART 4

The fourth section of "The Bear" also exemplifies a curious mixture of comedy and tragedy. The main vehicle for comedy is the ledger, with its faded, yellowing pages chronicling "a whole land in miniature," and ranging from the anecdotal entries describing "the anomaly calling itself Percival Brownlee" to the repeated cryptic notations about Eunice's drowning (292, 263). The humor in both cases derives partially from the laconic dialect spelling; however, whereas in the former entries the events narrated are basically humorous,[35] in the latter they are tragic and result in an almost grotesque comedy. As Harry

Campbell and Ruel Foster note, this is one of the techniques of Faulkner's "guarded style" by which he uses humor to give emotional ambivalence to a scene by creating a delayed reaction.[36] The suspense is further drawn out by Ike's poignant question, *"But why? But why?"*—even though he "knew what he was going to find before he found it" (267–68). The fact of his grandfather McCaslin's incest and miscegenation obsesses Ike's thoughts: *"His own daughter His own daughter. No No Not even him"* (270). However, his vision of Eunice's suicide transcends the knowable: "he seemed to see her actually walking into the icy creek on that Christmas day six months before her daughter's and her lover's (*Her first lover's* he thought. *Her first*) child was born" (271). It seems significant that Ike closes the ledger forever at the moment of his own romanticized recreation of reality.

Elements of subtle comedy also occur in the inconsistent, tangled arguments through which Ike attempts to justify his relinquishment to his cousin, Cass. He begins by stating that he can't repudiate the land because

> "it was never mine to repudiate. It was never Father's and Uncle Buddy's to bequeath me to repudiate because it was never Grand-father's to bequeath to them to bequeath to me to repudiate because it was never old Ikemotubbe's to sell to Grandfather. . . . because on the instant when Ikemotubbe discovered, realised, that he could sell it for money, on that instant it ceased ever to have been his forever . . . and the man who bought it bought nothing. (256–57)

Later, however, he contradicts himself that "'Grandfather did own the land nevertheless and notwithstanding'" (258). In another instance he uses God to explain the purpose behind substituting white tyranny of the land for the Indian's as a means of purging evil with evil and then proceeds to acknowledge that the "'men who transcribed His Book for Him were sometime liars'" (260). Cass deftly undercuts him on this issue by noting, "'I might answer that since you have taken to proving your points and disproving mine by the same text, I dont know'" (261).

The main function of the comic elements here is to further undermine the rationale behind Ike's actions. Both in the wilderness where he does not kill Old Ben even when he has a chance and later in relinquishing his heritage, Ike acts with a lack of self-knowledge and from overly idealistic and emotional premises. His assertion to Cass that " 'Yes. Sam Fathers set me free' " reverberates ironically against his mulatto kinswoman Fonsiba's cry, " 'I'm free,' " from the midst of utter desolation in Midnight, Arkansas (33, 280). This latter scene takes on further caustic comedy from the fact that Ike forces upon her part of the "tainted" legacy he himself eschews. The characterization of Fonsiba's husband, who wears lenseless, gold-framed spectacles and speaks in "his measured and sonorous imbecility of the boundless folly and the baseless hope . . . 'The curse you brought into this land has been lifted,' " is darkly satiric because it is Ike who bitterly reminds him that this is not freedom, not the new Canaan (279).

A last comic counterpoint to Ike's relinquishment is provided by the legacy from his uncle, Hubert Beauchamp, which turns out to be a tin coffee pot filled with I.O.U.'s. Ike not only lacks freedom—for he had "found long since that no man is ever free and probably could not bear it if he were"—but he also never had even a portion of the inheritance which he so grandiosely renounces (281). Many critics have found fault with the motivations behind Ike's actions.[37] Olga Vickery pungently asserts that Ike rejects sin but confuses the wilderness with Eden and sacrifices his life to it. Ironically, he stops short of the paradox of the Fortunate Fall and overlooks the necessity of returning to humanity to display his humanity.[38]

## "DELTA AUTUMN"

The failure of Ike's humanity becomes the central theme of "Delta Autumn." The tone throughout the chapter is bitter and sardonic. Terrible comic irony, for example, reverberates in the repetition of the "original sin" of old Carothers's miscegenation and belated legacy. As Bergson notes, the repetition of history is comic because of our recognition of coincidence; this comic effect is exaggerated if the situation is inverted.[39] Ike's participa-

tion in the sin as purveyor of the "conscience money" further
undermines the motivations behind his repudiation. Whereas in
the commissary he denounces Carother's actions and presents an
encomium to the Negro, in "Delta Autumn" he tacitly condones
Roth's equivalent act.[40]

Another trenchant irony involves General Compson's hunting
horn which Ike bequeaths to the girl. Although on the surface
his action can be seen as a chivalric gesture, it represents his
denial of the responsibility to "protect the does and fawns" (339).
Not a horn of hope and plenty, like Ike's own tin coffee pot, it
serves to remind the reader of the empty code which allows the
sacrifice of innocents. After the girl leaves, having accused Ike of
a failure of love, he retreats into his Christ role; however, he is a
mocking, obverse reflection of Christ because whereas Christ
gave up carpentering to serve humanity and die young, Ike takes
up carpentry, withdraws from humanity, and lives to be a useless
old man.[41] Roth's earlier sardonic question of Ike reverberates in
the reader's mind: " ' where have you been all the time you were
dead?' " (345).

## "GO DOWN, MOSES"

Finally, the comedy in the title story, "Go Down, Moses," is
almost totally fused with tragedy. The opening scene in the
Chicago jail parodies old Southwest humorist census dialogues
when Samuel Worsham Beauchamp sarcastically frustrates the
questions of the spectacled white young census taker.[42] The
apparent levity of his statement of occupation—" 'Getting rich
too fast' "—reflects ironically against the wilderness, which is
also dying because men wanted to get rich too fast. Unlike the
callous sheriff and his wife in "Pantaloon in Black," though, the
census taker is seemingly more moved than Samuel is by his own
plight: " 'If they dont know who you are here, how will they
know—how do you expect to get home?' " (370). Through a
mechanism that Freud terms "economy of sympathy," our "pity
is inhibited because we understand that he who is most concerned is indifferent to the situation."[43]

The rest of "Go Down, Moses" contains comedy but no humor. The basic situation is a bitter inversion of the traditional comic reintegration of society described by Northrop Frye in *Anatomy of Criticism*.[44] Instead of a wedding procession with the happy prospect of progeny, "Go Down, Moses" ends with a funeral procession and another dying out of the McCaslin line. The funeral itself presents grotesque comedy through the juxtaposition of Mollie's grief and the mechanical operations of the black undertaker's men who "lifted the gray-and-silver casket from the train and carried it to the hearse and snatched the wreaths and floral symbols of man's ultimate end briskly out and slid the casket in and flung the flowers back and clapped-to the door" (382). Unlike Rider who flung shovelfuls of dirt onto Mannie's grave to cover his inexpressible emotions, these men are professionals who feel nothing.

A second type of comedy associated with Gavin Stevens and the newspaper editor might be termed "comedy of misunderstanding."[45] The reader feels superior to the two white men who do not fully comprehend either their own motivations or the feelings of the old Negress, Mollie. Gavin organizes the elaborate funeral as a chivalric gesture to Miss Worsham, not Mollie, and cannot meaningfully participate in the ritual circle of grief around "the brick hearth on which the ancient symbol of human coherence and solidarity smoldered" (380).[46] The newspaper editor is involved in the funeral proceedings mainly for the novelty, as he has already promised Gavin not to print the copy, even though Mollie wishes it. Yet the situation takes on deep, tragic irony because of the misunderstanding of its import. Gavin's comic understatement—"'Come on. Let's get back to town. I haven't seen my desk in two days'"[47]—underscores his false belief that the formality of the funeral has eradicated the debt of racial injustice (283).

The comic elements in *Go Down, Moses* range the entire gamut from the genial "comedy of manners," satire of antiquated rituals, and mocking parodies and inversions of black-white behavior in "Was," "The Fire and the Hearth," and parts of "The

Old People" and "The Bear" to the sometimes savagely sardonic treatment of the tragic themes of repudiation and death and the motifs of the hunt and inheritance in the later stories. Finally, the comedy forms a nexus between idealism and irony—the wish for what perhaps was or might be and what is—for Faulkner, like Bergson, viewed comedy as a corrective to make us flexible and sane in a mechanical and sometimes mad society—in other words, fully human.[48]

## NOTES

1. Among the few early commentators who mention Faulkner's use of comedy is Aubrey Starke, who in a 1934 article, "An American Comedy: An Introduction to a Bibliography of Faulkner," *Colophon*, 5, pt. 19, [n.p.], states that Faulkner's purpose was to create comedy following the precedent of Balzac's *Comedie Humaine*. Malcolm Cowley, "William Faulkner's Human Comedy," *The New York Times Book Review* (October 29, 1944), 4, picks up and elaborates on this point. See also John Arthos, "Ritual and Humor in the Writing of William Faulkner," *Accent*, 9 (Autumn 1948), 17–30, who concludes, I feel erroneously, that if Faulkner had managed to balance outrage and humor better in the difficult works such as *Sanctuary* and *As I Lay Dying*, they would have been more integrated in the form of comedy which they seek; without this, they remain what Malraux terms *prèsque comique*. Richard Pearce, "Faulkner's One Ring Circus: *Light in August*," in *Stages of the Clown: Perspectives on Modern Fiction from Dostoyevsky to Beckett* (Carbondale: Southern Illinois University Press, 1970), 47, likewise overstates when he argues that "Faulkner's view of life was fundamentally comic." His treatment of the themes of rebellions against race, religion, and sex in relation to Bergson's views on comedy and recognition of the redemptive qualities of the comic are insightful. In contrast to these studies, this essay treats the comic elements in Faulkner's work as part of a unified tragicomic vision. See Warren Beck, *Man in Motion: Faulkner's Trilogy* (Madison: University of Wisconsin Press, 1969), 201. It is also deeply indebted to the sense of structural unity presented in the fine studies by Carol Harter, "The Diaphoric Structure and Unity of William Faulkner's *Go Down, Moses*" (Ph.D. diss., State University of New York at Binghamton, 1970), and Ronald Schleifer, "Faulkner's Storied Novels: *Go Down, Moses* and the Translation of Time," *Modern Fiction Studies*, 28 (Spring 1982), 109–27.

2. Cleanth Brooks, *William Faulkner: The Yoknapatawpha Country* (New Haven: Yale University Press, 1969), 245. See also Beck, 152.

3. Harry Campbell and Ruel Foster, "Humor," in *William Faulkner: A Critical Appraisal* (Norman: University of Oklahoma Press, 1951), 113.

4. William Faulkner, *Faulkner in the University: Class Conferences at the University of Virginia, 1957–1958*, ed. Frederick Gwynn and Joseph Blotner (New York: Random House, 1965), 39.

5. Henri Bergson, *Laughter: An Essay on the Meaning of the Comic*, trans. Cloudesley Brereton and Fred Rothwell (London: MacMillan, 1913), 10. Italics the author's.

6. Sigmund Freud, Book IV, "Wit and Its Relation to the Unconscious," in *The Basic Writings of Sigmund Freud*, trans. and ed. A. A. Brill (New York: Modern Library, 1965), 793–97, argues that children laugh from pure pleasure, whereas adults are consciously aware of superiority through comparison of themselves to others or within one's self. See also Herman Wilson, "A Study of Humor in the Fiction of William Faulkner" (Ph.D. diss., University of Southern California, 1956), 24.

7. Wilson, 364. A similar typology is developed by Campbell and Foster, 95–96, between frontier or native humor and "surrealistic" or atrabilious humor. See also Cowley, 4, in which he states that Faulkner combines the two dominant trends of American literature of the psychological horror story and realistic frontier humor: "If you imagine Huckleberry Finn living in the House of Usher and telling uproarious stories while the walls crumble about him, that will give you the double quality of Faulkner's work at its best."

8. Campbell and Foster, 112–13.

9. Bergson, 5.

10. Brooks, 245.

11. Nancy Posselt, "Images and Patterns: The Literary Uses of Cards and Card Games" (M.A. thesis, University of South Carolina, 1979), 24–34, contains an insightful section on the rituals associated with the hunt and card games in "Was." See also Lewis Dabney, "'Was': Faulkner's Classic Comedy of the Frontier," *The Southern Review,* n.s. 8 (1972), 736–48, which places "Was" in the context of the tall tale, vaudeville, funnies, and films. In *Faulkner in the University,* 39–40, Faulkner discusses the implications of placing Tomey's Turl on the same plane as the fox.

12. Karl Zender, "A Hand of Poker: Game and Ritual in Faulkner's 'Was,'" *Studies in Short Fiction,* 11 (1974), 53–60, gives the fullest treatment of this scene I have seen, though he doesn't treat the role of Tomey's Turl as dealer. See also Dabney, 747; *Go Down, Moses,* 300; and *Faulkner in the University,* 40. Harter, 36–37, shows how revisions from the typescript of "Was" emphasize Tomey's Turl's miscegenation and his filial relationship to the McCaslins rather than caricaturing him merely as a chronically rebellious slave.

13. Harter, 36–37, notes that the typescript of "Was" makes no reference to this semi-abolitionism.

14. Melvin Bradford, "All the Daughters of Eve: 'Was' and the Unity of *Go Down, Moses,*" *Arlington Quarterly,* 1 (Autumn 1967), 35–36. Two contrary misreadings of "Was" grow out of trying to see it either as totally comic or a sentimentalized myth of the Southern Edenic past or totally ironically by reading it reflexively from the viewpoint of "The Bear" and Ike's condemnation of slavery and its human costs. For the former reading, see, for example: John Longley, Jr., *The Tragic Mask: A Study of Faulkner's Heroes* (Chapel Hill: University of North Carolina Press, 1963), 105–6; Dabney, 736; and James Mellard, "The Biblical Rhythm of *Go Down, Moses,*" *Mississippi Quarterly,* 22 (Spring 1967), 137, 141, as well as his "Humor in Faulkner's Novels: Its Development, Forms, and Functions" (Ph.D. diss., University of Texas, 1964), 197–201. Stanley Tick, "The Unity of *Go Down, Moses,*" *Twentieth Century Literature,* 8 (July 1962), 72–73, argues that neither the nine-year-old Cass nor the adults see in the chase of Tomey's Turl any moral or social significance, but he feels that the novel as a whole is unified by its portrayal of the growth of moral consciousness from "Was" through the future in "Go Down, Moses." The most convincing treatment I have read concerning the relation of "Was" to the rest of the novel is Walter Taylor, "Horror and Nostalgia: The Double Perspective of Faulkner's 'Was,'" *Southern Humanities Review,* 8 (1974), 74–84, which asserts that Faulkner expected the reader "to hold conflicting opinions simultaneously in a kind of suspended judgement." The chase is inadvertently cruel, yet Uncles Buck and Buddy are genuinely doing the best they are capable of in regard to the fact of slavery; and "the situation is somehow very funny" (78). For relations of the hunt motif to the rest of the novel, see Schliefer, especially 124; and Olga Vickery, *The Novels of William Faulkner: A Critical Interpretation* (Baton Rouge: Louisiana State University Press, 1964), 164.

15. Faulkner, *Go Down, Moses* (New York: The Modern Library, 1955), 87. All subsequent references are incorporated in the text.

16. Irving Howe, *William Faulkner: A Critical Study* (New York: Random House, 1952), 91.

17. Jane Millgate, "Short Story into Novel: Faulkner's Reworking of 'Gold Is Not Always,'" *English Studies,* 44 (August 1964), 310–17. Less pronounced revisions occur

between the short stories "A Point of Law" and "Absolution" and the novel versions. See Harter, 57–65.

18. Longley, 23.

19. Howe, 90, overstates when he asserts that "The Fire and the Hearth" "is one of Faulkner's more dubious experiments in mating serious material with a tone so unevenly jocose that it allows him no secure narrative point of view."

20. The Snopes trilogy is filled with this type of "comedy of impotence." It is especially prevalent in *The Hamlet* and *The Mansion*, for example, in Houston's search for Ike Snopes and his cow, Mink Snopes's dealings with Houston over his barren cow, his "burial" and exhumation of Houston's body, and his long wait for Flem to get out of jail.

21. See *The Hamlet* (New York: Random House, 1940), 322, where Flem makes a similar gesture to Mrs. Armstid.

22. This misfiring can be compared with the more comic treatment of Boon's close call with a black whose gun misfires while he misses five times (*GDM*, 235–36). See also the version in *The Reivers* (New York: Random House, 1962), 14–15. Rider's murder of Birdsong might have been averted in the same manner, except that he used the Negro's natural weapon, the razor, and eliminated the element of mechanical error.

23. This scene is paralleled by the tragicomic one in which Roth is initiated into his white heritage. After having grown up side-by-side with Henry, as Zack and Lucas had done before them, he one day suddenly no longer can sleep in the same bed as the black. In a scene which serves as an obverse, mocking reflection of white behavior, Roth is forced to eat alone, ironically asking Henry if he is ashamed to eat with him. On one level this is comic; yet, on another, it is a tragic comment on racial injustice: "the old curse of [their] fathers, the old haughty ancestral pride based not on any value but on an accident of geography, stemmed not from courage and honor but from wrong and shame" (*GDM*, 111). Harter, 63, notes that the flashback scene was added after "A Point of Law."

24. Brooks, 248.

25. Harter, 59.

26. Harter, 94, notes that Faulkner revised from the *Harper's* version of "Pantaloon in Black" to "embellish and underscore" the sheriff's already "outrageous insensitivity." Edward Holmes, *Faulkner's Twice-Told Tales: His Re-Use of His Material* (The Hague: Mouton, 1966), 64–66, gives an interesting parallel in the treatments of white misunderstanding of the Negro in "Pantaloon in Black" to that in the New Orleans *Picayune* short story "Sunset." See also Temple Drake's rendition of Rider's imprisonment in *Requiem for a Nun* (New York: Random House, 1951), 198–99. In the latter, the jailer Tubb's sympathy and understanding for Nancy Mannigoe form an ironic foil to the other white characters' indifference.

27. Bobby Ray Dowell, "Faulkner's Comic Spirit," (Ph.D. diss., University of Denver, 1962), 43–45.

28. The close connection between laughing and crying can also be compared with the scene in which Ike McCaslin's wife, having just made her immemorial sacrifice and failed, lies "on her side, her back to the empty rented room, laughing and laughing" (*GDM*, 315). For a good discussion of this ambiguous scene, see Beck, *Faulkner: Essays by Warren Beck* (Madison: University of Wisconsin Press, 1976), 447. See also the description of Samuel Worsham Beauchamp with his teeth "fixed into something like furious laughter through the blood" when he is caught for breaking and entering (*GDM*, 372).

29. Bergson, 29; italics the author's.

30. In the short story "Lion," Lion is described in almost the exact terms: his topaz eyes "were as impenetrable as Boon's, as free of meanness or generosity or gentleness or viciousness but a good deal more intelligent." See *Harper's*, 172 (December 1935), 71; reprinted in Joseph Blotner, ed., *Uncollected Stories of William Faulkner* (New York: Random House, 1979), 190. In the novel, the equivalent description is muted so that Lion's eyes "were not fierce and there was nothing of petty malevolence in them, but a

cold and almost impersonal malignance like some natural force" (*GDM*, 218). As Harter notes, 120, the humanizing of Lion is eliminated in "The Bear," making him an embodiment of "an indifferent cosmic force—destructive and irrevocable."

31. In "Lion," the above quoted comment about Boon's inability to shoot reads, "He never had killed anything bigger than a squirrel that anybody knew of except that nigger that time." The sixteen-year-old narrator, Quentin Compson, then gratuitously comments, "They say he was a bad nigger, but I don't know." See "Lion," *Uncollected Stories*, 189.

32. There are similarities between Boon's relationship to Lion and those between Ike Snopes and the cow in *The Hamlet* and the Negro Sentry and the three-legged race horse in *A Fable*.

33. For two sympathetic treatments of the gum tree scene, see H. H. Bell, Jr., "A Footnote to Faulkner's 'The Bear,'" *College English*, 24 (December 1962), 179–83 and E. R. Hutchinson, "A Footnote to the Gum Tree Scene," *College English*, 24 (April 1963), 564–65.

34. See "Lion," *Uncollected Stories*, 200.

35. Bradford, 30, presents an interesting treatment of Percival Brownlee as Uncle Buck and Buddy's "spotted horse."

36. Campbell and Foster, 111.

37. See, for example, Richard Adams, *Faulkner: Myth and Motion* (Princeton: Princeton University Press, 1968), 137–54; Brooks, 244–78; Harter, 141–50; John Hunt, *William Faulkner: Art in Theological Tension* (Syracuse: Syracuse University Press, 1965), 137–68; W. R. Moses, "Where History Crosses Myth: Another Reading of 'The Bear,'" *Accent*, 13 (Winter 1953), 21–33; William Van O'Connor, *The Tangled Fire of William Faulkner* (Minneapolis: University of Minnesota Press, 1954), 125–54; Herbert Purluck, "The Heart's Driving Complexity: An Unromantic Reading of 'The Bear,'" *Accent*, 20 (Winter 1960), 23–46; Lyall H. Powers, *Faulkner's Yoknapatawpha Comedy* (Ann Arbor: University of Michigan Press, 1980), especially 174–91; Schleifer, 119–25; Stanley Sultan, "Call Me Ishmael: The Hagiography of Isaac McCaslin," *Texas Studies in Literature and Language*, 3 (Spring 1961), 50–66; and Vickery, 124–44.

38. Vickery, 48.

39. Bergson, 89–96. Bergson's third concept of reciprocal interference of a series may also come into play. See especially 96–98.

40. Like Henry Sutpen in *Absalom, Absalom!*, apparently it is "the miscegenation not the incest which he [Ike] cant bear"; *Absalom, Absalom!* (New York: Random House, 1964), 356. It is further interesting to note that Faulkner's early conceptions of the protagonist for *Go Down, Moses* were Bayard Sartoris (see the unpublished story "Almost," received by Faulkner's agent, Harold Ober, July 1, 1940), and Quentin Compson (see "Lion"). Although Faulkner had substituted an anonymous male persona for this role by the time he wrote the original version of "The Old People," Harter, 106, argues that there is a good deal of evidence that he was still fashioned upon Quentin, not Ike. See Michael Millgate, *The Achievement of William Faulkner* (New York: Random House, 1966), 227–28, for a comparison of Ike and the Corporal in *A Fable*; Abner Keen Butterworth, "A Critical and Textual Study of William Faulkner's *A Fable*" (Ph.D. diss. University of South Carolina, 1970), 82, 132–33, discusses the parallels between Ike and both the Runner and the old General.

41. See *GDM*, 365. See also Adams, 145; Harter, 151.

42. See, for example, the sketch by Johnson Jones Hooper in *Some Adventures of Captain Simon Suggs* (1846) and the anonymous vignette entitled "Taking the Census," in William T. Porter, ed., *A Quarter Race in Kentucky* (1846).

43. Freud, 299.

44. Northrop Frye, *Anatomy of Criticism* (Princeton: Princeton University Press, 1971), 43.

45. Harter, 46, notes that Gavin Stevens's stereotyping of Mollie when she tells him

that Hamp Worsham is her brother is no less facile and outrageous than Uncle Buck's in "Was" (see *GDM*, 372 and 19, respectively)—or, one might add, the sheriff's in "Pantaloon in Black."

46. For a fine treatment of the motif of the brick in "The Fire and the Hearth," which also pertains to "Go Down, Moses," see Schleifer, 115.

47. The complex interrelation between Is and Was is emphasized by the echoing of the end of "Was": "Uncle Buck said. 'Go on and start breakfast. It seems to me I've been away from home a whole damn month'" (30).

48. Bergson, 3, notes that "the comic does not exist outside the pale of what is strictly *human*." Italics the author's. See also his comment that "rigidity is the comic, and laughter is its corrective," 21; as well as 170–71. Bergson, 186, treats the relation between comedy and madness and comic absurdity, which he sees as of the same nature as dreams. Taylor, 81, insightfully links Faulkner's mixing of grotesque humor and tragedy with that of more contemporary Black Humorists such as Heller, Vonnegut, and Ellison. Perhaps an apt coda to *Go Down, Moses* is Ken Kesey's *One Flew Over the Cuckoo's Nest* in which McMurphy "knows you have to laugh at the things that hurt you just to keep yourself in balance, just to keep the world from running you plumb crazy. He knows there's a painful side . . . but he won't let the pain blot out the humor no mor'n he'll let the humor blot out the pain" (New York: The New American Library Signet Book ed., 1962, [212]).

# Twain and Faulkner: Miscegenation and the Comic Muse

## WILLIAM BEDFORD CLARK

In response to a question about William Faulkner's humor at the Faulkner and Yoknapatawpha Conference in 1976, Shelby Foote made a claim that even the most rock-ribbed Faulknerian might want to qualify: "I think Faulkner is . . . the greatest humorist since Mark Twain."[1] Regrettably, Foote declined to follow through with a more precise accounting for his enthusiasm in this regard, and I would certainly hesitate to put words in his most eloquent mouth, but if he meant that Faulkner shared with Twain a genius for subjecting even the darkest social and personal concerns to transfiguring comic scrutiny, I am prepared to go Shelby Foote one better. Despite what he has Young Satan say in the "Mysterious Stranger" manuscripts about the power of laughter to demolish the anguished absurdity of the human condition, Twain found that his sense of humor failed him at the end of his life, as he discovered himself awash in truncated fragments that explored but could not quite illuminate the Great Dark. In Faulkner on the other hand, the comic sense, always present, though often at first obscured by an ominous foreground, ultimately emerged triumphant. To put it another way, both authors courted the Comic Muse throughout their careers: She abandoned Twain when he needed her most, while she undertook a comfortable cohabitation with William Faulkner. I think I can best illustrate what I mean by comparing the radically disparate ways in which these two Southerners came to deal with one of the most tragic themes in Southern literature and history—miscegenation.

As early as 1789 Jedidiah Morse, author of *American Geography*, had observed that it was not uncommon in the South to see a mulatto child waiting on the table of the white man who was at once his father and master, and Morse clearly foresaw the immense literary potential of such a situation: "Choice food for satire! wide field for burlesque! noble game for wit! sad cause for pity to bleed, and for humanity to weep!"[2] While the Connecticut Yankee Morse initially pointed toward the bitter *comic* ironies inherent in the widespread mixing of blood that stemmed naturally from slavery, later writers have for the most part chosen to dwell at length on its more pathetic dimensions. Drawing upon a tradition that has its roots in the abolitionist rhetoric and antislavery fiction of the antebellum period, Southern writers since the Civil War have returned to the topic of mixed blood with an obsessive regularity. A "myth" of miscegenation has emerged, in which the prostitution of black women's bodies and the subsequent exploitation of one's own flesh and blood become metaphors for the South's legacy of racial guilt in the broadest sense, and in which the mulatto character, the living emblem of that guilt, becomes the avenging agent who brings the white man's wrongs home to roost.[3] Works as diverse as George Washington Cable's *The Grandissimes*, Allen Tate's *The Fathers*, and Carson McCullers's *Clock without Hands* spring from the same rich soil, as do Twain's *Pudd'nhead Wilson* and Faulkner's *Go Down, Moses*, the principal subjects of my remarks here. Both Twain and Faulkner recognized the tragic aspects of miscegenation, indeed seem to have felt them most intensely, but they attempted something few of their fellows dared; they enlisted the Comic Muse in an effort to come to terms with the perennial demon of the Southern imagination, the haunting figure of the wronged mulatto crying out for justice.

It is instructive to begin by recalling Twain's account of the genesis of *Pudd'nhead Wilson*. He originally set out, he tells us, to write a pure farce based on the slapstick misadventures of a pair of Siamese twins, but the appearance of certain characters on the scene, characters who took on a life of their own, turned

the farce in a decidedly tragic direction.[4] The novel that resulted, then, was the product of compelling inner motivations,
and its plot, taken in the abstract, is little more than a classic
restatement of the theme of miscegenation outlined above. Roxana, a beautiful mulatto slave, "heir to two centuries of unatoned
insult and outrage," has borne the child of a white "Virginian of
formidable calibre." Prompted by a desire to spare her son from
any possibility of ever being sold down river and in part by a
vaguely formulated sense of avenging herself upon the white
race, she switches the identities of her child and the white son of
a slaveholding aristocrat. Her son, "Tom," grows up to be the
dissolute scion of Dawson's Landing's preeminent family, while
the legitimate heir is conditioned into becoming the most abject
of slaves, until Tom, who has significantly blacked his face for
purposes of disguise, murders his supposed uncle and surrogate
father in the course of a robbery and is exposed through the
convoluted ratiocinations of the title character Wilson. When he
is then sold down river, Roxana's deepest fears are realized after
all. Tragic enough in the abstract, perhaps, but once this bare-
bones narrative line is reintegrated into the context of the novel
as a whole the effect is something quite different. Twain, it would
seem, has written a farce after all. The narrative voice that
dominates *Pudd'nhead Wilson* recounts the chain of events and
comments upon the motivations and actions of the characters
from a stance of wry, ironic, at times brutally contemptuous,
condescension.[5] As readers, we of necessity look down, both
figuratively and literally, upon the tribulations of these blind
fools who are puppets of a cosmic determinism with something
of the cruel relish usually associated with pratfall humor. We are
moved to laughter, however bitter, rather than to pity and fear.
As Aristotle knew, and as Thomas Hobbes recognized with cynical accuracy, we tend to laugh from a superior vantage point.
The ability to laugh implies transcendence.

If *Pudd'nhead Wilson* is approached as both an expression of
the Southern literary imagination *and* of its author's most inti-
mate inner compulsions (Twain's painful ambivalence towards

the South and feelings of guilt over slavery are well known), it is
tempting to look upon the novel as a personal, as well as artistic,
triumph. The "black" humor (in both senses of the term) which
Twain brings to bear on the tenderest spot on his region's
wounded psyche would seem to argue for a kind of breakthrough
on the author's part. If the South's heritage of racial wrongs is but
one more example of the absurd perfidy of "the damned human
race," then the very fact that Twain can subject such folly to
scornful ridicule is an indication of the degree to which he has
succeeded in extricating himself from the communal shame; it is,
indeed, an act of self-absolution. The extent to which such a
process represents a defensiveness on the jokester's part is not to
be gainsayed. Norman Holland, in a recent, witty book on
laughter, quotes Freud to the effect that "humor has in it a
*liberating* element. . . . It refuses to be hurt by the arrows of
reality or to be compelled to suffer. It insists that it is impervious
to wounds dealt by the outside world, in fact that these are
merely occasions for affording it pleasure."[6]

One need not be a confirmed Freudian to see how nicely such
an observation seems to fit the circumstances out of which
*Pudd'nhead Wilson* emerged and assumed its final shape. But
the sad fact remains that even if Twain did succeed in laughing
certain ghosts to rest in the very process of writing his novel,
they did not stay down for long. When Twain again recreated the
lost Hannibal of his youth in "Indiantown" and other brooding,
fantastical fragments written over the last decade or so of his life,
the spectres of slavery and racial injustice loom forever in the
not-too-distant background.[7] The gratuitous black minstrel
humor that intrudes briefly onto the scene in "No. 44, The
Mysterious Stranger" strikes a distinctly false note, seems indeed to represent a kind of whistling in the dark, compared to
more disturbing vestiges of Twain's sense of racial injustice in his
later work—most tellingly perhaps in an unfinished novel entitled "Which Was It?" That especially suggestive example of the
diffuse and dreamlike process pieces Twain was reduced to writing at the end is set in a seemingly idyllic Southern village where

the slaves are ostensibly as contented as those in the fiction of the un-Reconstructed Southern apologist Thomas Nelson Page. Like *Pudd'nhead Wilson*, "Which Was It?" gradually evolves into a murder mystery, a tale of hidden crime that must be ferreted out, but the differences between these two narrative projections of Twain's inner turmoil are shocking and profound. Here the murderer is a white Southern gentleman and his nemesis, the only character who knows of his guilt, is the man's cousin—a *mulatto* with "a long bill agin he lowdorn ornery white race"— who blackmails his white kinsmen into becoming *his* slave in an ironic reversal of racial roles that evokes horror more than laughter. Twain's protagonist is trapped by the South's ancestral curse, but so too is the author who cannot proceed with his narrative once miscegenation has reasserted itself. The transcendent, sardonic laughter of *Pudd'nhead Wilson* did not signal a valid exorcism; it provided only a temporary evasion.

Mark Twain's quandary at the point at which his story breaks off is strikingly like that Faulkner's Isaac McCaslin faces toward the end of *Go Down, Moses*. Uncle Ike too has sought to distance himself from his region's communal guilt, symbolized by a heritage of mixed blood (and in this case incest), through standing above the sordidness. His renunciation of his birthright, like Twain's transcendent laughter, is premature and evasive. Even more importantly, it is doomed to failure, as Isaac learns when the twin evils of miscegenation and incest return to confront him in the supposed safety of his beloved wilderness itself. But it should be emphasized that it is the character, not the author, who is trapped in *Go Down, Moses*. In spite of the elegiac gloom that pervades the best-known sections of that novel (for my purposes here I am prepared to accept Faulkner's word that it is a novel), *Go Down, Moses* is often a remarkably humorous book. And some of the most hilarious passages touch upon the very tragic motif that dominates the narrative—miscegenation as the symbol of Southern racial sin.

The high hilarity of "Was," the narrative unit that introduces the McCaslin saga, sets the novel moving at a frenetic pace and presents an admirable illustration of the old critical truism that the essential difference between tragedy and comedy is one of perspective.[8] Here we have a literal manhunt in which a mulatto slave is pursued by his white half-brother and a pack of hounds. Yet the focus is not upon the terror of the runaway (indeed he feels none), but on the exasperated frustration of his pursuing kinsman Uncle Buck, who finds slavery more trouble than it is worth. Things are so ajumble in "Was" that the real manhunt turns out to be one orchestrated by the mulatto Turl and the old-maid Miss Sophonsiba for their respective romantic ends, and, in a variation on one of the hoariest jokes in folk tradition, Uncle Buck, the pursuer as pursued, a bachelor and misogynist, is caught quite literally with his pants down in a spinster's bed. At the very core of this spirited chase remains the fact of blood ties across the color line, but that fact is merely one element in a garish comic pattern that embraces human activity on its own terms without stooping to judgments enforced from without.

Indeed, the celebrated fourth section of "The Bear," the focal piece of *Go Down, Moses,* which details Isaac McCaslin's struggles to extricate himself from his family's tainted heritage, has its share of stubborn comic ironies, though Ike's obsessive and finally self-indulgent preoccupation with the triangular curse of slavery, miscegenation, and incest brought upon the land by his grandfather Carothers McCaslin precludes his taking a joke where the reader finds it. The same plantation ledgers that reveal old Carothers's misdeeds to his grandson also sketch out the fragmentary chronicle of the androgynous Percival Brownlee, a slave whose fecklessness gives a new dimension to the phrase "the burden of Southern history," as well as to the thwarted efforts of Uncle Buck and Uncle Buddy McCaslin to *"Get shut of him."* Even when freed, this clownish slave (a universal human, not racial type) is loath to leave the old plantation, not out of loyalty to his white folks as in the novels of Page, but out of a parasitic determination to mind the main chance. The final irony is that Brownlee, once set on ministering to his people's spiritual needs as a jackleg evangelist, ends up as the

proprietor of "a select New Orleans brothel" presumably cater-
ing to a white clientele and stocked with mulatto "fancy gals" like
the genuinely pathetic slave Eunice, bought by the patriarch
Carothers McCaslin in New Orleans back in 1807 and eventually
the mother of the daughter whom he subsequently violated. In
this same connection, the reader would do well to ponder the
humorous implications of the flashback scene in which Miss
Sophonsiba, who has finally realized her dream of a match with
Buck McCaslin, takes her young son Isaac to visit his Uncle
Hubert Beauchamp and finds a mulatto seductress established in
her late mother's house and wearing one of her own cast-off
dresses. At first the startled Hubert reacts like a little boy
surprised with his hand in the cookie jar, or rather honey pot.
He tries in vain to pass the girl off as his new cook, and his effort
to assuage his sister's wrath with the thought that blacks are now
free and therefore " 'folks too just like we are' " stands the Mc-
Caslin family curse on its head.[9]

Our recognition of this comic material (whether brought to
our attention by close reading or otherwise) inevitably serves to
distance us from Ike's dilemma, though in no way does it undercut the deadly serious nature of slavery and the sexual abuse of
black women that provokes Ike's rightful indignation and informs
his personal myth of his region's collective past. Indeed, it can be
argued that taken in the abstract these elements underscore the
pervasiveness of miscegenation in the South, but that is precisely the point. Viewed as concrete and specific components of
Faulkner's total fictive construct or, to soften the figure somewhat, as integral if secondary strands in the overall narrative
pattern or "design" of Go Down, Moses, Uncle Buck's pursuit of
Tomey's Turl, Percival Brownlee's pandering, and lonely old
Hubert Beauchamp's desire for a "cook" reveal humor at work in
the novel in a much more profound way than that afforded by
conventional comic relief. This humor is anything but gratuitous;
it emerges organically from the darker vision that surrounds it.
What is all the more remarkable, however, is that it is essentially
healthy—one is tempted to say "good-natured"—a far cry from

the embittered glee of *Pudd'nhead Wilson*. It provokes a benign smile rather than a spiteful snicker. There is about it a kind of pragmatic earthiness not unlike that we find throughout the humor of the Old Southwest Faulkner so obviously admired,[10] and like much of that humor it seems to spring from an acceptance of the absurdities and contradictions of the human experience and an urge to revel in them for their own sake.

In *Go Down, Moses,* humor is never evasive, nor combative and satirical. It is rather an important sign of Faulkner's ability to embrace and affirm the human condition as he finds it, in keeping with the principles he would later outline so unmistakably in the Nobel Prize acceptance speech. Walter Brylowski comes close to putting his finger on the source of the underlying comic spirit of the novel when he makes the Kierkegaardian observation that in *Go Down, Moses* Faulkner "has captured the psyche in its turn from the religious-ethical mode of consciousness."[11] There is a dimension of the comic perspective that partakes of the sacramental, a level of merriment that, if not precisely Godlike, is by its very nature of a different order from the explicitly Satanic laughter of the late Twain. This kind of humor derives not from a will, conscious or otherwise, to rise above what Yeats calls "the foul rag-and-bone shop of the heart" or, broadly speaking, the human predicament generally. Rather it arises from a recognition of the resilient bedrock of man's indestructibility at the very bottom of tragedy's abyss.[12] In Faulknerian terms, it bolsters a sense of human kind's capacity to endure and ultimately prevail.

Such is the vision that finally informs *Go Down, Moses,* but Faulkner did not arrive at it comfortably. It represents what Robert Penn Warren might call an "earned vision." Twain's attempt to laugh away the regional curse of miscegenation in *Pudd'nhead Wilson* involved a precipitous transcendental leap, too rapid an abdication of the tragic perspective in favor of the comic. Faulkner's driving creative imagination allowed him no such luxury. Before he could enable himself to explore the comic ironies and implications of illicit sexual relations across the color

line, he had to confront the tragic side of the equation in all its
unmitigated darkness. He did just that, of course, in *Absalom,
Absalom!*

Students of Faulkner all but universally agree that *Absalom,*
which appeared in 1936, a full six years before the author published the segments of *Go Down, Moses* in book form, is his
purest and most extensive achievement in the tragic mode. Like
Twain's *Pudd'nhead Wilson,* it was a novel that the author
claimed he had to write. It underwent a long gestation period
and progress was slow. At one point, Faulkner set the manuscript
aside and wrote an altogether different kind of novel, *Pylon,* but,
he would later confess, "The story still wouldn't let me alone."[13]
Judith Bryant Wittenberg has argued persuasively for the importance of *Absalom, Absalom!* as an intensely personal document
into which Faulkner poured "a century of family history and
nearly forty years of his own experience."[14] I would add that
*Absalom* is also a most telling expression of the Southern collective conscience. The tale of the rise and fall of the House of
Sutpen is *the* quintessential realization of the myth of miscegenation and its dire consequences that Southern writers have
wrestled with ever since the Civil War freed them from the
obligation to act as apologists for slavery. In the pages of that
book, Faulkner coerced himself into confronting the most
shameful images of his region's guilt with an honesty and
ruthless determination reflected in the manic preoccupation
with which his character Quentin Compson reconstructs the
Sutpen tragedy for his roommate Shreve. Significantly, *Absalom*
is "almost completely unleavened by the humor found in
Faulkner's other novels."[15] Even a passage like that in which
Wash Jones and Sutpen get drunk together in the scuppernong
arbor is steeped in a dramatic irony that never allows it to rise
above the level of gallows humor.

By now, the thrust of my argument should be clear. In the
process of writing *Absalom, Absalom!* Faulkner undertook a
descent into the abyss. He charted the depths of nightmare and
taboo. But as students of the genre know, tragedy is nothing if it

is not cathartic, and the novel's creator emerged from the crumbling and charred ruins of the Sutpen mansion with a thing of value denied his protagonist Quentin, a fuller grasp on the polar ironies of human experience and a lasting conviction that the tragic mode alone could not do full justice to the human predicament, that humor "is a part of man too" and "even tragedy" walks "a tightrope between the ridiculous . . . and the terrible."[16]

There is no more forceful index to Faulkner's success in laying the ghost of miscegenation to rest than his portrayal of Lucas Beauchamp in *Go Down, Moses.* Despite the fact that he can and does choose to immerse himself in the stereotypical (and inscrutable) role of "Negro" when it suits his purposes, Lucas is so fully human that we recognize ourselves in him from the beginning. Indeed, the black writer Ralph Ellison has singled out Faulkner's characterization of Lucas for special praise.[17] It is only when we step back from the text for a moment that we begin to see Lucas's literary antecedents. In terms of Faulkner's own work, we can trace his lineage back to Joe Christmas in *Light in August* and Charles Bon in *Absalom, Absalom!*,[18] who are in turn the fictional descendants of a long line of mulatto characters whose genealogy goes back to early nineteenth-century American literature. Such characters are victims of a split identity, torn between the white world that rejects them and the black world they too often reject with disdain. They are frequently angels of wrath who bring the ancient curse of miscegenation down on the heads of their white kin. In what we see retrospectively of Lucas as a young man, there is ample evidence of these traits at work, but Lucas outgrows and outlives them after his own descent into the abyss—the nearly tragic encounter with his white cousin Zack Edmonds over the latter's supposed sexual exploitation of his wife. For the new Lucas, his identity as a "man" supersedes any racial pigeonholing. He is a vibrant creation of the Comic Muse as he tries to outwit his daughter and future son-in-law, who threaten his moonshine business, and Faulkner's answer to Erskine Caldwell's Ty Ty

Walton as he quixotically digs for imaginary treasure on the McCaslin place. We laugh at Lucas not because he is beneath us, but because he *is* us, an embodiment of our all-too-human hopes, frustrations, fears, and stubborn pride. Resurrected again in *Intruder in the Dust*, this walking incarnation of sexual relations between the races does indeed stand forth as "tyrant" over the "conscience" of the white community, not unlike Joe Christmas in *Light in August*. But Lucas assumes that role not by becoming a tragic scapegoat, though he is threatened for a time with lynching, but by emerging as an uncompromised and uncompromising *comic* victor, whose vindication somehow vindicates the South herself.

Lest my remarks be in anyway misconstrued, I wish to close by stressing the obvious fact that Faulkner, in wrestling with the thorny problem of miscegenation in his fiction—and winning, did not permit his final comic vision to obscure the realities of racial injustice in the South's past. They were there, just as Quentin Compson and Isaac McCaslin found them, but they were only part of the panoramic human picture.[19] Faulkner's awareness of this crucial fact gave him not only the conviction that old wrongs should be righted but the eventual courage to do what he could in that direction, even given his discomfort in the public arena. In the end, laughter is indeed liberating; it enables us to get on with the work before us.

## NOTES

1. In *The South and Faulkner's Yoknapatawpha: The Actual and the Apocryphal*, ed. Evans Harrington and Ann J. Abadie (Jackson: University Press of Mississippi, 1977), 61.

2. Quoted in Louis Ruchames, ed., *Racial Thought in America: From the Puritans to Lincoln* (Amherst: University of Massachusetts Press, 1964), 198.

3. I have dealt with the origins and aspects of the myth of miscegenation at some length in "The Serpent of Lust in the Southern Garden," *Southern Review*, n.s. 10 (1974), 805–22.

4. See Twain's preface to "Those Extraordinary Twins" in the Norton Critical Edition of *Pudd'nhead Wilson*, ed. Sidney E. Berger (New York, 1980), 119–20. *Pudd'nhead Wilson* remains one of the most problematic works in the Twain canon. Indispensable to understanding it is Robert Rowlette's *Twain's "Pudd'nhead Wilson": The Development and Design* (Bowling Green: Bowling Green University Press, 1971).

5. Frank C. Cronin is quite right when he calls attention to the overriding importance of the narrative voice in the novel. See "The Ultimate Perspective in *Pudd'nhead Wilson*," *Mark Twain Journal*, 16, no. 1 (1971–72), 14–16. James W. Gargano is more attuned to the vital role humor plays in the novel than Cronin, but I would differ with him on what he identifies as the "genial" nature of that humor. See "*Pudd'nhead Wilson:* Mark Twain as Genial Satan," *South Atlantic Quarterly*, 74 (1975), 365–75.

6. *Laughing: A Psychology of Humor* (Ithaca: Cornell University Press, 1982), 52.

7. The best and most extensive, though by no means definitive, account of Twain's lifelong obsession with the problems of race is found in Arthur G. Pettit's *Mark Twain and the South* (Lexington: University Press of Kentucky, 1974).

8. Lyall H. Powers, in *Faulkner's Yoknapatawpha Comedy* (Ann Arbor: University of Michigan Press, 1980), 164, is one of the more recent critics to note the sinister undercurrents at work in "Was," but he seems too intent upon emphasizing the fundamental "horror" of the story. Despite the title of his book, Powers at times appears to undervalue the comic mode. Walter Taylor has written a particularly fine essay on "Was": "Horror and Nostalgia: The Double Perspective of Faulkner's 'Was,'" *Southern Humanities Review*, 8 (1974), 74–84. It is more difficult to agree with Stuart James, who acknowledges the presence of humor in *Go Down, Moses*, but maintains that it is still Faulkner's "most despairing work." See "The Ironic Voices of Faulkner's *Go Down, Moses*," *South Dakota Review*, 16, no. 1 (1978), 80–101.

9. I have heard it suggested that this episode is a parody of old Carothers McCaslin's misdeeds. Indeed, it seems fair enough to see Mr. Hubert as Carothers's comic foil. He too would pass on a legacy to Isaac, but he squanders the money and Isaac is finally left with nothing. Hubert Beauchamp is a character out of classic comedy—the sad but foolish old man, *senex amans*.

10. For an overview of Faulkner's use of this brand of humor, see Robert D. Jacobs, "Faulkner's Humor," in *The Comic Imagination in American Literature*, ed. Louis D. Rubin, Jr. (New Brunswick: Rutgers University Press, 1973), 305–18.

11. *Faulkner's Olympian Laugh* (Detroit: Wayne State University Press, 1968), 166. George C. Bedell's remarks in *Faulkner and Kierkegaard* (Baton Rouge: Louisiana State University Press, 1972), 85, are likewise germane here.

12. My thinking on the nature of the tragic and comic as modalities of literary expression is deeply indebted to the work of the Jesuit critic William F. Lynch, as brilliantly presented in his book *Christ and Apollo: The Dimensions of the Literary Imagination* (New York: Sheed and Ward, 1960).

13. *Faulkner at the University*, ed. Frederick L. Gwynn and Joseph L. Blotner (Charlottesville: University of Virginia Press, 1959), 281.

14. *Faulkner: The Transfiguration of Biography* (Lincoln: University of Nebraska Press, 1979), 131.

15. Ibid., 141. This dearth of humor in *Absalom, Absalom!*, so uncharacteristic of Faulkner, has puzzled critics almost from the beginning of systematic discussion of Faulkner's writing. See for example Harry Modean Campbell and Ruel E. Foster, *William Faulkner: A Critical Appraisal* (Norman: University of Oklahoma Press, 1951), 94.

16. *Faulkner at the University*, 39.

17. See his discussion of the film version of *Intruder in the Dust* in *Shadow and Act* (New York: Vintage, 1972), 273–81, and his remark in an interview with Robert Penn Warren reprinted in *Robert Penn Warren: A Collection of Critical Essays*, ed. John Lewis Longley, Jr. (New York: New York University Press, 1965), 43.

18. Eric J. Sundquist links Lucas with Christmas and Bon in *Faulkner: The House Divided* (Baltimore: The Johns Hopkins University Press, 1983), 155–56, but he does not recognize the extent to which Faulkner's comic transformation of the tragic mulatto stereotype is integral to understanding the vision embodied by *Go Down, Moses* on its own terms. *Go Down, Moses* is not *Absalom, Absalom!*, nor was it meant to be. For all my admiration for Sundquist's book, I cannot help but feel he falls into the trap many

Faulknerians find themselves in when he downplays humor and comedy as less "serious" than the tragic mode.

19. Ronald Schleifer suggests that Lucas's refusal to become a victim of the past like his kinsman Isaac McCaslin parallels Faulkner's attitudes toward the problem of history. See "Faulkner's Storied Novel: *Go Down, Moses* and the Translation of Time," *Modern Fiction Studies*, 28 (1982), 109–27.

# What Faulkner Learned from the Tall Tale

## Thomas L. McHaney

In 1918, with the connivance of Phil Stone, William Faulkner affected an English accent, invented a British vicar named Twimberly-Thorndike, wrote letters in the vicar's name declaring himself to be a "god-fearing young Christian gentleman," and successfully lied his way into the Royal Air Force-Canada. When in Toronto he gave information for his Certificate of Service, he put the "u" into his name, said his birthplace was Middlesex, and allotted himself a birthday not in September, as he should have, but in one of his favorite months, May, and in a year subsequent to his actual nativity. He seems to have given people in Toronto the impression that he was a former Yale student. In 1919 he wore the unearned wings of a British aviator, began telling people he had crashed a plane or two, and used a cane and strong whiskey, he would explain, to compensate for his war wounds, which shifted, as did the location of Yoknapatawpha County later, to whatever site suited the author's purposes. In 1925 he not only told Sherwood Anderson about his war experiences but also left Anderson convinced that Faulkner believed a child conceived between white and black would be impotent, like a mule.[1] In 1931 William Faulkner told Marshall Smith of the Memphis *Press-Scimitar* (the sensational evening Memphis paper which his Auntee read with relish), that his parents were a Negro slave and an alligator, that his brothers were Eagle Rock, an airplane, and Dr. Walter E. Traprock (pseudonym of *Vanity Fair* author George Shepard Chappell, who wrote parodies of popular novel forms and whose *Cruise of the Kawa* Phil Stone had ordered from New Haven in 1922).[2] In 1932 Faulkner wrote in the introduction to the Modern Library *Sanctuary* that he had never known nor lived among people who wrote novels and stories and "I suppose I did not know that people got money for them"—this after he had published seven books, sojourned in New Haven, New York, New Orleans, Paris, and even attended the 1931 Southern Writers Conference in Charlottesville.[3] In 1936, apparently suffering *delerium tremens* after a bout of drinking, he frightened Meta Carpenter by crying that the German airplanes of his war years were after him again.[4] At another time, possibly in the 1930s, according to his brother John, Faulkner was so impossibly drunk that his mother was called to Rowan Oak to care for him.

> For two days she fed Bill iced tea, first with a little whiskey in it and then less and less till he was drinking straight iced tea. For twelve hours Bill didn't have anything but tea. Mother knew that by then he ought to be sober enough to talk, anyhow. She drew a chair up beside his bed.
>
> "Billie, don't you think it's about time you got up and went to work?" she said.
>
> "I can't," Bill mumbled. "I'm drunk."
>
> "If you are, you're drunk on iced tea," Mother said. "That's all you've had for the last twelve hours."
>
> Bill shifted his eyes from the ceiling to her, then sat up on the edge of the bed. He said, as pleasant as you please, "Well, I believe I'll get up and go to work then."[5]

This is the same man who, in 1940, delivered the moving and genuine funeral sermon for Caroline Barr, called Mammie Callie, who had raised him, extolling her virtues and giving her credit for a few of his own: "From her, I learned to tell the truth."[6]

I do not dispute that memory. Faulkner did learn to tell the truth, something his worldwide reputation corroborates sufficiently to need no validation from me, though the Nobel Prize did not make him any less shifty in new country, to invoke roughly the motto of Johnson Jones Hooper's Captain Simon Suggs. In 1951, shortly after his moving Nobel Prize Acceptance Speech and on the Saturday morning following the presentation of the Medal of the French Legion of Honor in New Orleans, which he accepted in French, praising the French literary spirit, he told a reporter for the *Times-Picayune*, "I'm a farmer. . . . I ain't a writer. . . . Why I don't even know any writers."[7] Subsequent interviews with him and anecdotes about his life during the post-Nobel period show that he remained as creative in front of a live audience, whether of one or one hundred, as he was when alone with pen and paper.

Stretching the longbow was and is an American tradition, though obviously not something we can claim as unique. But given our Puritan heritage it is a tradition that we should regard with wonder and pride, for despite unpromising beginnings and regardless of all admonitions and warnings, this country has made progress in the matter of lying, though we have had setbacks in other areas, and William Faulkner should be set down, right along with some of our presidents, as one of the great practitioners. In fact, much of Faulkner's personal humor, like much of his fictional humor, springs from his ability to tell what Huck Finn called stretchers, what we call tall tales, and what a great many fastidious puritans might call lies.

The conventional wisdom about this, I believe, is that Faulkner, as Southerner, was to the manner born, but it is interesting that he seems not to have accepted this heritage into his writing until his late twenties, busy as he was during his youth trying to appear " 'different' in a small town"[8] by affecting some of the exotic personal styles with which you are doubtless familiar—the ones that resulted in his being called "Count No 'Count" or the "Marquis de Lafayette"—and working within the traditions of late romantic poetry, especially the decadent and symbolists modes. As a matter of fact, at that time Faulkner disdained one of the major literary transmitters of the tall tale tradition in American writing, Mark Twain, whom he judged, in 1922, to be "a hack writer who would not have been considered fourth rate in Europe, who tricked out a few of the old proven 'sure fire' literary skeletons with sufficient local color to intrigue the superficial and the lazy."[9] (This point of view regarding Twain was shared, oddly, by Sherwood Anderson, in whose 1925 novel *Dark Laughter*, written in New Orleans with Faulkner around, Twain is condemned for pulling his literary punches in what he wrote about the river because of his submission to American Puritanism and materialism. Anderson, like some other writers of the period, perhaps even Faulkner, appears to have taken Van Wyck Brooks's 1920 view of Twain quite seriously. Hemingway's famous statement about *Huckleberry Finn*'s role as the beginning of all American literature does not come until *Green Hills of Africa*, in 1935, three years after Bernard DeVoto's 1932 "corrective" to Brooks's presentation of Twain.)

Faulkner's known preference for the late romantic and his rejection of Twain's material and method have led me to wonder when and how Faulkner changed—if that is the right word— from the man who wrote "L'après midi d'une faune" (the title of his first published poem, stolen in a friendly manner from Mallarmé) to the man who wrote "L'après midi d'une vache," or, as it was titled in English and eventually published under the authorship of one Ernest V. Trueblood, "Afternoon of a Cow."[10] How did he work his way from the fin de siècle decadents to, or back to, the antebellum Southern humorists? How did he get through the affectations of mannered, imitative poetry to become, in his prose, "poetically the most accurate man alive"[11] when it came to using the rhythms of the vernacular tale in modernist fiction?

One ironical explanation is that Faulkner found his way back to the paradoxical exaggeration of old Southwestern realism—a paradox noted, for example, by Thomas Bangs Thorpe when he claimed that the exaggerated tales merely reflected the exaggerated lives lived in the exaggerated circumstances of the Old Southwest's big woods—not despite the decadent material with which he experimented so heavily in his youth and young manhood, but through it.

Like so many young writers, Faulkner was, in more than one way, fleeing his own experience, attempting to be "different" in a small town not merely in how he behaved but in what and how he wrote. Doing that, he may have fled his native materials and their voices right into the arms of his own best manner. We know, for example, that in the Edwardian Housman Faulkner found materials congenial to his own experience and a poetic voice that had eluded him in the work of his modernist contemporaries. In the symbolist poets and impressionist painters and writers he discovered the ideal of art and the models for manipulating abstractions that he could not yet discern in things closer to hand. He may have found in the prose of Oscar Wilde, also, an admonition to untruth that touched his imagination. "The Decay of Lying" by Wilde is a debate between two young aesthetes about the relative merits of art and nature. The central point is Vivian's reading of his essay, also entitled "The Decay of Lying":

> "One of the chief causes that can be assigned for the curiously commonplace character of most of the literature of our age is undoubtedly the decay of Lying as an art, a science, and a social pleasure. The ancient historians gave us delightful fiction in the form of fact; the modern novelist presents us with dull facts under the guise of fiction. The Blue-Book is rapidly becoming his ideal both for method and manner. He has his tedious 'document humain,' his miserable little 'coin de la creation,' into which he peers with his microscope. He is to be found at the Librarie Nationale, or at the British Museum, shamelessly reading up his subject. He has not even the courage of other people's ideas, but insists on going directly to life for everything, and, ultimately, between encyclopedias and personal experience, he comes to the ground, having drawn his types from the family circle or from the weekly washerwoman, and having acquired an amount of useful information from which never, even in his most meditative moments, can he thoroughly free himself.
>
> "The loss that results to literature in general from this false ideal of our time can hardly be over-estimated. People have a careless way of talking about a 'born liar,' just as they talk about a 'born poet.' But in both cases they are wrong. Lying and poetry are arts—arts, as Plato saw, not unconnected with each other—and they require the most careful study, the most disinterested devotion. Indeed, they have their technique, just as the more material arts of painting and sculpture have, their subtle secrets of form and colour, their craft-mysteries, their deliberate artistic methods. As one knows the poet

by his fine music, so one can recognise the liar by his rich rhythmic utterance, and in neither case will the causal inspiration of the moment suffice. Here, as elsewhere, practice must precede perfection. But in modern days, while the fashion of writing poetry has become far too common, and should, if possible, be discouraged, the fashion of lying has almost fallen into disrepute. Many a young man starts in life with a natural gift for exaggeration which, if nurtured in congenial and sympathetic surroundings, or by the imitation of the best models, might grow into something really great and wonderful. But as a rule, he comes to nothing. He either falls into careless habits of accuracy, or takes to frequenting the society of the aged and the well-informed. Both things are equally fatal to his imagination, as indeed they would be fatal to the imagination of anybody, and in a short time he develops a morbid and unhealthy faculty of truth-telling, begins to verify all statements made in his presence, has no hesitation in contradicting people who are much younger than himself, and often ends by writing novels which are so like his life that no one can possibly believe in their probability."[12]

This witty but serious passage from Wilde is in much the same precious voice that Faulkner used when writing his essays in *The Mississippian:* "A national literature cannot spring from folk lore," he wrote in 1922, the same year he low-rated Twain, "though heaven knows, such a forcing has been tried often enough—for America is too big and there are too many folk lores."[13] Or compare Wilde's remarks on Henry James—"Mr. Henry James writes fiction as if it were a painful duty, and wastes upon mean motives and imperceptible 'points of view' his neat literary style, his felicitous phrases, his swift and caustic satire"[14]—with Faulkner on Amy Lowell: "Miss Amy Lowell tried a polyphonic prose which, in spite of the fact that she has created some delightful statuettes of perfectly blown glass, is merely a literary flatuency; and it has left her, reed in hand, staring in naive surprise at the air whence her bubbles have burst."[15]

Whether Faulkner read Wilde's essay or not I cannot say, though plenty of evidence exists, cited by Brooks, Millgate, Blotner, and others, that he read a good deal of Wilde, and whether he needed to read it in order to come to proper terms with lying is perhaps moot. His decadent poses—like some of his later ones—showed, as I have already suggested, practiced skill in pulling the longbow, even if the bow was at that point Pre-Raphaelite purple or symbolist yellow. I do think he would have found the essay encouraging. The backwoods version of Vivian's dictum is, perhaps, V. K. Ratliff's "if it aint complicated up enough, it aint right."[16] But conversely, one can see today, I hope, that the tall tale style people like Ratliff inherited, carefully filtered through a consciousness created by absorbing Conrad, Eliot, Freud, Frazer, Bergson, Einstein, Joyce, Jung, Anderson, Cézanne, Picasso, and Matisse, becomes a fine-edged tool in the modernist artist's battle against the regimentation, dull empiricism, and everydayness of modern times.

Whatever Faulkner might have recognized if he read "The Decay of Lying," he would have recognized himself, for at the end of the piece Vivian invites Cyril to join him on the terrace where "'droops the milk-white peacock like a ghost,' while the evening star 'washes the dusk with silver,'" demonstrating, he says, that at "twilight nature becomes a wonderfully suggestive effect . . . though perhaps its chief use is to illustrate quotations from poets"[17]—poets, one notes immediately, whom Faulkner was imitating for all he was worth, in his early twenties, right down to the peacocks and silver dusks and poignant twilights.

By the time Faulkner reached New Orleans and the important orbit of Sherwood Anderson and the other famous Creoles, on his way to Paris, doubtless bent on ploughing the latest decadence for all it was worth, he appears to have suffered a sea change as writer, and not only under the tutelage of Anderson. New Orleans, with its connection to the river, its French Quarter characters, its interesting newspaper crowd, housed Roark Bradford, whose *Ol' Man Adam an' His Chillen* would become *Green Pastures;* Lyle Saxon, a chronicler of the city and the river's past; and the *Double Dealer,* a little magazine whose title suggests some affinity with the tradition of the tall tale. It was, in a sense, the birthplace of the half-horse half-alligator frontier legend epitomized in Andrew Jackson's swamp-fighters and apotheosized, for Faulkner and Anderson, in the equestrian statue of Jackson in Jackson Square with its enormous boots. The gigantic boots, they speculated, concealed some terrible secret. The brief but marvelous work Faulkner created in the tall tale tradition while in New Orleans is now well known: the fabulous adventures of the Jackson family, especially the piece now in *Uncollected Stories* about the metamorphosis of Claude, who attempts to harvest the family's sheep, rapidly turning into first beavers and then alligators as they float on cane life preservers in the bayous, and whose exploits in the water lead to his becoming a shark that bothers the plump blonde lady bathers along the Gulf Coast.

Some of the Al Jackson material would find its way into *Mosquitoes,* where it is juxtaposed with an anthology of late nineteenth- and early twentieth-century styles and forms, including some of the purple passages retrieved from Faulkner's more aesthetic period. The combination of decadence and tall tale humor may be farfetched, but it seems to have been a congenial mode for Faulkner, whose next work, after the New Orleans sojourn and before the composition of *Mosquitoes,* was done in Paris and includes "Elmer," that equally mixed-mode Portrait of the Artist as a Young Arkansas Hick.

Once he had returned home from Europe, Faulkner took up *Father Abraham,* the early version of Flem Snopes's machinations in Frenchman's Bend. The voice of *Father Abraham,* however, is not what we should expect from the material, nor do the allusions seem altogether appropriate to the subject matter:

> He [the reference is to Flem Snopes] is a living example of the astonishing byblows of man's utopian dreams actually functioning; in this case the dream is Democracy. He will become legendary in time, but he has always been symbolic. Legendary as Roland and as symbolic of a form of behavior; as symbolic of an age and a region as his predecessor . . . as symbolic and as typical of a frame of mind as Buddha is today. . . . As Buddha, through a blending of successive avatars, was in the beginning Complete and will be Complete when thought has long since progressed logically into a frigid region

without sight nor sound where amid sunless space the I become a sightless eye contemplates itself in timeless unsurprise, so with him.[18]

Faulkner's point of view in the germ of the opening scene of *The Hamlet* appears to derive from Balzac and Emerson, with the condescension of A. B. Longstreet, but later passages in this piece of apprentice work are as decadent as anything he wrote: "They tiptoed through the dark hallway and onto the veranda, into the pallid refulgence of the moon. The apple tree raised its virginal transience, haunting as a forgotten strain of music frozen into fragile and fleeting permanence, still as a dream, as austere and passionate and fine."[19] And if this is where *The Hamlet* began, it seems appropriate that what would become the *closing* episode of the first Snopes novel appeared in embryonic form in *Saturday Evening Post* only six years later, in 1932, written in a more appropriate voice but bearing a title from that great decadent battle piece, Fitzgerald's rendering of *The Rubáiyát*. "Lizards in Jamshyd's Courtyard," once titled, Blotner tells us, "Omar's Eighteenth Quatrain,"[20] comes from a passage—"They say the Lion and the Lizard keep/The courtyards where Jamshýd gloried and drank deep"—that directly precedes the passage, "I sometimes think that never blows so red/The rose as where some buried Caesar bled," from which Stark Young borrowed the title of his 1934 novel.

Though he did not have an ear for it yet in *Father Abraham*, the juxtaposition of frontier exaggeration and fin de siècle color proved not to be a bad idea for Faulkner, as many of his novels testify, including *Light in August, Absalom, Absalom!*, and, of course, *The Hamlet*, where Swinburne and Mallarmé roam with Ike Snopes, Wagner watches over Eula Varner on the evening of the spotted horses, and the ponies themselves might have erupted from work by a postimpressionist or cubist or even one of the old predecessors such as Rimbaud, whose poem *Ornieres* (wheel ruts) in *Illuminations* evokes "twenty spotted circus horses" and juxtaposes them, as would *As I Lay Dying*, with "Coffins, too, . . . rolling along to the trot of large blue and black mares," and whose *Parade* (Circus) in the same volume reminds the critic Robert Greer Cohn, at least, with its "Virile men! Eyes deadened, like a summer's night, red and black, tricolored, of steel spotted with golden stars," of Buck Hipps and Popeye.[21]

We know pretty much where Faulkner imbibed his fin de siècle images, pure from Symons's symbolist volume, from Swinburne and Beardsley and Wilde, or filtered through such modernist poets as Eliot, Cummings, or Conrad Aiken. And we have a good deal of evidence about some of the personal as well as the primary literary sources for his use of the traditions of native American humor: travels through the countryside of north Mississippi alone or with his Uncle John to campaign for county office, tale swapping with, among others, Anderson and Phil Stone, and some early reading in Longstreet, G. W. Harris, T. B. Thorpe, and others (it's hard to imagine a young man of his generation missing out on *Mark Twain's Library of Humor*).

But, for all the possible, even local connections (Longstreet was president of the University of Mississippi and is buried in the same cemetery as Faulkner), for quite some time in his young literary career Faulkner seems to have put the tradition of native humor and realism behind him, and even when he first takes up the Snopes material in *Father Abraham*, as we have seen, the voice he uses is a curious combination of A. B. Longstreet's distant and disdainful gentleman narrator and Ralph Waldo Emerson. When he takes up the material of the antebellum backwoods Southerners again, however, in the mid-1930s, everything seems to work, culminating at the end of the decade in those two masterpieces, twin crowns of the tall tale tradition in America, *The Hamlet* and *Go Down, Moses*.

It is not as if Faulkner had lost his sense of humor between 1926 and 1932, of course, for there is humor, usually mordant, slashed into all his novels, including his most serious ones—*The Sound and the Fury, Light in August, Sanctuary*, and *Absalom, Absalom!* But it does seem likely that a series of publishing events transpired during this period to reawaken Faulkner's interest in the tall tale tradition, to renew its marketability at a time when he needed to consider the literary market carefully, and to reinspire his attempts to practice the art of lying in that peculiarly Southwestern mode, though he would tinge his work still with the color and formal arrangements of symbolism, impressionism, or cubism and infuse it not with references to Buddha but to such analogous modern spirits as Bergson, Freud, and Jung.

Faulkner, as many have noted, appears to have read the works of the antebellum writers Longstreet, Hooper, George Washington Harris, Henry Clay Lewis, and Thomas Bangs Thorpe. He came to admire Mark Twain, though in 1947 he says merely that people will read *Huck Finn* for a long time, adding that "Twain has never really written a novel, however. His work is too loose. We'll assume that a novel has set rules. His work is a mass of stuff—just a series of events."[22]

It is unnecessary for me to list specific examples of what Faulkner got from the antebellum humorists, especially in view of what has been written on the subject, so I will only summarize a few points germane to my special purposes. Longstreet created a scurrilous backwoods character named Ransy Sniffle who became sufficiently famous in his time for the name—run together—to become generic; it was listed, however briefly, in a dictionary of American slang, thus becoming, whether with influence on Faulkner and Phil Stone or not I cannot say, a suggestive study in the kind of onomatopoeonymy—to coin a doubtful term a big liar would envy—that gave us Flem Snopes.

Hooper gave us Simon Suggs—a tag name with imputations of simony on the one hand and something viscous on the other, another fitting predecessor of Flem, Eck, and other catarrhal Snopes nomenclature. As a recent writer on Mark Twain's Victorianism has reminded us, Hooper also pushed the sexual humor of the nineteenth-century genre to its limits. Leland Krauth notes in the staid pages of *American Literature* that the camp meeting scene in *The Adventures of Captain Simon Suggs, Late of the Tallapoosa Volunteers*, from which Twain may have found inspiration for some of the exploits of the Duke and the

Dauphin in *Huckleberry Finn*, is heavy with sexual innuendo—
if innuendo isn't too weak a word where we find men and women
rolling about on the ground or sobbing in "promiscuous heaps,"
where we hear a "sensual seeming man" exhorting, "Keep the
thing warm, breethring," as he lavishes caresses on a "bevy of
young women" and croons, "Come to the Lord, honey!"—I
don't know how Leslie Fiedler missed that—and where a huge
woman shouts "Gl-o-ree!" before she has a fit of the jerks and
falls "across a diminutive old man in a little round hat"—*that's* as
nice a pre-Freudian touch as is the response: "'Good Lord, have
mercy!' ejaculated the little man."[23]

George Washington Harris gave us the prototypical frontier
iconoclast, Sut Lovingood, an example in his own person—
natural born durned fool—as well as in his exploits (turning
bulls, hornets, lizards loose at inappropriate times and places or
pursuing those "tearing" gals, Sal Yardley and Sicily Burns), as
Noel Polk has proved to my satisfaction, of the dangerous release
of animal nature.[24]

These images are not, in their way, unsuited to the fin de
siècle material in which Faulkner had immersed himself between what must have been a lot of youthful reading of Southern
humor and his rediscovery of its importance for his own writing.
Much of that late nineteenth-century work also dramatizes re-
pressed sexuality and the dangers of animal nature, but in decadent or symbolist imagery (cf., Beardsley, Swinburne,
Mallarmé, or, for that matter, Picasso). It really isn't so surprising, finally, that Faulkner could link stock diddling and, say,
Swinburne's "In the Orchard" ("Ah God, Ah God, that day
should come so soon") or Flem Snopes and the *Rubáiyát* ("Lizards in Jamshyd's Courtyard").

Thomas Bangs Thorpe gave us the Big Bear of Arkansas, Jim
Doggett, and the "unhuntable creation bear" that he ironically
pursues with his "inexpressibles" around his ankles because he
has been out answering the call of nature—one never mentioned
by Emerson and Thoreau—when the bear had walked through
his fence. Touched by the tragic imagination, Faulkner managed

to hunt Thorpe's bear with the majesty of Melville and the dramatic variety of Shakespeare, using one of literature's odd couples, Boon Hogganbeck and his sleeping companion, Lion, all in the context of a number of sexual and racial travesties.

A litany of Faulkner's more obvious potential sources could go on and on, including Mark Twain, whose celebrated frog, linguistically gifted blue jay, tree-climbing buffaloes, and humorously pragmatic Huck Finn testify to Twain's own fortunate immersion in and transcendence of the tradition—if also, as Krauth has observed, his not infrequent dilution of it. One of Twain's great achievements was that he took both the tall tale and the high-flying marvelously inventive language in which it was told and converted both to literary use germane to the serious philosophical and artistic currents of his time, a double-edged success that appears to have escaped Sherwood Anderson but which made Faulkner and Hemingway finally claim Twain as the founder of American literature, their literary grandfather.

A frog that can perform like Jim Smiley's frog, or rather fail to perform because he is loaded with buckshot by one of Twain's perennial mysterious strangers, may be decadent, shrugging in his impotence "like a Frenchman, so," may even be Freudian, though that is in another country, but he certainly leads us naturally to a horse that can be repainted and blown up with a bicycle pump to sour Ab Snopes on horse trading and turn him to the antisocial behavior that paves the way for his son Flem's reinvention of fire insurance, the credit system, and nepotism. A frog like Jim Smiley's also leads to a lesser known episode in another American classic, which I cite because it illustrates that there are several conduits besides the antebellum writers and Twain by which the tall tale tradition may have reached Faulkner's lumber room. Owen Wister's *The Virginian* (1902), as James B. Meriwether pointed out in a talk at Georgia Tech in 1976, contains an episode that links Jim Smiley's frog to Faulkner and Sherwood Anderson's large-booted Jackson clan. In Wister's novel the Virginian and some others are stranded in a swampy area when their train breaks down. The region is so poor that no food is available to buy. But the resourceful Virginian catches frogs in the nearby swamps and the stranded travelers enjoy a fine meal of frogs' legs. Then he begins to talk about the unresourceful people in the nearby town who, surrounded by a wealth they don't recognize, are poor and hungry.

"I've been where there was big money in frawgs, and they ain't been," he says. "The trouble," he explains, "is that this is cattle country. They're all cattle hyeh. Talk cattle, think cattle, and they're bankrupt in consequence." They haven't noticed that the swamps, filled with frogs, are a natural resource. Why in Tulare, California, he exclaims, folks have gotten into frog ranching in a big way, "put up big capital and went into it scientific, gettin' advice from the government Fish Commission," and selling the frogs from San Francisco to New York. In Tulare, he says, they talk frogs the way they talk steers and crops other places, and "till yu' got accustomed to it, it would give 'most anybody a shock to hear 'em speak about herdin' the bulls into a pasture by themselves." The work paid well, too, he explained, because you risked rheumatism, it being so muddy and wet in the swamps, and it wasn't easy: sometimes, if a pelican got after the frogs, they'd stampede and break the fence—a wire net strung along a ditch. But like cattle herding, frog ranching had its romance: "yu've heard the mournful, mixedup sound a big bunch of cattle will make? Well, seh, as yu' druv from the railroad to the Tulare frawg ranch, yu' could hear 'em a mile. Springtime they'd sing like girls in the organ loft, and by August they were about ready to hire out for bass." There were "frawg trains tearing acrosst Arizona—big glass tanks with wire over 'em." But as for the hands, there's one problem: the herders who worked in the pastures, the Virginian explains, keep their feet hidden. If you ever see a man that hides his feet and won't take off his socks in company, he has worked in the swamps and caught the disease. "Catch him wadin', and yu'll find he's web-footed."[25] And that, of course, is also why the statue of Andrew Jackson, swamp-fighter, according to Anderson and Faulkner, has such large boots.

In regard to the invention of the Jackson clan—with their clear connection to the seventeenth president—as well as the Snopeses, it is worth noting that a good bit of Old Southwest humor was anti-Jacksonian—*The Adventues of Captain Simon Suggs*, for example, was a mock-campaign biography of the commoners' president. We may suppose that, in its way, so was the original invention of the Snopes clan, as related for us in the opening of *Father Abraham* with its description of Flem as the "living example of the astonishing by-blows of man's utopian dreams actually functioning; in this case the dream is Democracy."[26] One of the most significant things about Faulkner's use of the tradition is that he worked his way through the anti-Jacksonian, anti-democratic sentiment and came to a sympathetic appreciation of the rural folk of the South, including some Snopeses. Faulkner's growing sympathy for the rural poor reflects, in one sense, a national concern fostered by the first Roosevelt administration for the Nation's Number One Economic Problem, the South.[27] He probably did not fail to notice that his material was politically and economically timely, but I suspect that he was also aware of some literary events in the early 1930s that could have helped to establish a basis for the popularity of both his Snopes stories and the hunting materials in *Go Down, Moses,* too. The literary South benefited from the political and economic attention of the New Deal in several ways, not least of which was the Federal Writers' Project and its sponsorship of state travel guides, the collection of local histories, photographs, and so on. Visibility in newspapers and magazines helped give currency to Southern stories. Faulkner's correspondence with the *Saturday Evening Post* and with *Scribner's* shows their eager interest in the Snopes material. "We like your Mississippi stories better than anything else," wrote a *Scribner's* assistant editor in 1931, referring to "Spotted Horses." "I am still hopeful that you are going to do a little more with the monumental character, Flem Snopes."[28] The *Post* responded similarly to "Lizards in Jamshyd's Courtyard," and though we don't have the records yet, I suspect similar response was made to the parts of

*Go Down, Moses* that Faulkner beefed from the corral of his imagination. The success of Southern writers of this period did not occur simply because they were talented; timeliness played an important role, and between writing what someone wants and nothing, even a serious writer will usually prefer to work on those conceptions that promise an audience.

Not merely contemporary Southern life, but the South-western humor tradition itself received some important publishing attention at the same time that Faulkner began to gather up his own materials. The uniqueness of this attention can be illustrated, perhaps, by a look at the recent past. When I began to study American literature only twenty-five years ago, the standard guide to the study of American literature, Clarence Gohdes's 1959 *Bibliographical Guide*, had a nineteen-item section entitled "Essay, Humor and Other Minor Types." Under the category of humor were listed two books by Walter Blair, Constance Rourke's dry *American Humor* (which rates the Southwesterners low) and Tandy's *Crackerbox Philosophers*. Jay B. Hubbell's magisterial *The South in American Literature* (1954) devoted only a few pages to the Old Southwestern tradition which we now find so important. Academia always lags behind the artist, one supposes, and this situation is now happily changed, so that in Louis D. Rubin's 1969 *Bibliographical Guide to the Study of Southern Literature*, Milton Rickels lists nearly a hundred items on the humorists of the Old Southwest alone. But the conditions only twenty years ago illustrate indirectly the void in which Faulkner and his contemporaries might have labored in the 1920s. Conditions for them were also soon to change, however, without long-lasting effect upon academia, so that between 1930 and 1940 many popular treatments of the backwoods tradition appeared, including Franklin Meine's *Tall Tales of the Old Southwest* (1930), Robert Coates's book about the Natchez Trace, *The Outlaw Years* (1930), Blair's book on Mike Fink (1933) and his *Native American Humor* (1937), DeVoto's 1929 *Saturday Review* essay identifying "The Big Bear School of Literature" and his *Mark Twain's America* (1932). Of particular importance, however, are two books by an old acquaintance of Faulkner's, Arthur Palmer Hudson, who taught at the University of Mississippi from 1919 until 1930, married a daughter of Professor Calvin Brown, whose family was close to Faulkner in several ways, and whose Oxford wife, Grace, was one of Phil Stone's secretaries and typed Faulkner's manuscripts. Hudson left Mississippi in 1930 in the wake of the Bilbo purges. He went to the University of North Carolina at Chapel Hill, where he had studied before— like Thomas Wolfe, he had even written a folk play under "Prof" Koch of the Carolina Playmakers—and where he taught from 1930 until his retirement in 1961. But before he left Mississippi, Hudson had completed work on his *Folksongs of Mississippi and Their Background*, parts of which he self-published at Oxford in typescript.[29] The book itself was accepted by the University of North Carolina Press, though it was not published for six years because of the economic restrictions during the Depression. When it came out in 1936, it appeared alongside Hudson's two-volume *Humor of the Old Deep South*, also published by North Carolina, a *vade mecum* to the vital colonial and antebellum writing produced in what Hudson calls "Misslouala," an imaginary country centered on Mississippi but including parts of her neighboring states. While working on his *Humor* book, Hudson and his wife returned to Mississippi on research grants during the summers of 1934 and 1935. Whether they visited Faulkner at those times is not recorded, and Faulkner was much occupied in Hollywood during this period, but it seems likely—given all the local connections—that he was aware of Hudson's continuing work. He corresponded with Hudson in August of 1945, and in 1951, Blotner recounts, the Hudsons did visit the Faulkners and carried their tape recorder inside to play for Faulkner some of their collected material.[30]

Arthur Palmer Hudson's *Folksongs of Mississippi* is a collection of Mississippi versions of traditional ballads and songs. Hudson prefaces the collection with narratives about the people and their stories. Among the anecdotes Hudson recounts are several that would have interested Faulkner, including the story of "Brother" Brasher of Calhoun County, "still living" when Hudson was doing his book. Brother Brasher was a backwoods hard-shell Baptist from near Bruce, not far from Oxford; he had once been a rowdy and leader of the Skuna River gang but after he got religion, he was converted into a fearsome battling lay minister who simply whipped the rest of the county rowdies and moonshiners into his church.[31] A character strikingly similar to him appears, moved to Wylie's Crossing, in Faulkner's essay "Mississippi." Several other episodes and anecdotes in Hudson's books seem to be echoed in Faulkner, and even among those that do not necessarily ring bells are some that would certainly have inspired Faulkner's own bold flights of controlled rhetoric. For example, in the *Folksong* book Hudson cites—and in *Humor of the Old Deep South* anthologizes—the work of J. F. H. Claiborne, antebellum Mississippi journalist and historian. One of Claiborne's many writing achievements is his account of travel through the piney woods region of the state.

Claiborne's travel account, as reprinted from the Natchez *Free Trader and Daily Gazette* of 1841–42 in the *Publications of the Mississippi Historical Society*, volume 9, edited at the University of Mississippi in 1905, ends with three excellent examples of antebellum Southern realism: two accounts of pursuit by wolves—"his horse had taken a stoney path leading down a long descent; his iron hooves fell fast and sharp and left a train of fire behind him. For half an hour he continued his flight, bearing hard upon the bit, bounding forward like a deer and quivering with alarm at the fire that burst from beneath his feet"—and a charming report of Claiborne's sojourn at the piney woods cabin of an aged widow with four daughters and three absent sons.

On this farm, he relates, the "main crop is the sweet potato" (probably the white sweet potato that Faulkner favored). "Some nations boast of their palm tree which supplies them with food, oil, light, fuel, shelter and clothing, but it will be seen that we have in the potato a staple article scarcely inferior to it. It will grow upon soils too thin to produce corn and with little culture. It may be converted into a valuable manure. For forage it is excellent. Hogs and cows thrive on it exceedingly. An acre properly cultivated will yield from three to five hundred bushels. Its farinacious properties make it almost equal to bread and it supplies some of the most delicious dishes for the desert."

Proving the writer's point, the widow's place is well supplied with potatoes. In the widow's barn, he finds a trough "filled with potatoes and the rack [filled] with hay made of the dry [potato] vines." At supper,

> almost every dish was composed of potatoes dressed in many various ways. There were baked potatoes and fried potatoes—bacon and potatoes boiled together—a fine loin of beef was flanked round with potatoes nicely browned and swimming in gravy. A hash of wild turkey was garnished with potatoes mixed up in it. A roast fowl was stuffed with potatoes; beside us stood a plate of potato biscuit, as light as sponge; the coffee, which was strong and well flavored, was made of potatoes, and one of the girls drew from the corner cupboard a rich potato pie. In about an hour a charming blue-eyed girl brought us a tumbler of potato beer that sparkled like champagne and rather archly intimated that there were hot potatoes in the ashes if we felt like eating one. The beer was admirable, and we were told that good whiskey, molasses and vinegar were sometimes made of potatoes.
>
> At length we turned in. The little chamber we were shown to was the perfection of neatness. . . . The pillows were bordered with fringed network and the sheets as white as the untrod snow; but the bed itself, though soft and pleasant, was made of potato vines. Either from over fatigue, our late and hearty supper, or from our imagination being somewhat excited, we rested badly; the night-mare brooded over us; we dreamed that we had turned into a big potato, and that some one was digging us up. Perspiring, struggling, we clinched the bed and finally leaped up gasping for breath. It was some time before the horrid idea would quit us. In the morning, owing to the drenching of the previous day, we were an invalid and threatened with fever and sore throat. The kind old lady insisted on our remaining in bed and she immediately bound a mashed roasted potato, just from the ashes, moisted with warm vinegar, to our neck and gave profusely a hot tea made of dried potato vines. . . .

Finally, healed, he leaves, his pockets filled with biscuits, venison, and "*potato chips.*"[32]

It would be good to know whether this account, especially hinting sexuality as it does, like the camp meeting rhetoric in *The Adventures of Simon Suggs*, has anything to do with the potato-eating propensities of Eula Varner in *The Hamlet*, and with no more hope of establishing a connection, I will also observe that this vegetarian *idée fixe* in the piney woods is paralleled, in a way, by the rural scene witnessed when Will Varner visits Labove's home and finds, one by one, that all the members of the Ole Miss athlete's family clack around in cleated football shoes.

I offer these examples not as sources, however, but as types brought close to Faulkner at an appropriate time, the time when he was returning to the tall tale tradition. Hudson's *Humor of the Old Deep South* is, to me, an even richer resource than the *Folksong* book. It contains narratives of Mississippi history that move, like the Compson Appendix, from 1699 to the present, with contents and even rhythms of the sort that would appear in Faulkner's chronicle writing, especially *Requiem for a Nun* and the essay "Mississippi."

A standard or at least widespread interpretation of Faulkner's use of the tall tale tradition and related materials is that it reflects his connection to the agrarian literary illusion or even betrays his primitivism. Happily, several critics have already gone beyond the naiveté of such a view. In 1971 Hans Bungert published, in German, a book that still appears to be too little known. He observed that Faulkner would have found in the tradition "realism, functional application of the vernacular, the proximity of humor and horror and violence; adaptations of frame-narratives and other distancing devices; and a freeing of the imagination that is perfectly in accord with Faulkner's already established hyperbolic humor."[33] These, of course, are modernist tools, and one might say that getting away from, and then coming back to, such traditional material may have served Faulkner as well as it did someone like Picasso, who might have remained a good Andalusian academy painter, but whose encounters in other parts of the world, notably Paris, freed his local bulls, as much as similar experiences freed Faulkner's cows and horses, for the modernist expression of primitive energies.

In "Humor and America: The Southwestern Bear Hunt, Mrs. Stowe, and Mark Twain" James Cox reaches toward another aspect of the tall tale that makes it congenial with modernism. *The Adventures of Huckleberry Finn*, he writes, is "a lie, a tall tale, a stretcher, and does not, like a serious novel, represent or even reflect the truth, but deviates from it, because language simply cannot tell the truth. Insofar as we see the lie and the lying of Huck—and here I mean the whole marvelous magic of his language—we begin to get the humor and lose the meaning."[34]

I don't want to summarize—or misstate—Cox's full argument, which goes on to contrast the way in which our critical seriousness changes the book, whereupon we lose the humor and get the meaning, but I do want to use the statement I've just quoted for a point of my own: I am not so sure that we lose the meaning when we perceive the humor of the lie: I rather think we are in the position of the wise provincial hearing an old tale being perpetrated upon an unwitting and literal-minded stranger—someone like that character Twain put into so many of his pieces just to emphasize the point: the narrator of the jumping frog tale or of Jim Blaine's grandfather's ram or the townsmen of Dawson's Landing who don't get David Wilson's joke and so rename *him* Pudd'nhead, when it is they who are the "Simon-pure labricks" and "dam-fools." In other words, if we are initiated into the tradition, we perceive the irony.

The meaning of *The Adventures of Huckleberry Finn* has always been wrapped up in its humor, a point supremely overlooked by the various libraries and schools that have banned the book for its linguistic or social viciousness, surely missing the point. Whether or not Huck has had the experience and missed the meaning, the reader who has caught Twain's irony has not and is nevermore a stranger to the book. Agreeing with Professor Cox about what is implied in the story's character as lie, I would say that Huck has simply masked and rhetorically distanced the power of his own experience and realization.

What Albert Guerard has said about the composition—the use
of rhetoric and the manipulation of point of view—in *The Hamlet*
is also, I think, a telling argument against the view of Faulkner as
naive, primitive, shamanistic oral storyteller and one that sup-
ports my contention that the stylistic qualities of the tall tale
were inspirational for a modernist writer.[35] Michael Millgate, in
his summary view of Faulkner's achievement, has also written
perceptively of Faulkner's adaptation of the tall tale: "when
Faulkner employs the tall tale he does so with precisely calcu-
lated literary objectives in view: he uses it with a full view of its
antecedents and with a sophisticated awareness of its contribu-
tion to the elaborate interplay of traditional and experimental
features which constitutes the complex multiple presentation of
his novels . . . it remains only one of many devices which he can
deploy and manipulate at will."[36]

Though our greatest examples are literary and come from the
hands of some of the fine nineteenth-century writers mentioned
in this essay, the view that the tall tale itself remained a naive
form is apparently as seductive as the view that Faulkner was
only "demon driven," to the point of excluding art. And the
person who has read very little Faulkner might say, Why not let
him be a vessel for the muse? Why not accept the personal
fictions he also created and embellished: Faulkner the un-
tutored—"an old eighth grade man"—the unread—"Bible and
Shakespeare"—the unliterary: "I had never known nor lived
among people who wrote novels and stories."

One reason the serious reader of Faulkner cannot accept these
fictions is that now we know better. But we can interpret them.
These personal fictions, especially the recurrent one about his
nonexistent World War I flying experience, served Faulkner in a
number of ways when he was young and unlikely looking and not
very productive as an artist. But with the passing of time, with
the attainment of mastery and fame, they were—especially the
ones about being a farmer who did not have the wit or interest to
answer questions about "linear discreteness" in his work—as
much a way to keep the public at bay as Huck's reply to Aunt
Sally's questions about the steamboat wreck: "Anybody hurt,"

she says. "N'om. Killed a nigger." One imagines Aunt Sally's
eyes going blank with the burden of contradiction in her sentimentally Christian society as she replies, "Well, it's lucky; because sometimes people do get hurt."[37] Huck has skillfully
elicited from her subconscious something about how things will
fare with Jim here down the river, what kind of society this is,
despite appearances. Obviously, Twain also obtains closure to a
scene that he does not want to prolong any more than Huck
does, but Huck's ploy is in perfect accord with what he has done
all down the river: one can shut people up by pitching them lies
so monstrously appropriate that they won't question them. (Perhaps, if I am not being too cute a "cricket," as John Seelye's
Huck calls us, the evasion sequence thus tells us without specifically saying so that Jim will never be free.)

Telling his lies, Faulkner enacted an evasion sequence of his
own, behind which he could often work in peace—the marvelous, and apparently not quite verisimilar anecdote about
requesting from the Hollywood people the right to work at
home, and then going back to Oxford, is both parable and
example. One of the beauties of the backwoods tradition of
exaggeration is the way that it protects a wise provincialism: the
big lie pretends to fool people and the insiders pretend to be
fooled—an important aspect of the tradition that is often overlooked. Hints are dropped liberally all along that a tall tale is tall,
but an outsider may not pick them up. Thus the tradition contains a sort of backwoods dramatic irony, one expressed in the
words of an old saying from my native state, Arkansas: We always
lie to strangers. As dramatic irony, the backwoods lie separates
the local from the outsider and gives power to the provincial in
the face of money, travel, experience, and sophistication. And
because the insider can tell the difference, he knows who he is
and what is important.

Faulkner's open liberties with the truth may have hurt a few
feelings now and again—Sherwood Anderson was apparently
offended when he learned how hard his leg had been pulled—
but they seem to have been mainly forms of self-protection, often

wry, rather than attempts to betray anyone. Like the tall convict in *The Wild Palms*, perhaps Faulkner had the "hill-man's sober and jealous respect not for truth but for the power, the strength, of lying—not to be niggard with lying but rather to use it with respect and care, delicate quick and strong, like a fine and fatal blade."[38]

What Faulkner discovered in the tall tale, then, in addition to its pleasures, which tickled him, and its usefulness, which masked him, were its rhythms, its fund of distancing devices (narrators within narrators, ironic voices, self-interruptions, false innocence), its deliberate exaggeration to get to the truth, and its appropriateness to his own place and experience. As I have said, the tall tale, especially in its traditional literary form, is a good modernist tool, and the Arkansas motto I quoted earlier—We always lie to strangers—might be a modernist or even postmodernist manifesto, for how else can one speak to a stranger?

Faulkner also recognized that the native tall tale was one with other great stories he admired, most of them cited in *Notes on a Horsethief*, from Eve and the Snake to Androcles and the Lion to Mary and the Lamb to Ahab and the Whale, matchless models of human longing and the human spectacle, "and all the celestial zoology of horse and goat and swan and bull . . . the firmament of man's history."[39]

In lying, he discovered, is much truth. It is not without significance that among Faulkner's first experiments in prose— the short sketches he wrote in New Orleans in 1925—one is about a man on the front gallery of a country store telling a tale to a group of friends and one stranger. Before the story is quite over, the stranger pulls a gun and shoots the storyteller, fleeing onto a passing freight train, because the story has pointed to him as a murderer. The storyteller, who survives, swears he was only making it up. The story is called "The Liar." And that's the truth.

NOTES

1. Joseph Blotner, *Faulkner: A Biography* (New York: Random House, 1974), 1:206–7, 210–11, 369 ff., 498.

2. Joseph Blotner, *William Faulkner's Library: A Catalogue* (Charlottesville: University of Virginia Press, 1964), 124.

3. *Essays, Speeches, and Public Letters by William Faulkner*, ed. James B. Meriwether (New York: Random House, 1965), 176.

4. Meta Carpenter Wilde and Orin Borsten, *A Loving Gentleman* (New York: Simon and Schuster, 1976), 143–44.

5. John Faulkner, *My Brother Bill* (New York: Trident Press, 1963), 149.

6. *Essays, Speeches, and Public Letters*, 117.

7. *Lion in the Garden: Interviews with William Faulkner, 1926–1962*, ed. James B. Meriwether and Michael Millgate (New York: Random House, 1968), 64.

8. *William Faulkner: Early Prose and Poetry*, ed. Carvel Collins (London: Jonathan Cape, 1963), 115.

9. *Early Prose and Poetry*, 94.

10. *Uncollected Stories of William Faulkner*, ed. Joseph Blotner (New York: Random House, 1979), 702–3.

11. The phrase comes from Randall Stewart, "Poetically the Most Accurate Man Alive," *Modern Age*, 6 (Winter 1962), 81–90.

12. Oscar Wilde, "The Decay of Lying," *The Writings of Oscar Wilde*, Uniform Edition (London & New York: A. R. Keller, 1907), 6:12–15.

13. *Early Prose and Poetry*, 89.

14. "The Decay of Lying," *The Writings of Oscar Wilde*, 6:15–16.

15. *Early Prose and Poetry*, 76.

16. William Faulkner, *The Town* (New York: Random House, 1957), 296.

17. "The Decay of Lying," *The Writings of Oscar Wilde*, 6:63.

18. William Faulkner, *Father Abraham*, ed. James B. Meriwether (n.p.: Red Ozier Press, 1983), 13.

19. Ibid., 60.

20. *Uncollected Stories*, 686.

21. *Rimbaud: Complete Works, Selected Letters*, trans. Wallace Fowlie (Chicago: University of Chicago Press, 1966), 238–39, 224–25; Robert Greer Cohn, *The Poetry of Rimbaud* (Princeton: Princeton University Press, 1973), 272.

22. *Lion in the Garden*, 56.

23. Quoted by Krauth, "Mark Twain: The Victorianism of Southwestern Humor," *American Literature*, 54 (1982), 371–72.

24. Noel Polk, "The Blind Bull, Human Nature: Sut Lovingood and the Damned Human Race," in *Gyascutus*, ed. James L. W. West III (Atlantic Highlands, N.J.: Humanities Press, 1978), 13–49.

25. Owen Wister, *The Virginian* (New York: Macmillan, 1902), 191–200.

26. *Father Abraham*, 13.

27. Cf. Victor Strandberg, "Transition: From Freud to Marx," in *A Faulkner Overview: Six Perspectives* (Port Washington, N.Y.: Kennikat Press, 1981), 56–88. In "Southwestern Humor and Faulkner's View of Man," *William Faulkner: Materials, Studies and Criticism*, 7 (April 1985), 38–46, Jean Rouberol makes a similar point about Faulkner's divergence from the anti-Jacksonian sentiments of the humorists.

28. Letter of 9 July 1931, in James B. Meriwether, "Faulkner's Correspondence with *Scribner's Magazine*," *Proof*, 3 (1973), 267.

29. Relevant portions of Hudson's papers are in the Mississippi Collection, University of Mississippi, where I examined the typescript versions of the folksong collections and other materials.

30. *Selected Letters of William Faulkner*, ed. Joseph Blotner (New York: Random House, 1977), 198; Blotner, *Faulkner*, 2:1389–90.

31. Arthur Palmer Hudson, *Folksongs of Mississippi and Their Background* (Chapel Hill: University of North Carolina Press, 1936), 37–38.

32. J. F. H. Claiborne, "A Trip Through the Piney Woods," *Publications of the Mississippi Historical Society,* ed. Franklin L. Riley, Volume 9 (Oxford, Miss.: Printed for the Society, 1906), 533–35. Along with two other passages from Claiborne's "A Trip Through the Piney Woods," the potato episode is reprinted, condensed, in Hudson's *Humor of the Old Deep South* (Chapel Hill: University of North Carolina Press, 1936), 540.

33. Hans Bungert, *William Faulkner und die humoristische Tradition des amerikanischen Südens* (Heidelberg: Carl Winter Universitaetsverlag, 1971), 237 [from Bungert's English-language summary of his book].

34. James M. Cox, "Humor and America: The Southwestern Bear Hunt, Mrs. Stowe, and Mark Twain," *Sewanee Review,* 83 (Fall 1975), 600.

35. Albert J. Guerard, *The Triumph of the Novel: Dickens, Dostoevsky, Faulkner* (New York: Oxford University Press, 1976), 212–20. In this section of his book Guerard discusses Faulkner's "artful modulation" of styles, his manipulation of distancing devices, and especially "his success [in *The Hamlet*] blending disparate modes, tones, feelings." His final evaluation is that the first Snopes novel deserves more and better attention "as an essentially poetic achievement."

36. Michael Millgate, *The Achievement of William Faulkner* (New York: Random House, 1966), 291.

37. Mark Twain, *The Adventures of Huckleberry Finn,* ed. Henry Nash Smith (Boston: Houghton Mifflin, 1958), 185–86.

38. William Faulkner, *The Wild Palms* (New York: Random House, 1936), 276.

39. William Faulkner, *Notes on a Horsethief* (Greenville, Miss.: The Levee Press, 1950), 19; *A Fable* (New York: Random House, 1954), 161.

# Faulkner's Humor: A European View

## HANS BUNGERT

Let me begin by agreeing with Walter Blair and Hamlin Hill that "writers who are foolhardy enough to discuss . . . humor . . . are an endangered species." They are "kicked around for allegedly proving that they themselves have no humor whatever" and are regarded as "unamusing nitpickers."[1] On the other hand, anticipating this reproach they may deal with their subject matter in too light a vein.

German scholars discussing humor are an even more endangered species, for everybody knows that Germans have no sense of humor—which is why I did not have to begin my lecture with a joke.

As the subtitle of my paper is "A European View," I shall first make some remarks about European, especially German, reactions to Southern humor in general and Faulkner's humor in particular, thus placing the reception of Faulkner as a humorist in a historical context. When I then turn to a discussion of Faulkner as a humorous writer I am not going to look at his works and achievements from a deliberately European perspective—though my views, like those of any scholar in the humanities, may be tinged by my own particular cultural matrix.

The reception of Southern literary humor in the German-speaking countries began at a surprisingly early stage. Representative examples of Southwestern humor were available in German translations in the 1850s. *The Hive of the Bee-Hunter* by T. B. Thorpe, published in New York in 1854, appeared in a German translation in 1856. A German version of *Odd Leaves from the Life of a Louisiana "Swamp Doctor"* by Henry Clay

Lewis came out five years after the publication, in 1850, of the American original. Nineteenth-century critics, reviewers, and literary historians in Austria and Germany were remarkably well-informed about American humor and American humorists, and in their attempts at general characterization and evaluation they arrived at results similar to those of their British colleagues, seeing, for example, exaggeration and tall tales as distinctive features of American and especially Southwestern humor.

Very early, critics and reviewers in the German-speaking countries regarded Mark Twain as a culminating point in the history of American humor, and at the end of the nineteenth century he was already considered to be a writer who not only amuses, but also instructs and exerts a morally invigorating influence. By the turn of the century, according to Edgar H. Hemminghaus, the chief chronicler of Mark Twain's German reception, he was enjoying a popularity in Germany that "had attained a height unprecedented in the history of the literary invasion from this side of the ocean."[2] But as early as 1878 Thomas Wentworth Higginson had made the following entry in his journal during a visit to a German city: "As for Mark Twain, they all quote him before they have spoken with you fifteen minutes and always give him a place so much higher in literature than we do. I don't think any English prose writer is so universally read."[3] Mark Twain's popularity has remained undiminished to this day, and he still may well be the best-known American author in Germany, whereas in France, for example, he has never achieved such a high degree of popularity.

In Justin Kaplan's words, the relationship between Mark Twain and the German-speaking countries, where he stayed for three extended periods, was a "requited love affair."[4] Part of this love affair was the successive and successful translation of the author's works into German, which, beginning with *The Celebrated Jumping Frog of Calaveras County and Other Sketches*, appeared in large numbers. It was, however, not only through translations that Mark Twain's works became known in Germany and other countries of continental Europe. Many of his books were published in English in the Tauchnitz Publishing Company's famous "Collection of British and American Authors," and an interesting incident in the publishing history of *Adventures of Huckleberry Finn* is that the Tauchnitz edition of Mark Twain's masterpiece appeared in Leipzig a few weeks before the book came out in the United States.

Having proved receptive of Mark Twain's humor, the German-speaking countries seem to have been prepared to discover the comic spirit in Faulkner's writings, too. This hypothesis is borne out by the fact that the two books in which Faulkner comes closest to Mark Twain, *The Unvanquished* and *The Reivers*, occupy a special status in the history of the reception of Faulkner's works in Germany. Like *Adventures of Huckleberry Finn, The Unvanquished* was published in English by Tauchnitz in Leipzig; it appeared as volume 384 of "The Albatross Modern Continental Library" in the same year as the original Random House edition (1938).[5] *The Reivers* reached a particularly large number of readers because this is Faulkner's only novel to be serialized in a German newspaper; between April 4 and June 29, 1964, it ran in a leading national newspaper, the *Frankfurter Allgemeine Zeitung*.

In the history of the growth of Faulkner's reputation, German writers, critics, and reviewers certainly did not play as remarkable a role as their French colleagues. Still, even during the Nazi era, when three of his novels and several of his short stories were translated, Faulkner began to be ranked as the most significant contemporary American novelist after Thomas Wolfe. In the German-speaking countries there was no Maurice Coindreau, no André Malraux, no Maurice Le Breton, no Jean-Paul Sartre to acclaim Faulkner as a powerful new voice in world literature and praise him as a model for fledgling native writers, but among the authors who, by reviewing the German translation of *Light in August* in 1935, helped to establish Faulkner's reputation in Germany, Switzerland, and Austria was Nobel Prize winner Hermann Hesse; and one of Faulkner's early translators was

Georg Goyert, who had rendered James Joyce's *Ulysses* into German.

In his article "William Faulkner's Works in Germany to 1940: Translations and Criticism," William W. Pusey comes to the conclusion that German readers seemed to be particularly interested in "Faulkner's inexorable treatment of basic moral problems, his sociological picture of the South, his skillful psychology and his stylistic innovations."[6] The French critics' and writers' emphasis on existential despair and *fatalité* which they detected in Faulkner's work finds no parallel in pre-World War II German reviews and essays, and though after the war German reviewers and critics were influenced by French as well as American Faulkner criticism, by and large they did not fail to see the comic elements in Faulkner's work. In fact, one reviewer, in a mild attempt at witticism, went so far as to call the author "Mark Faulkner" and "William Twain."[7]

Faulkner's humor was, for example, noted in many reviews of the German translations of *The Hamlet* and *The Reivers*. It was not until 1957 that the first volume of the Snopes trilogy appeared in Germany. For German readers, this long delay had the advantage that they could get to know the trilogy as an entity, because the publication of the translation of *The Hamlet* was quickly followed by that of *The Town* and *The Mansion*, both of which came out only one year after their publication in the United States, that is, in 1958 and 1960 respectively.

Most reviewers of *The Hamlet* failed to recognize the structural and thematic complexity of the novel, fascinated as they were by Flem Snopes and the world of Frenchman's Bend. The humor in the novel was defined and evaluated in a variety of ways. Reviewers spoke of Faulkner's "regal humor," of elements of rural farce, of amusing roguery, of broad comedy, and of *The Hamlet* as an entirely humorous book. More sophisticated reviewers, who compared the novel with other books by Faulkner, saw the humor keeping a precarious balance between laughter and horror and judged the humor to be an instrument for over-

coming the demons of the puritanical denial of worldliness. A
prominent publisher expressed the opinion that in this novel
doom and the terrors of fate were at least partly dissolved in
serenity, and he concluded that, appropriately, Faulkner no
longer believed in the downfall of mankind. One of the leading
newspaper critics saw the novel as a proof of the hypothesis that
only a tragic writer can also be a true humorist. The author of
*The Hamlet* was also regarded as a folk raconteur, and it was
pointed out that the novel demonstrated how writers can find
fascinating material by keeping away from cities and living in the
country.[8]

Judging from the number of issues and editions as well as the
number of reviews, *The Reivers* in German translation was probably more of an immediate success with the general reader than
any other novel by Faulkner. The book was not considered to be
a major work and actually puzzled some reviewers, but it defi-
nitely settled Faulkner's reputation as a humorist. It was compared with Thomas Mann's *Felix Krull*, and one reviewer called
the author "a genial Münchhausen."[9] The author's humor was
felt to be warmer than in his other books, but several reviewers
detected elements of melancholy, nostalgia, and romanticism
underneath the cheerfulness and humor.

Like the reviewers referred to in this brief and fragmentary
survey of Faulkner's reception in the German-speaking countries, writers and scholars in many parts of the world and especially, of course, in the United States have long since
recognized the importance of the comic mode in Faulkner's
works. Thus Katherine Anne Porter said in an interview in 1950:
Faulkner "is one of the funniest men in the world. . . . I love
Mark Twain and I never forget him really; but when you speak of
humor, he's my standard";[10] and in 1948 she wrote in a letter:
"William Faulkner has the deepest and most serious humor in
this country at present."[11] Similarly, John Hawkes declared in an
interview: "Obviously Faulkner was one of the greatest of all
comic writers."[12] Scholars were somewhat slow in taking up the
challenge presented by remarks that Malcolm Cowley and

Robert Penn Warren made about Faulkner's humor in 1946, but by now a considerable, though still not sufficiently large, amount of scholarship exists on the subject.

Dealing with Faulkner's (or any other writer's) humor, a scholar is confronted with various problems of a methodological nature. One of the problems is that "the study of comedy is so often a method of categorization rather than analysis," as Fred Miller Robinson complains in his recent book, *The Comedy of Language*, which includes a chapter on *As I Lay Dying*.[13] The neat categories and simple typologies one comes across in some unpublished doctoral dissertations on Faulkner's humor prove that some scholars are not aware of this pitfall. Another problem is that some studies of Faulkner's comic mode tend to be predominantly descriptive and occasionally almost limited to an enumeration and retelling of funny episodes. The largest problem results from the absence of a fully satisfactory theory of comedy or theory of humor. This lack of a generally accepted, valid theory may lead to reductionism in studies of Faulkner insofar as certain individual theories are tested by being applied to the author and his work; in other words, Faulkner may become merely a test case.

In view of this last problem I do not plan to base my brief discussion of Faulkner as a humorist on a theory. Still, for reasons that I hope will become clear at the end of this paper, I want to quote three theoretical statements on humor.

The first quotation is from an early essay by Thomas Carlyle. In this essay, Carlyle defines humor in the following way:

> It is . . . the bloom and perfume, the purest effluence of a deep, fine and loving nature; a nature in harmony with itself, reconciled to the world and its stintedness and contradiction, nay finding in this very contradiction new elements of beauty as well as goodness.[14]

The essay in which this passage occurs is on the German Writer Jean Paul. Jean Paul himself, in his *Vorschule der Ästhetik* (Prolegomena to Esthetics), has this definition of humor:

It diminishes what is great, but unlike parody, in order to place it side by side with what is small, and enlarges what is small, but unlike irony, in order to place it side by side with what is great, thus destroying both, because all things are equal and nothing vis-à-vis infinity.[15]

The definition implies that a true humorist sees insufficiencies, inadequacies, and failings *sub specie aeternitatis.*

In a comparable way the Danish philosopher Harald Höffding regards the humorist as somebody who does not close his eyes to disharmony and misfortune and does not lose the feeling of being part of the *Weltstrom,* the world current, though he witnesses much suffering and the destruction of much that is beautiful and great. "The humorist," writes Höffding, "does not retreat into the desert because his dreams did not all become true."[16]

Obviously such definitions are too general and also too idealistic to let us come to grips with the humor of a writer who is conscious of and perturbed by the complexity, irritancy, and disorder of the modern world and of human history. They clearly indicate, however, that humor is much more than buffoonery and being funny and that it is related to what can be broadly termed humanism.

In a very general way, the few remarks that Faulkner in his later years made about humor can also be regarded as those of a humanist. When asked by a student at the University of Virginia whether he looked at his humor as a more relaxing kind of work, he contradicted rather vehemently and declared humor to be "a part of man, too . . . a part of life,"[17] and at West Point, shortly before his death, he made it clear that for him writing about people meant writing about "man in his comic . . . human condition" as well as his tragic condition.[18]

The importance Faulkner attached to humor became evident early in his career when in the foreword to his and William Spratling's book *Sherwood Anderson & Other Famous Creoles* he wrote: "We have one priceless universal trait, we Americans. That trait is our humor. What a pity it is that it is not more

prevalent in our art."[19] This early statement is almost program-
matic. It is, therefore, surprising that for a long time critics saw
and often still see Faulkner's humor as a phenomenon of his later
years, and that they are unable to discover it in his early writings. One of the reasons for this error and oversight may be the
exclusive emphasis that is usually put on folk humor and characters representing this brand of humor in Faulkner's novels and
short stories.

There can, of course, be no doubt that the author is deeply
indebted to the tradition of folk humor and to the literary
tradition that began with the Southwestern humorists.
Faulkner's folk humor abounds with situations of the trickster
tricked, episodes of trade and swapping, and tall tales all the way
from his early novel, *Mosquitoes,* to his last one, *The Reivers.* As
in Southern folk humor and the writings of the Southwestern
humorists, exaggeration is one of the distinctive features of
Faulkner's humor or, more precisely, this type of his humor.
There are, however, significant differences between Faulkner's
hyperbolic humor and that of his predecessors.

For one thing, Faulkner uses hyperbole in plots and narrative
contexts where it comes unexpectedly. The comedy of exaggeration is not confined to the Yoknapatawpha cycle either, but also
permeates such stories about World War I as "Turnabout." A
second difference is that Faulkner "epicizes" tall tales. They do
not remain anecdotal and incidental in his fiction, but are epi-
cally expanded and integrated into larger thematic and structural
contexts. They usually add to the complexity of a work and in
many cases make for a heterogeneous homogeneity, as it were.
Finally, hyperbole or "the distortions of humor," as Robert Penn
Warren calls it,[20] must be regarded as part of a more general
strategy in Faulkner's art. As the author himself said, "the artist's
prerogative, I think, is to emphasize, to underline, to blow up
facts in order to state a truth."[21] Consequently, comedy of
exaggeration also is a means of establishing a more powerful
fictional reality and coming closer to truth.

It is not only facts that Faulkner blows up, emphasizes, and distorts, but he also employs this strategy as a humorous method of characterization. As a result of this strategy, some of his comic characters—Eula Varner, Flem Snopes, and the protagonist of "Old Man," for example—are no longer mere human beings of flesh and blood, but assume legendary and mythical proportions. This method of characterization has led critics to the conclusions that in Faulkner's works man "is hyperbolized into pure quality"[22] and that his major characters are "supreme expressions of particular aspects of the human personality."[23] While the partial validity of such conclusions cannot be doubted, one should not overlook the presence of so many realistically portrayed comic characters in Faulkner's fiction, characters that are not mythicized or blown up, but remain breathing human beings. In fact, one aspect of the many-faceted tension in Faulkner's fiction is the very contrast between these two types of characters that appear side by side in many of his novels, as for instance in *Light in August* and *The Hamlet*.

The realistically drawn comic figures, who often have a sense of humor themselves, tend to be characterized in and associated with a vernacular style. Faulkner is, of course, a writer of many styles, but while his oxymoronic, convoluted, syntactically complicated style has often been analyzed, his colloquial style has not been given the attention it deserves. Symptomatically, Faulkner is not discussed in Robert Bridgman's study, *The Colloquial Style in America*.[24]

The vernacular style, of which Faulkner is a great master, very often is a source of comedy. For comic effects, Faulkner does not rely on excessive dialect, puns, or misspellings the way the "phunny phellows," that is, the literary comedians, and occasionally also Mark Twain did. Faulkner's verbal comedy is appropriate to the character and results from observing speech habits and transforming these into art. As far as distortions of individual words or funny folk etymologies are concerned, it is sometimes difficult for the non-Southern reader to know whether certain words were invented by the author or taken over from empirical linguistic reality. The famous "sour deans" (for "sardines") in *The Reivers*, "and-bush" (for "ambush"), and "he telefoamed" (for "he telephoned") are a few of many examples one finds in Faulkner. It also is in character when a black woman in "The Devil Beats His Wife," who does not know the words "telegram" and "cable," uses the word "soon letter" instead, or when in the final section of *As I Lay Dying* Cash speaks of the "graphophone" that Anse's new wife owns. It should be noted that Faulkner never—or almost never—reverts to conventional malapropisms.

In the use of metaphors and similes he is both humorous and realistic inasmuch as they are fitting for the respective situation, setting, and narrator. Ratliff's speeches and narratives are full of such similes. He describes the lightfootedness of one of the spotted horses by saying: "It . . . jumped the banisters and the lot fence like a hen-hawk."[25] Elsewhere, he comments on some-body's clumsiness by remarking: "Hit was like a fahr—the fellows with the water hose done the most part of the damage."[26] In *The Mansion* he does not refer to Flem Snopes's greed in abstract terms, but talks of "his pure and simple nose for money like a preacher's for sin and fried chicken."[27] Ratliff's style appears as particularly humorous in *The Mansion* and also *The Town* because it is contrasted with the intellectual rhetoric of Gavin Stevens, whom one critic has called "the greatest windbag in American literature."[28]

Closely related to verbal comedy or, indeed, part of it is the comedy of names in Faulkner's fiction. Faulkner is one of the great inventors of character names in world literature. One of his happiest inventions—and so he thought himself—was the name "Snopes" with the whole cluster of first names for members of the clan, including Wallstreet Panic, Montgomery Ward, and Watkins Products, though, of course, "Snopes" is not merely a funny name. The importance a name may have for bringing about comic complications becomes particularly clear in the short story "My Grandmother Millard and General Bedford Forrest and the Battle of Harrykin Creek," which in its narrative technique, characters, and setting is closely linked with *The Unvanquished*. The amusing story would not exist were it not for the name of one of the characters.

The action takes place on the Sartoris plantation during the Civil War. The story deals with love at first sight, but the first glance that the man, a young Confederate officer, casts on the girl finds her in an unusual and delicate situation. Melisandre is sitting in the outhouse, the privy, trying to save the family silver from a detachment of Union troops by hiding it under her skirts. The Yankee soldiers have long been familiar with this trick and are not going to keep away from the privy. At this juncture, the young Confederate officer enters the scene to act as an embarrassing rescuer.

When shortly afterwards the lieutenant, who has won the girl's affection at once, introduces himself, his family name turns out to be Backhouse, a name unfortunately reminiscent of the place of their first meeting. This revelation leads to a hysterical fit on Melisandre's part and to a number of other complications, but this obstacle on the road to matrimony is finally removed when the commanding general orders the name Backhouse to be changed to Backus—a change that incidentally conforms to the laws of the historical development of the English language, that is, English phonology.

Thematically, the story thrives on a contrast between romantic and realistic elements. This contrast is also evidenced by the names Melisandre and Backhouse. More important, however, is the function the officer's name has for the plot. The name brings about the complication and the dramatic climax of the girl's hysterical fit, and it is only through the change of the name that the happy ending is made possible.[29]

The humor in "My Grandmother Millard and General Bedford Forrest and the Battle of Harrykin Creek" also derives from the narrative perspective, which is that of a boy and a realist. A surprisingly large number of Faulkner's most humorous short stories and novels are narrated from a child's or adolescent's point of view. "Shingles for the Lord," "Uncle Willy," "Was," *The*

*Reivers*, and the greater part of *The Unvanquished* are some examples. In these texts, the narrative perspective of a child is one of the constituents of comedy. Faulkner was well aware of this; when at the University of Virginia he was asked why he had used Charles Mallison as one of the narrators in *The Town*, he replied: "I thought it would be more amusing as told through the innocence of a child that knew what he was seeing but had no particular judgment about it."[30] On the basis of this statement, the comedy in the short stories and novels I have mentioned could be termed "comedy of limited perception."

However, both in *The Reivers* and *The Unvanquished* the situation is not as simple as that, because in both novels there actually are two narrative perspectives of first-person narrators. In *The Reivers* the predominant voice is that of Lucius Priest as a boy, but every so often the voice of Lucius Priest as an experienced, almost philosophical grandfather interferes and brings about a dialectic tension in the book. In *The Unvanquished*, comedy prevails as long as Bayard is a boy of limited understanding, a boy who sees the war as a sequence of exciting adventures, but is unaware of its horrors and of the moral dilemmas he, his father, and Miss Rosa become increasingly involved in. In the last chapter, in "An Odor of Verbena," when Bayard has reached the age of twenty-four, there is no room left for comedy any more. The serious moral and social theme of the book, which has, of course, been there from the beginning, is finally recognized by the reader, and the shock of recognition he experiences is the more powerful because he has been deceived and misled by what seemed to be light and purely humorous early chapters. In *The Unvanquished*, comedy functions as a method of concealment and is part of a strategy of initially misleading the reader in order to intensify the noncomic final impact.

*Go Down, Moses* can be read in a similar way. The first chapter or story, "Was," is not simply a prelude, but introduces in a deceptively humorous manner profoundly serious themes, the themes of relations between blacks and whites, of private versus communal ownership, and of man's attitude towards nature. A major difference between *The Unvanquished* and *Go Down, Moses* is that in the latter (and later) book the pivoting point is already reached in the second chapter, "The Fire and the Hearth," because it is here that comedy turns into and is replaced by seriousness. Still, the novel is another example of comedy of deception and of the method of withheld meaning.

Another category in my incomplete typology of functions of Faulkner's humor is what I propose to call "contrapuntal comedy." In composing and structuring his books, Faulkner employed counterpoint in a variety of ways, and within this contrapuntal method comedy has its place, too. In several interviews, the term "counterpoint" was used by the author himself. About *The Wild Palms* he said:

> The story I was trying to tell was the story of Charlotte and Harry Wilbourne. . . . I decided that it needed a contrapuntal quality like music. And so I wrote the other story simply to underline the story of Charlotte and Harry. . . . I'd write the chapter of one and then I would write the chapter of the other just as the musician . . . puts counterpoint behind the theme that he is working with.[31]

"Old Man" is a comic counterpoint to the story "Wild Palms," and taken together these two stories convincingly illustrate Faulkner's general intention to write about man in his comic and tragic human condition.

Whereas the novel *The Wild Palms* is strictly symmetrical in structure, the contrapuntal comedy is quantitatively less prominent in other novels. In *Light in August*, the action revolving around Lena Grove and Byron Bunch is a humorous antithesis to the tragedy, brutality, and horror prevailing in the other strands of action. As a "makeweight to the terrible," to borrow a phrase from Cleanth Brooks,[32] the comedy centering around Lena Grove is given a notable position because among the major characters she is the one that the reader sees at the very beginning and at the end of the novel. Maurice Coindreau has called *The Sound and the Fury* a "symphonie démoniaque où ne manque que la gaîté d'un scherzo."[33] This is an untenable view, for the Jason section is a scherzo or, in my terminology, contrapuntal comedy.

This type of comedy can even be detected in the macrostructure of the volume of Faulkner's *Collected Stories*. While he was preparing this volume for publication, Faulkner wrote in a letter to Malcolm Cowley: "even to a collection of short stories, form, integration, is as important as to a novel"; and in this context he used the phrase "contrapuntal in integration."[34] A detailed analysis, especially of the sections "The Country" and "The Wasteland," would show that humorous short stories serve as counterpoints to serious ones. At the beginning of the volume, for example, "Shingles for the Lord" is such a counterpoint to the closely related story "Barn Burning," and in the last section of the book, in "Beyond," the story "Divorce in Naples" provides a comic antithesis to the stories preceding and following it.[35]

The term "antithesis" is useful for interpreting individual works. It would, however, be misleading to regard Faulkner altogether as a writer for whom the comic mode is generally an antithesis to the tragic mode. Actually, in his world view Faulkner is unable to make a neat distinction and draw a sharp line between the comic and the tragic. He certainly is not a humorist of the kind described by Carlyle, namely "a fine and loving nature . . . in harmony with himself [and] reconciled to the world." His humor does, however, enable him to observe man coping with his fate and to strike a balance between despair and hope, pessimism and optimism. To come back to Harald Höffding's definition of humor, Faulkner does not close his eyes to disharmony and misfortune and does not retreat into the desert because his dreams did not all become true.

In this respect, Faulkner's humor has moral and anthropological dimensions. It also has an epistemological function. Without disregarding the problem of subjectivity and the difficulty of perceiving truth, Faulkner tries to see reality as a continuum and as a totality. In his endeavour to come closer to an objective or rather intersubjective view of reality and human life, the tragic and the comic mode are two ways of looking at a blackbird.

NOTES

1. Walter Blair and Hamlin Hill, *America's Humor* (New York: Oxford University Press, 1978), vii.

2. Edgar H. Hemminghaus, *Mark Twain in Germany* (New York: Columbia University Press, 1939; rpt. New York: AMS Press, 1966), 47.

3. *Letters and Journals 1846–1906*, ed. Mary Thatcher Higginson (Boston: Houghton Mifflin, 1921; rpt. New York: Negro Universities Press, 1969), 300.

4. Justin Kaplan, *Mr. Clemens and Mark Twain: A Biography* (New York: Simon and Schuster, 1966), 215.

5. The Albatross, originally an independent firm, had merged with Tauchnitz. *Pylon* appeared as volume 293 of "The Albatross Modern Continental Library" in 1935.

6. *Germanic Review*, 30 (1955), 226.

7. Jürgen Lütge, "Gute alte Spitzbubenzeit," *Münchner Merkur*, 28/29 December 1963, quoted by Edith Zindel, *William Faulkner in den deutschsprachigen Ländern Europas: Untersuchungen zur Aufnahme seiner Werke nach 1945* (Hamburg: Hartmut Lüdke, 1972), 442. Zindel's doctoral dissertation is the most extensive and detailed discussion of the reception of Faulkner's works in the German-speaking countries.

8. For a fuller treatment of the reception of *The Hamlet*, see Zindel, 387–401. Most of the material presented in this paragraph has been culled from Zindel's book.

9. Klas Ewert Everwyn, "Faulkners glückliches Yoknapatawpha," *Rheinische Post*, 4 January 1964, quoted by Zindel, 435.

10. Interview, "Camera Three," WCBS-TV; quoted from page 5 of the photocopy of a transcript in the Linton R. Massey Collection, Alderman Library, University of Virginia.

11. Letter to Edwin Seaver, quoted by Edwin Seaver, ed., *Pageant of American Humor* (Cleveland and New York: World Publishing Co., 1948), 17.

12. John Enck, "John Hawkes: An Interview," *Wisconsin Studies in Contemporary Literature*, 6 (1965), 146.

13. *The Comedy of Language: Studies in Modern Comic Literature* (Amherst: University of Massachusetts Press, 1980), x.

14. "Jean Paul Friedrich Richter," in *Critical and Miscellaneous Essays* (London: Chapman and Hall, 1872), 1, 14f.

15. My translation. The original reads: "Er erniedrigt das Große, aber ungleich der Parodie—um ihm das Kleine, und erhöht das Kleine, aber ungleich der Ironie—um ihm das Große an die Seite zu setzen und so beide zu vernichten, weil vor der Unendlichkeit alles gleich ist und nichts." *Vorschule der Ästhetik*, ed. Josef Müller (Leipzig: Felix Meiner, 1923), 125.

16. "Der Humorist flüchtet nicht in die Wüste, weil nicht alle Blütenträume reiften." *Humor als Lebensgefühl* (Leipzig and Berlin: Teubner, 1918), 97.

17. Frederick L. Gwynn and Joseph L. Blotner, eds., *Faulkner in the University: Class Conferences at the University of Virginia, 1957–1958* (Charlottesville: University of Virginia Press, 1959), 39.

18. Joseph L. Fant III and Robert Ashley, eds., *Faulkner at West Point* (New York: Random House, 1964), 97.

19. (New Orleans: The Pelican Bookshop Press, 1926), n. pag.

20. "William Faulkner," in *William Faulkner: Three Decades of Criticism*, ed. Frederick J. Hoffman and Olga W. Vickery (New York: Harcourt, Brace & World, 1963), 118.

21. *Faulkner in the University*, 282.

22. Florence Leaver, "Faulkner: The Word as Principle and Power," in *William Faulkner: Three Decades of Criticism*, 203.

23. Edmond L. Volpe, *A Reader's Guide to William Faulkner* (London: Thames and Hudson, 1964), 287.

24. (New York: Oxford University Press, 1966).

25. "Spotted Horses," *Scribner's Magazine*, 89 (June 1931), 592.

26. "A Bear Hunt," in *Collected Stories* (New York: Random House, 1950), 67.

27. (New York: Random House, 1959), 56.

28. Irving Howe, *William Faulkner: A Critical Study*, 2nd ed. (New York: Vintage Books, 1962), 286.

29. This story is also discussed in Hans Bungert, "Functions of Character Names in American Fiction," in *The Origins and Originality of American Culture*, ed. Tibor Frank (Budapest: Hungarian Academy of Sciences, 1984), 165–75.

30. *Faulkner in the University*, 116.

31. Ibid., 171.

32. *William Faulkner: The Yoknapatawpha Country* (New Haven and London: Yale University Press, 1963), 71.

33. "Préface," *Le Bruit et la Fureur* (Paris: Gallimard, [1938]), 12.

34. Malcolm Cowley, *The Faulkner-Cowley File: Letters and Memories, 1944–1962* (New York: Viking, 1966), 115f.

35. For a more extensive treatment of the structure of *Collected Stories*, of contrapuntal comedy, and other types of comedy in Faulkner's works, see Hans Bungert, *William Faulkner und die humoristische Tradition des amerikanischen Südens* (Heidelberg: Carl Winter, 1971), especially part 3.

# Faulkner Reads the Funny Papers

## M. Thomas Inge

In assessing the work of a great writer of the twentieth century, it can be informative to examine the cultural context in which the author lived and worked. No writer works entirely in a vacuum, and a work of literature relates to and is influenced by the things the writer reads, sees, and experiences. Since this century has witnessed the complex development of a massive media environment and new forms of popular culture that reach people at all social and economic levels in all regions, it is necessary to examine not only the classics and so-called "high" culture of a writer's time but the popular and mass culture as well.

Of all the popular arts, the comic strip is considered the most inconsequential. Produced by a daily deadline, read quickly and thrown out with the trash, and considered primarily to be a childish amusement, this uniquely American derived art form has been accorded little appreciation, even though at present more than 100 million people follow the daily adventures of their favorite characters and, at certain points in the history of journalism, comic strips have spelled the financial success or failure of a newspaper. Some fine works of the imagination and visual artistry have appeared in the comics in the course of their development, but they have been lost to cultural history because of their impermanent format. There is evidence that William Faulkner—himself once an aspiring cartoonist—had a fondness for the funny papers and that this fondness is reflected in his fiction.

Through the tutoring of his mother, young William Faulkner

learned to read the newspapers before he entered school, and the Memphis *Commercial Appeal* was among them.[1] A major Southern daily since its beginning in 1839, the *Commercial Appeal* carried then a Sunday color comic section featuring such strips as *The Katzenjammer Kids* by Rudolph Dirks, *Happy Hooligan* by Fredrick Burr Opper, *Little Jimmy* by James Swinnerton, *Buster Brown* by Richard Felton Outcault, *Foxy Grandpa* by "Bunny" (Carl Edward Schultze), and other favorites of the time. As daily comic strips became available (Bud Fisher's *Mutt and Jeff,* beginning on November 15, 1907, was the first regularly published daily comic strip), these were added to the columns of the daily issues of the *Commercial Appeal.* Another source of the comics could have been the Hearst *Chicago American,* which was advertised in the October 30, 1902, issue of the Oxford *Eagle* as available through local newsdealers by subscription and containing on Sundays "A Humorous Weekly Printed in Colors." Most of America's favorite strips were available to Faulkner throughout his life, and his references to at least two specific titles in his fiction, as well as allusions to several others, demonstrate that he paid them some attention.

It is also important to note that as a child Faulkner had an interest in drawing, which almost certainly would have led his eyes to the bright colorful pages of the funnies. He gave his first-grade teacher a watercolor sketch and once spent his time during a sermon in the Baptist church drawing a carefully detailed train in the hymnal, a subject which he repeated in his first-grade reader. His artistic abilities attracted the attention of his teachers, who would send him to the blackboard when an illustration was needed.[2] He once astonished his mother when he had rushed home to tell about a new sprinkler wagon he had seen in the streets of Oxford, but unable to describe it in words, he produced a highly detailed drawing of the machine.[3]

While he had always had his mind set on becoming a writer, he also illustrated some of his own childhood stories and apparently entertained the idea of a professional career in art. When he was fourteen, he submitted an entry to a *St. Nicholas* magazine drawing contest, and he drew cartoons for classmates as well as for an eleventh-grade yearbook that remained unpublished. After leaving school and on trips away from home, Faulkner wrote family and friends letters that often included drawings; and while he was in training with the RAF in Canada in 1918, his class notebook included precise renderings of the trainer planes and sketches of other cadets, officers, and scenes both real and imagined. In the 1920s he produced several illustrated, hand-lettered booklets including a 1920 set of poems called *The Lilacs*, the 1920 play *Marionettes*, and the 1926 chivalric allegory *Mayday* written for Helen Baird, a woman he was courting. During the time he spent in New York City in 1921, Faulkner planned to take some art classes and hoped to earn money from his art while perfecting his skills as a writer. Long after he gave up his artistic ambitions, he would entertain close friends and family with cartoons, caricatures, and sketches.[4]

The only Faulkner drawings to see print during his lifetime, at least that we know about, were the twenty-one cartoons and sketches he produced primarily for local publication—fourteen for five editions of the University of Mississippi yearbook, *Ole Miss*, issued between 1917 and 1922; four for the University humor magazine *The Scream* in 1925; and three for the May 1925 issue of *The Double Dealer* in New Orleans. These are not the drawings of an amateur but rather those of an artist who knows how to control a line for maximum effect, to suggest in a few lines a more complex scene or idea, and to suggest through controlled caricature the humorous side of the people around him, swept up in the latest fashions, fads, and attitudes encouraged by the jazz age. These drawings are carefully balanced in design, make effective use of blacks and whites, and are restrained in style. Faulkner had full control of his pen and ink.

The artist who influenced Faulkner's work most profoundly was Aubrey Beardsley (1872–98), whose sensually shocking illustrations in the 1890s came to symbolize the decadent movement in England. Beardsley is mentioned in at least three of Faulkner's novels—*Soldiers' Pay, Light in August,* and *Absalom,*

*Absalom!* In the most thorough analysis of this influence, Addison C. Bross suggested that Faulkner was attracted by Beardsley's "playful whimsy, his extravagant grotesqueness, his eternal suggestiveness—often erotic, often hinting at perversity, but always suave, always self-contained. A Beardsley drawing seems to hide, just beyond the observer's awareness, a sinister and abominably fascinating story."[5]

In several of his *Ole Miss* drawings, particularly the border decoration for his poem "Nocturne" in the 1920–21 volume and the introductory illustration for the Social Activities section in the 1919–20 volume, the evidence of Beardsley's influence is fairly obvious, especially in the second where Faulkner appropriates the earlier artist's trademark—the candelabrum. (Figure 1.) It is in the fiction, however, rather than in the drawings that the full ethos of Beardsley was to have its effect, such as the hints of corruption, sensuality, and decadence or the use of the grotesque.[6]

The other artist with whom Faulkner has been compared in his style was mentioned by Faulkner himself in a passage in *Mosquitoes*. Julius Kauffman is speaking, but the sarcasm about college students affecting the latest attitudes and aping the jazz age stereotypes was probably shared by the writer himself:

> A few years ago a so-called commercial artist . . . named John Held began to caricature college life, cloistered and otherwise, in the magazines; ever since then college life, cloistered and otherwise, has been busy caricaturing John Held.[7]

John Held, Jr., was probably one of the most widely recognized cartoonists of the 1920s. His thin, flat-chested, unconventional women gave full visual form to what became known as the flappers; and his pseudosophisticated, booze-drinking, racoon-coated men gave new meaning to the Joe College caricature. Faulkner could have seen Held's work in *Life*, *Vanity Fair*, the *New Yorker*, or any number of popular magazines of the period, or even in his Hearst syndicated newspaper comic strip feature *Oh! Margy!* If F. Scott Fitzgerald was the literary spokesman for

# SOCIAL ACTIVITIES

*Figure 1.* William Faulkner, *Ole Miss,* 1919–1920.

the jazz age, Held was its illustrator, so it was a most appropriate collaboration when he did the drawings for Fitzgerald's *Tales of the Jazz Age* in 1922. Hardly any artist since Held who has set out to portray the Roaring Twenties was able to escape his influence, Faulkner included. (Figures 2–5.) Held's thin and nervous line, the angular attitudes of his figures, his ability to capture the energy of dance and music, and the inherent satire of his detached point of view—all of these are characteristic of Faulkner's cartoons as well.[8]

*Figure 2*. From *The Most of John Held, Jr.*

*Figure 3*. William Faulkner, *Ole Miss*, 1916–1917.

*Figure 4.* From *The Most of John Held, Jr.*

*Figure 5.* William Faulkner, *Ole Miss*, 1919–1920.

*Figure 6*. George McManus, *Bringing Up Father*. © King Features Syndicate.

*Figure 7*. William Faulkner, *Ole Miss*, 1920–1921.

In addition to Held, there are other popular cartoonists of the time who might easily have had an influence on Faulkner's style. One was George McManus, best known for his classic tale of the nouveau riche, *Bringing Up Father* (beginning in 1913), in which Maggie tried to rise above her origin as a washerwoman after winning the Irish sweepstakes while Jiggs continually slipped back into the former world of his cronies in Dinty Moore's tavern for a serving of corn beef and cabbage. McManus achieved a clean line in his comic strip panels with stylized fashions, art nouveau backgrounds, and neatly detailed architecture, directions in which Faulkner seemed to be working. (Figures 6 and 7.)

Another cartoonist of possible influence was Cliff Sterrett, whose *Polly and Her Pals* (beginning in 1912) began as a type of college humor strip focusing on Maw and Paw Perkins, their attractive daughter Polly, and the dozens of collegiate suitors who pursue her affections. Sterrett began to experiment with the visual potential of comic art and was soon incorporating in the 1920s striking patterns of abstraction much in the style of cubism and surrealism. Faulkner too demonstrated an interest in such nonrealistic patterns and a similar preference for design over characterization. (Figures 8 and 9.) Other cartoonists whose

*Figure 8.* Cliff Sterrett, *Polly and Her Pals.* © King Features Syndicate.

*Figure 9.* William Faulkner, *Ole Miss,* 1917–1918.

work bears artistic similarities with Faulkner's include Bud Fisher, whose classic adventures of the comic team *Mutt and Jeff* became the longest running daily American comic strip, and Billy De Beck, whose sporting life feature *Barney Google* (beginning in 1919) kept the nation involved in the picaresque adventures of this pint-sized hero. (Figures 10 and 11.)

Finally, however, it should be noted that none of these creative artists—Beardsley, Held, McManus, Sterrett, Fisher, or De Beck—is a direct source of imitation for Faulkner. The Mississippian may have observed and learned from them and others as well, but he was working in a vein that is distinctly his own. He was no copyist. His sense of design, his satirical point of view, his effective arrangement of blacks and symmetrical patterns, his ability to suggest with a few lines rather than include details—these might have matured into a comic style suitable for the humor magazines and funny papers of the time. (Figure 12.) If Faulkner was, as he described himself, a "failed poet," one might say that before that he was a "failed cartoonist."

It is in his fiction that the influence of popular comic art was to linger. One can see it in the early unpublished short story of 1925 called "Frankie and Johnny." Were it not for the fact that the chronology prohibits it, one might guess that Faulkner was inspired by the set of block prints called *The Saga of Frankie and Johnny* begun by a young John Held, Jr., in 1916 but not published until 1930.[9] (Figure 13.) Faulkner's version has recast and revised the American folk ballad in the form of a series of bold vignettes and rough prints much in the style of Held's unrefined woodcuts. The cast of characters has been expanded, the mother rather than Frankie is the prostitute, and the ending has been changed, or rather we are not witness to Johnny's death, which is likely to follow upon the tragic events.

Faulkner invests the story with a certain degree of psychological subtlety by focusing upon Frankie's relationship with her mother and Frankie's plight as the archetypical wronged woman likely to follow in her mother's footsteps. For the most part, however, the story is told through exaggerated caricature (such

*Figure 10.* Bud Fisher, *Mutt and Jeff.*

*Figure 11.* Billy De Beck, *Barney Google.* © King Features Syndicate.

C'est horrible! – Quel donc? – Le mal de mer de ma fiancée.
La, pourquoi ne trouvez-vous pas une amie qui est onpheline?

*Figure 12.* William Faulkner, *Ole Miss*, 1922.

*Figure 13.* From *The Most of John Held, Jr.*

as the father who drowns saving the fat lady at the beach, a scene taken directly from hundreds of comic post card drawings of the period) and bittersweet comic detail (such as the prostitute mother whose sense of decency is offended by what people will think of her pregnant unwed daughter). The stereotypes of comic strip art—the domineering, strong-willed mother who never realizes the hypocrisy of her own actions, the dominated father who is all kind-hearted boast, the delicate heroine who can pack a mean punch in the style of Little Orphan Annie, and the posturing Johnny who sees himself as a bold Hairbreadth Harry who comes to Frankie's rescue—these are set in the naturalistic context of a *Maggie* by Stephen Crane or *Sister Carrie* by Theodore Dreiser. In the contrast and melodramatic juxtaposition lies the brilliance of Faulkner's story. Frankie says, "Gee, at times Johnny was worse than a movie," and she might as easily have said, "Johnny was worse than the funny papers."[10]

Also noteworthy is Faulkner's slightly stilted use of urban backstreet dialect and criminal slang, although such lines as "Beat it, Bum; or I'll slam you for a row" and "Hit me, baby, I

*Figure 14*. Richard Felton Outcault, *The Yellow Kid*.

like it"[11] sound like dialogue from the later gangster films of the
1930s. Crane and Dreiser had made attempts at such language,
but before Crane went public with *Maggie* in 1896 (an edition
was printed privately in 1893), Richard Felton Outcault had
already originated a form of urban slang in his comic feature
begun on May 5, 1895, *Hogan's Alley*, better known as *The
Yellow Kid*, in which a street urchin spoke in crude language by
way of words printed on his yellow nightshirt. (Figure 14.) The
influence of the character was such that parents and guardians of
propriety soon brought such pressure and notoriety to Outcault
that he abandoned the feature in 1898 and created in 1902 the
more proper *Buster Brown*, but *The Yellow Kid* lingered on into
the new century in the form of book reprints, magazines, adver-
tisements, games, and toys, all of which Faulkner could have
encountered as a child.

   The one novel by Faulkner with a character whose name is
most closely associated with comic strips is *Sanctuary*. Popeye
Vitelli was, of course, partly modeled after the Memphis gangster Neal Karens Pumphrey, also known as "Popeye," who had

subjected a young woman to much the same treatment accorded Temple Drake in *Sanctuary*.[12] Before then the adjective "popeyed," meaning open-eyed with surprise, expectation, and wonder, had been around a long time, at least as far back as the early nineteenth century in America (*A Dictionary of Americanisms on Historical Principles* by Mitford Mathews takes it back to 1824 in print), and Faulkner used it twice in application to the character Major Ayers in *Mosquitoes* in 1927 before there was a comic strip Popeye.[13] Thus, we cannot argue that the only source of the name could be the comic strip, although other evidence suggests a connection.

Faulkner's Popeye first appeared in an unpublished short story written around the same time as *Sanctuary*. In "The Big Shot" he is described in the style of a stark comic strip image: "a slight man with a dead face and dead black hair and eyes and a delicate hooked little nose and no chin, crouching snarling behind the neat blue automatic. He was a little dead-looking bird in a tight black suit like a vaudeville actor of twenty years ago, with a savage falsetto voice like a choir-boy."[14] An identification with a comic strip character even appears quite intentional here when two pages later Faulkner describes him as "a little, cold, still, quiet man that looked like he might have had ink in his veins."[15] Indeed, all comic strip characters have nothing but ink in their veins.

Faulkner continued to use these stylized caricaturelike descriptions of Popeye in the opening pages of *Sanctuary*:

> He [Horace Benbow] saw, facing him across the spring, a man of under size, his hands in his coat pockets, a cigarette slanted from his chin. His suit was black, with a tight, high-waisted coat. . . . His face had a queer, bloodless color, as though seen by electric light; against the sunny silence, in his slanted straw hat and his slightly akimbo arms, he had that vicious depthless quality of stamped tin. . . .
>
> Across the spring Popeye appeared to contemplate him with two knobs of soft black rubber. . . . The cigarette wreathed its faint plume across Popeye's face, one side of his face squinted against the smoke like a mask carved into two simultaneous expressions. . . .

His skin had a dead, dark pallor. His nose was faintly aquiline, and he had no chin at all. His face just went away, like the face of a wax doll set too near a hot fire and forgotten. . . .

Popeye's eyes looked like rubber knobs, like they'd give to the touch and then recover with the whorled smudge of the thumb on them. . . . Ahead of him Popeye walked, his tight suit and stiff hat all angles, like a modernistic lampstand.[16]

The black knobby eyes and ghostly white skin, the distorted features, the figure he strikes when he stands or walks, like a piece of stamped tin or a modernistic lamp for the living room— all are reminders of a character in a black and white cartoon or comic strip. Popeye also demonstrates the strength of a comic strip superhero, as when he plucks Temple Drake from the ground:

His hand closed upon the back of her neck, his fingers like steel, yet cold and light as aluminum. She could hear the vertebrae grating faintly together. . . . Suddenly she felt herself lifted bodily aside, Popeye's small arms light and rigid as aluminum.[17]

Usually this sort of thing can only happen in the fantasy world of the comics, and many a time the comic strip Popeye has been known to pick up a struggling Olive Oyl in just this manner.

Any recent reader who has picked up *Sanctuary*, which appeared in print on February 9, 1931, has found it necessary to go through a process of dissassociation as it becomes evident that Faulkner's Popeye seems to have nothing to do with the beloved Popeye of comic strip and animated film fame. The selection of that name could have been a little joke at the expense of the reader, just another amusing perversity from an author who delights sometimes in affronting his readers. It was not until 1971 that a critic even dared to note the relation between the two figures, this in a footnote to an essay on the mythological sources of *Sanctuary* by Thomas L. McHaney, who noted "Elzie C. Segar's popular comic strip, 'Thimble Theatre,' had introduced the now-famous Popeye on January 17, 1929, and within a few weeks he had attained great popularity. The sailor replaced Ham Gravy as Olive Oyl's perpetual suitor. . . . The comic dialogue

between Popeye's grandmother and the chauffeur [in chapter 31]
clearly resembles the humor of Segar's strip."[18]

Then in 1973 in a brief article, the first to address the matter of
Faulkner's use of the comic strips, Pat M. Esslinger expanded on
the connection McHaney had made:

> Popeye may be the symbol of evil and the Pluto figure who
> sweeps Judge Drake's teasing daughter into the recessed Hades of
> Miss Reba's place, but he might also be the Popeye of E. C. Segar's
> comic strip. In the much disputed last chapter of *Sanctuary*, which
> was inserted only in the revised version of the novel, Faulkner
> carefully includes his clue to the joke. He prepares a long, elaborate,
> and seemingly irrelevant passage on how the child Popeye, who
> can't walk or talk and who has a great similarity to the crawling baby
> Swee'-pea of the comic strip, was raised on olive oil. The baby's eggs
> had to be cooked in it, and the incident of the broken bottle of olive
> oil led to the house burning which left Popeye impotent. It is this
> association of Faulkner's Popeye with olive oil that leads the reader
> to Segar's "Thimble Theatre" and the parallels between the comic
> strip and the *Sanctuary* Popeye. The obvious parallels occur in both
> characters' diminutive stature, the ubiquitous dangling cigarette that
> replaces the corncob pipe, the one knobby eye of each closed against
> the cigarette smoke, and the impotency, or in the comic strip
> counterpart, the weakness, which can be overcome only by an
> outside force such as a corncob or a magical dose of spinach. *Sanctu-*
> *ary's* Popeye is seen in an omnipresent, black, skin-tight suit, black
> rather than the white the comic strip character wore, but its sailor
> overtones are established when Temple asks, "What river did you
> fall in and with that suit on?" The black suit and the constant
> reference to Popeye as "that black man" also merge the little gang-
> ster with the black man of the comic strip, Bluto, the black evil or
> Pluto force who always carries off the fair maiden Persephone figure,
> Olive Oyl. And the short little Memphis bootlegger may have, as the
> opening page of the novel indicates, "that vicious depthless quality
> of stamped tin," but he also has that pale flatness of a cartoon
> snipped from the Sunday funnies.[19]

Two corrections are in order here. Faulkner could not have
intended any association between his infant Popeye and
Swee'pea since that infant character did not appear in Segar's

comic strip until July 28, 1933, nor could he have intended any reference to Popeye's nemesis Bluto, later known as Brutus, since he appeared in a comic strip sequence beginning in June of 1933 and thereafter appeared primarily in the animated films first distributed that same year. (Figures 15 and 16.) Both Swee'pea and Bluto, then, came into being over two years after the publication of *Sanctuary*. It should also be noted that the Popeye Faulkner may have seen in the funny papers did not yet derive his strength from spinach but rather from having stroked the three hairs on the head of the magical "whiffle hen." His corncob pipe was never a source of his superhero strength, and only for the first four weeks of his existence did he wear an all-white sailor suit, to be replaced by the blue pants and black jersey with red collar, an outfit he has worn for over fifty-five years. It is interesting to note that in a 1933 promotional piece in which Segar traced the early years of Popeye, he is shown as a young man in one drawing, "The Sailor as a Young Rake," dressed in just the sort of tight black suit Faulkner's Popeye wore. (Figure 17.)

I do not mean to question the possibility that Faulkner may have recalled Segar's comic strip sailor when he named his character, only these inaccurate details. Popeye became famous immediately after his creation, and *Thimble Theatre* soon became the most widely circulated comic strip in the United States, making some knowledge on Faulkner's part almost unavoidable. What the errors do suggest is the cavalier attitude scholars take when they choose to discuss comic art. They tend to bank on vague memories; assume that comic strips do not develop, change, and add characters during the course of their histories; and avoid the truly hard labor of going through newspaper collections on microfilm or locating reprints to check the accuracy of their impressions and assumptions.

Faulkner's mention of olive oil does remain a strong clue that he had Segar's character partly in mind, but there are other ways in which the worlds of *Thimble Theatre* and *Sanctuary* are alike—through the presence of violence, an atmosphere of ter-

*Figure 15. (Figures 15–29. Elzie Crisler Segar, Thimble Theatre. ©*
King Features Syndicate.)

*Figure 16.*

**The Four Ages of Popeye** (*from a King Features promotional series of 1933*).

1. The Infink Popeye.

2. The Childhood Slugger in Action.

3. The Sailor as a Young Rake.

4. The Adulk Mariner in a Characteristic Pose.

*Figure 17.*

ror, and graveyard humor. These are elements lost to the contemporary reader because those who produced the Popeye
comic strip after Segar's early death on October 13, 1938, moved
into more innocent story lines and reshaped the character into a
less complex figure more compatible with the interests of
younger readers. Segar's *Thimble Theatre* was a comic strip
largely adult in content and orientation.

*Thimble Theatre* had been in progress for almost a decade
before Popeye came on the scene. Designed partly as competition for Ed Whelan's popular feature satirizing the film world,
*Midget Movies* and later *Minute Movies*, *Thimble Theatre* inten-
tionally had a changing cast of characters but primarily featured a
nondescript comic hero named Ham Gravy, his gangly but ultra-
feminine girlfriend Olive Oyl, her contentious and bad-tem-
pered brother Castor Oyl, and their parents, Cole and Nana
Oyl. Beginning as a very simply drawn gag-a-day feature satirizing stage melodrama, Segar began to develop continuity and
interplay among his characters and moved the feature in the
direction of fantasy and adventure. Through imaginative and
narrative skill, and an adept hand at creating mystery and suspense, Segar was taking the comic strip in new directions of
storytelling power and adult interest.

The tone and tenor of Segar's distinctive approach to comic
strip narrative is evident in the preceding eighteen weeks of the
story in which Popeye was to make his first appearance.[20] On
September 10, 1928, Castor and Olive's Uncle Lubry Kent Oyl
returns from Africa with a rare and magical creature called the
whiffle hen, which he has named Bernice. When challenged by
Uncle Lubry to kill Bernice for a $1,000 prize, Castor engages in
twenty-six straight days of unsuccessful efforts to murder the
fowl by every conceivable method of mayhem—guns, axes, poison, cannons, drowning, hanging, starvation, dynamite, electricity, gas, feeding it to a shark, and sending after her a
murderous bird called the arrow hawk intent on impaling her
brain. (Figure 18.) Despite this violence, Bernice becomes fond
of Castor and becomes his constant but annoying companion.

Unaware that rubbing the three hairs on the head of the whiffle hen brings consistent good luck, Castor is soon beset by enormous offers of money to purchase the hen from strange men, as well as a woman fully draped in black sent by the criminal kingpen Mr. Fadewell. (Figure 19.) The competition for possession becomes so keen that Castor is subjected to several murderous threats, is finally knocked out, and is buried alive in a state of delirium. (Figure 20.) He survives, however, to witness the probable deaths of his would-be assassins. (Figure 21.) This is very unusual and strong fare for comic strips but representative of the kind of intriguing and powerful narratives created by Segar. The comic distance, the dark humor, and the obvious fantasy keep the horror in perspective and allow the reader to view the story as one would a gothic tale or detective yarn,

Figure 18.

Figure 19.

Figure 20.

*Figure 21.*

specifically designed to play upon our delight in being playfully frightened.

Castor decides to sail for Dice Island, the largest gambling resort in the world and owned by Fadewell, to break the bank with the luck the whiffle hen will bring. When he, with Olive and Ham Gravy, go to buy a boat, it is at this point that they go in search of a sailor to manage the vessel and find Popeye, as ugly and unlikely a figure to become an internationally admired hero as one can imagine. (Figure 22.) He is completely aloof and independent, speaks his own mind (although in a bizarre and ungrammatical dialect), and has a temper that cannot be controlled. It was probably his incorrigibility that made him so

*Figure 22.*

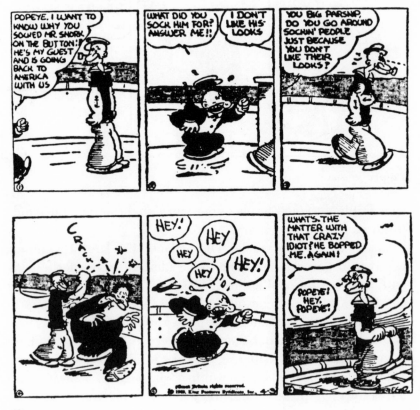

*Figure 23.*

*Figure 24.*

attractive to funny paper readers at a time when most comic pages were still dominated by naughty children, whimsical animals, domestic comedy, and melodrama.

Popeye's penchant for extreme violence was demonstrated ten weeks after his appearance when he socks a deceitful character named Snork simply because he does not like his looks. (Figure 23.) His special powers for survival, which antedate those of Superman by nine years, are demonstrated when the unarmed Popeye is attacked by Snork with a gun. Although riddled with bullets, Popeye still stands, and the incredulous Snork exclaims, "Why don't you drop? I've shot you a dozen times—are you a demon?!!"[21] (Figure 24.) He finally collapses and crawls off into the dark of the ship's hold where he survives apparently by

*Figure 25.*

*Figure 26.*

rubbing the head of the whiffle hen. After a long night of
recuperation, he finally emerges from hiding for one more crack
at Snork's jaw and finds the criminal brutalizing Olive Oyl.
(Figure 25.) When Popeye downs Snork for the final time, his
bravery elicits Olive's admiration who muses, "He's a man all
right! If he wasn't such a funny lookin' thing, I'd give him a
kiss."[22] (Figure 26.) This is the first sign of a romance which will
push Ham Gravy out of Olive's life and *Thimble Theatre* altogether. Five months later, on November 11, 1929, to be exact,
Segar would come across the phrase that would best epitomize
his creation's integrity, self-knowledge, and independence of
mind. When an exasperated Castor Oyl asks, "Fighting! Always
fighting! What kind of an egg are you anyway?" Popeye replies,
"I yam what I yam and that's what I yam."[23] (Figure 27.) This

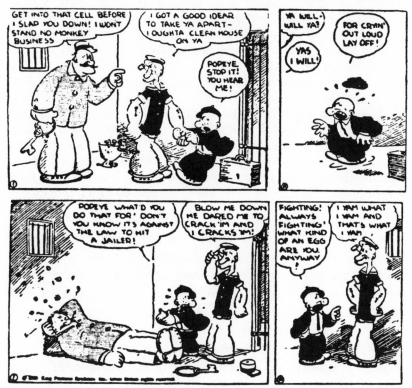

*Figure 27.*

would remain Popeye's sole creed (later modified to read "I yam what I yam, an' tha's all I yam"), an aid in times of distress, as Temple Drake would discover when cringing in fear in the corncrib as she later reported it to Horace Benbow: "So I'd hold my eyes tight shut and say Now I am. I am now."[24]

As comic art scholar Bill Blackbeard has summarized his nature,

> Segar's Popeye is a character compounded of vulgarity and compassion, raw aggression, and protective gentleness, violent waterfront humor and genuine "senskibiliky," thickheaded stubbornness and imaginative leadership, brutal enmity and warm friendship, who can knock out a "horsk" in rage and nurse a baby carefully while it is suffering a fever that makes thermometers pop. He is no paranoid daydream, but a realistic, complex, often wrong but determined man of action who suffers continual agonies of decision, who pursues what he believes to be right far beyond the bounds of cop-interpreted law and order, who has to fight his very way to comprehensibility through the warp and woof of an English language that is often almost too much for him. . . .
>
> Popeye—human, smelly, capable of disastrous mistakes, able to slug a woman, pursue likely looking chicks with lusty interest, swear a blue streak when "irrikated," able to be cheerfully cynical about almost everything dear to the proper, from patriotism to making money, and with a capacity to look as sloppy as he behaved—was certainly more of an *anti*-superhero than anything else. Yet it was his jaunty character and behavior that wowed the public and made them turn to *Thimble Theatre* first among the comics for a full decade.[25]

These comments, of course, simply go to show that the Popeye of the funny papers was a complex, multifaceted character with more of the bizarre and antisocial in his nature than most people today are likely to know about. (Figure 28.) It is in this context, therefore, that Faulkner's use of the name becomes most appropriate. His mean-spirited, pugnacious, violence-prone, independent, and aggressive Popeye has none of his namesake's redeeming qualities but all of his terrifying features turned to purely criminal purposes. Women find both attractive, perhaps because they are rebels and outsiders, and both live life on their own terms. Popeye Vitelli, however, places himself

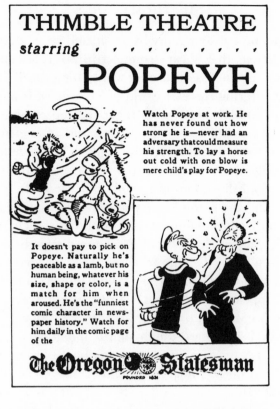

*Figure 28.*

*Figure 29.*

beyond any human sympathy by a cold and immoral cruelty. But the associations that Segar's comic strip world of violent humor would have for the reader of 1931 would serve as effective preparation for entering the evil world of *Sanctuary*. It might also be noted that both Faulkner and Segar created complete fictional communities populated by recurring and often family-related characters, took liberties with the English language in the name of stretching its creative potential (Segar contributed two new words to English—*goon* and *jeep*), and successfully combined the tragic and the comic in revealing parables of life that reflect on the complexities of human conflict and existence. (Figure 29.)

The other major character in Faulkner's fiction besides Popeye who bears a name famous in comic strip history is Jiggs, the mechanic who is a part of the Shumann expanded family in *Pylon*. In appearance he bears a strong resemblance to the Jiggs of George McManus's *Bringing Up Father*.[26] (Figure 30.) We are told that he has a "hard tough shortchinned face" with a "bald spot neat as a tonsure" on top of his head, has a "short thick musclebound body," wears skintight pants "enclosing a pair of short stocky thick legs," and walks fast with a "short bouncing curiously stiffkneed gait."[27] Also like the browbeaten Jiggs, dominated by his wife Maggie, so too does Faulkner's Jiggs have a henpecked background. He tells the bus driver in chapter 1 how he ran out on his wife in Kansas because she would grab the money he earned before he had a chance to tell his employer the job was finished.[28]

Here the similarities end, but as the narrative develops, Faulkner surrounds Jiggs with other types of comic references, particularly to animated films and vaudeville or stage comedy. When he puts his hand into his pocket for the money with which to make a down payment on the boots he wishes to purchase, the clerks "could follow it, fingernail and knuckle, the entire length of the pocket like watching the ostrich in the movie cartoon swallow the alarm clock," and Jiggs is also described as a "cartoon comedy centaur."[29] When he boards the bus in the beginning, he soon finds himself involved in a scene resembling "that comic stage one where the entire army enters one taxicab and drives away."[30] When Jiggs meets with the unnamed reporter, Faulkner says,

> As they stood side by side and looked at one another they resembled the tall and the short man of the orthodox and unfailing comic team—the one looking like a cadaver out of a medical school vat and dressed for the moment in garments out of a floodrefugee warehouse, the other filling his clothing without any fraction of surplus cloth which might be pinched between two fingers, with that trim vicious economy of wrestlers' tights.[31]

*Figure 30.* George McManus, *Bringing Up Father.* © King Features Syndicate.

Another apt comparison, of course, would have been the classic tall and short team of the comics, Mutt and Jeff, themselves based on the duos of stage tradition to which Faulkner refers.

The word most frequently associated with Jiggs, aside from the comic strip practice of reducing the affirmative "yes" to an irritatingly repetitive corruption "yair," is the verb to "bounce." Everything he does and everywhere he goes is with a bounce. Possessed by the boots on which he bounces, Jiggs becomes the comically singular character whose devotion to an object or action warps him into an exaggerated stereotype. This is a standard source of humor in the comic strip and stage comedy.

What Faulkner seems to be about here in using various references from comic strips, animated films, and vaudeville or the stage is to invest Jiggs with his dramatic role as a comic chorus or witness to the tragic events of the novel. Finally the reporter begins to laugh at the absurd actions of the characters, including his own, and tells Jiggs that what started out to be a "good orthodox Italian tragedy" has now "turned into a comedy."[32] The reporter has achieved a cynical distance on the extreme behavior and exaggerated actions of the characters, a perspective they all lack, but like them he proves unable to resist following out the fated impulses that possess them even into the jaws of death. Defiant laughter is the answer to the meaninglessness of life and death. The forlorn central figures of the novel at one point are described as forming "a tableau reminiscent . . . of the cartoon pictures of city anarchists."[33]

Given that one of the major settings of the novel is the world of journalism and the newspaper, references to comic strips are not surprising, but one wonders whether or not the thoughts of the reporter were shared by Faulkner when he describes the newspaper as a "fragile web of ink and paper, assertive, proclamative; profound and irrevocable if only in the sense of being profoundly and irrevocably unimportant . . . the dead instant's fruit of forty tons of machinery and an entire nation's antic delusion."[34] Of his work, the reporter says, "We got to eat, and the rest of them have got to read. And if they ever abolish fornication and blood,

*Figure 31.* Zack Mosley, *Smilin' Jack*. Reprinted by permission: Tribune Media Services.

where in the hell will we all be?"[35] These are not positive views of what was then the most influential of the nation's mass media.

Given the other major physical setting, the airport where the airmeet takes place, it is surprising not to find any references to the several popular aviation comic strips of the period: *Tailspin Tommy* by Hal Forrest and Glen Chaffin (beginning in 1928), so popular that it became the first adventure comic strip to be adapted as a weekly movie serial released in 1934; Lyman Young's *Tim Tyler's Luck* (1928); *Scorchy Smith* by John Terry (1930), but rendered brilliantly after 1933 by Noel Sickles; Roy Crane's *Captain Easy* (1933), which grew out of the earlier *Wash Tubbs* (1924); and Zack Mosely's *Smilin' Jack* (1933). All of these adventure strips dwelt lovingly on the romance of flying and the minute details of aircraft construction, realistic detail being the standard for the latter. They dealt with airmeets, barnstorming, and death-defying feats of the sort depicted in *Pylon*. But Faulkner chose not to draw on any of these popular figures or their images, unless we are to find in Laverne and her erotic stunt in the airplane with Shumann, with her skirts flapping in the breeze, some suggestion of the curvaceously rendered women of *Smilin' Jack* called by the artist "de-icers." (Figure 31.)

As best I have been able to determine, only two comic strips are specifically mentioned in Faulkner's fiction, one by name and the other by description, both in *Light in August*. Mrs. Hines's appearance in the courthouse in Mottstown is reminiscent, we are told, of a scene out of "the Katzenjammer kids in the funny paper"; and at the conclusion, when Byron Bunch and the traveling furniture repairer who tells the story to his wife compete for the position of who will sleep on the ground, "It was like those two fellows that used to be in the funny papers, those two Frenchmen that were always bowing and scraping at the other one to go first."[36] The last reference is to *Alphonse and Gaston,* a short-lived Sunday newspaper feature of 1902–1904 by Frederick Burr Opper, who dropped it to devote more attention to his better known strips *Happy Hooligan* and *Maude the Mule*. Alphonse and Gaston are extremely polite Frenchmen who have carried good manners to such an extreme that they are both immobilized and unable to act as disaster occurs around them: "You first, my dear Alphonse!" "No, no—*you* first, my dear Gaston!"[37] (Figure 32.) They reside more in the popular consciousness and language as representatives of excessive politeness rather than as comic strip characters. In both cases in *Light in August,* Faulkner seems merely to be using the two comic strips as idiomatic references since they have no integral relationship to the plot or action.

Of course, some of the children in Faulkner's fiction conduct themselves after the fashion of the eternally troublesome pranksters Hans and Fritz in the Rudolph Dirks comic strip *Katzenjammer Kids,* which began in 1897. (Figure 33.) For example, the activities of young Malcolm and James Faulkner in setting the pasture afire in the 1937 comic sketch "Afternoon of a Cow" are not unlike the typical mischief of the *Katzenjammer Kids*, except for the addition of the cook's son, Grover, who is equally culpable. The comic strip was based on the German verse tales of Wilhelm Busch, *Max und Moritz* (1865), and interestingly enough in the original tales, the young hell-raisers burn the schoolmaster by putting gunpowder in his pipe and are themselves burned when they fall into dough and are cooked in the baker's oven.[38] There is no evidence, however, that Faulkner knew the work of Wilhelm Busch, although translations of the grim moral fables were available.

Besides Popeye and Jiggs there are several characters whose names could conceivably have been inspired by comic strips of

*Figure 32.* Frederick Burr Opper, *Alphonse and Gaston.*

*Figure 33.* Rudolph Dirks, *The Katzenjammer Kids.* © King Features Syndicate.

the time: Hawkshaw the barber of the stories "Hair" and "Dry September" after Gus Mager's *Hawkshaw the Detective* (beginning in 1913); the reporter Smitty in *Pylon* after Walter Brandt's office boy strip *Smitty* (1922); the squatter Wash Jones of *Absalom, Absalom!* and the Jefferson jailer Euphus Tubbs of several novels after Roy Crane's comic adventurer *Wash Tubbs* (1924); the treacherous horse trader and father of Flem, Abner Snopes, after Al Capp's hillbilly strip *Li'l Abner* (1934); and the mentally deficient criminal known as Monk in the story of that name in *Knight's Gambit* after Gus Mager's *Monk* series of comic strips (1904) featuring apelike humans performing wacky deeds (such as *Knocko the Monk, Groucho the Monk,* or *Sherlocko the Monk*—which served to inspire the names of the Marx Brothers in 1918). But these are mere borrowings or simply incidental uses of the same names. Occasionally Faulkner picks up a word originated in the comics, such as "twenty-three skidoo," repeated several times in *The Reivers* by Carrie's nephew Otis and the deputy Butch Lovemaiden, a coinage by political cartoonist Tad Dorgan who was popular in the first two decades of the century.[39]

This examination of Faulkner's fiction for comic strip references suggests that he looked to the funnies as a source of names for some of his characters, but rather than appropriate them in any direct way, he used the contexts of their associations in indirect ways to reflect on the situations and natures of the figures to whom they are applied. Faulkner read the funny papers, but perhaps a little more deeply and seriously than most people would suspect. But then this was the man who wanted, when he first went to Hollywood in 1932, to write film scripts for Mickey Mouse cartoons.[40] My guess is that he was not thinking about the mild-mannered Mickey of the Disney animated films but rather the courageous, hell-raising adventures of Mickey as depicted in the breathtaking adventure comic strip version that master artist-writer Floyd Gottfredson produced from 1930 to 1932. When Faulkner read the funny papers, he laughed, but more wisely and appreciatively than most critics might imagine.

NOTES

1. Joseph Blotner, *Faulkner: A Biography* (New York: Random House, 1974), 92–93. John Faulkner tells a different story in *My Brother Bill* (New York: Trident Press, 1963), 34–36, where he recalls their father reading the funny papers to the gathered children every Sunday in the Falkner household and their disappointment when Bill returned home after his first day at school unable to read the funnies on his own.

2. Blotner, 94–95.

3. Carvel Collins, "Introduction," *Mayday* by William Faulkner (Notre Dame: University of Notre Dame Press, 1978), 9–10.

4. Ibid., 5, 10–11; Blotner, 165, 315–16, 345–46, 941. For a detailed study of Faulkner's drawings in the context of "a complex, far reaching artistic movement spanning the late nineteenth and early twentieth centuries," see Lothar Hönnighausen, "Faulkner's Graphic Work in Historical Context," in *Faulkner: International Perspectives*, ed. Doreen Folwer and Ann J. Abadie (Jackson: University Press of Mississippi, 1984), 139–73.

5. Addison C. Bross, "*Soldiers' Pay* and the Art of Aubrey Beardsley," *American Quarterly*, 19 (Spring 1967), 5.

6. Ibid., 3–23. Bross focuses primarily on *Soldiers' Pay*. In "Beardsley and Faulkner," *Journal of Modern Literature*, 9 (September 1976), 339–56, Timothy K. Conley summarizes Bross and expands the discussion of Beardsley's influence to include later novels.

7. William Faulkner, *Mosquitoes* (New York: Boni & Liveright, 1927), 230.

8. For a selection of Held's characteristic work, see *The Most of John Held* (Brattleboro, Vermont: The Stephen Greene Press, 1972).

9. See John Held, Jr., *The Saga of Frankie & Johnny* (New York: Clarkson N. Potter, 1972), which reprints the 1930 edition.

10. *Uncollected Stories of William Faulkner*, ed. Joseph Blotner (New York: Random House, 1979), 345.

11. Ibid., 339.

12. Blotner, 492–93, 607–8.

13. Faulkner, *Mosquitoes*, 178, 282.

14. *Uncollected Stories*, 504.

15. Ibid., 506.

16. William Faulkner, *Sanctuary* (New York: Jonathan Cape & Harrison Smith, 1931), 3–6.

17. Ibid., 227–28.

18. Thomas L. McHaney, "*Sanctuary* and Frazer's Slain Kings," *Mississippi Quarterly*, 24 (Summer 1971), 237, note 25.

19. Pat M. Esslinger, "No Spinach in *Sanctuary*," *Modern Fiction Studies*, 18 (Winter 1973), 556–57. Esslinger also draws some parallels between Temple/Popeye and Little Orphan Annie/Daddy Warbucks, but they are too strained to hold up. There are far too many differences between the independent, feisty, self-sufficient Annie and the dependent, passive, easily dominated Temple for any connections to be meaningful, in spite of Temple's frequently blank eyes.

20. An almost complete run of the daily comic strip from September 10, 1928, to May 12, 1930, is reprinted in Bill Blackbeard's edition of *Thimble Theatre Introducing Popeye* by Elzie C. Segar (Westport, Connecticut: Hyperion Press, 1977).

21. Ibid., 70.

22. Ibid., 80.

23. Ibid., 120.

24. *Sanctuary*, 210.

25. Bill Blackbeard, "The First (arf, arf) Superhero of Them All," *All in Color for a Dime*, ed. Dick Lupoff and Don Thompson (New Rochelle, New York: Arlington House, 1970), 98, 117–18. This is the best appreciation of Segar's achievement, which Blackbeard

views as one of the masterpieces of comic strip art. See also Blackbeard's introductions to *Thimble Theatre Starring Popeye the Sailor* by E. C. Segar (Franklin Square, New York: Nostalgia Press, 1971) and *Thimble Theatre Introducing Popeye* by Elzie C. Segar (Westport, Connecticut: Hyperion Press, 1977). For other interpretations see Bud Sagendorf, *Popeye: The First Fifty Years* (New York: Workman Publishing, 1979), and Alan Gowans, *Prophetic Allegory: Popeye and the American Dream* (Watkins Glen, New York: American Life Books, 1983).

26. For a selection of this comic strip spanning its forty-two years under McManus's hand, see George McManus, *Bringing Up Father Starring Maggie and Jiggs* (New York: Charles Scribner's Sons, 1973).

27. William Faulkner, *Pylon* (New York: Harrison Smith and Robert Haas, 1935), 8, 11, 56.

28. Ibid., 16.

29. Ibid., 10, 270.

30. Ibid., 15.

31. Ibid., 56.

32. Ibid., 279.

33. Ibid., 81.

34. Ibid., 111.

35. Ibid., 239.

36. William Faulkner, *Light in August* (New York: Harrison Smith and Robert Haas, 1932), 375, 473.

37. Richard A. Milum, in "Faulkner and the Comic Perspective of Frederick Burr Opper," *Journal of Popular Culture*, 16 (Winter 1982), 139–50, finds in *Alphonse and Gaston* "an exasperating and unrelenting dedication to chivalry" which he applies to numerous characters in Faulkner's fiction, but the relationship is too tenuous to bear such broad interpretation. His entire essay, which is intended to demonstrate the influence of the comics on Faulkner, never establishes a specific connection between the two beyond this reference.

38. See *The Genius of Wilhelm Busch*, ed. and trans. Walter Arndt (Berkeley: University of California Press, 1982), 29–34.

39. M. Thomas Inge, "The Comics and American Language," *Inklings* (Museum of Cartoon Art), Number 4 (Summer 1976), 3–4, 10.

40. Blotner, 772. For an exploration of similarities between Faulkner's comic literary techniques and those found in animated films, see D. M. Murray, "Faulkner, the Silent Comedies, and the Animated Cartoon," *Southern Humanities Review*, 9 (Summer 1975), 241–57.

# Faulkner and the Small Man

## Barry Hannah

I live in Oxford and I am a smallish man like Faulkner. Like Faulkner, I write, sometimes for a living. I take my friends sometimes over to his place, Rowan Oak, which is a shrine now because he won the Nobel Prize. I let my dogs run through the woods as I posture around like a squire waiting for them to return. There is a satisfying enraptured green and brown about the grounds that is holy and earthly at the same time, especially when there's nobody else around and you are left with your own quiet dreams and forget about what the next jerk you meet is going to want from you.

Unlike Faulkner, I don't have the Charlie Chaplin mustache and the baggy trousers and the ducklike walk that his niece Dean Wells recalls about him. I'm as full of myself as the next man, but I think what the small man, Faulkner, had was a Napoleonic complex with nothing but a pencil to bring it off. None of us know when we guess about the dead. It's just sometimes fun, and as writers know, the less accurate the merrier. In a way I think Faulkner wanted to own the world, or at least Lafayette County, so badly that, without enough money, all he could do was write about it, his "tiny postage stamp of land."

He *was* a postman. My father, who was at Ole Miss the same time as Faulkner, told me an anecdote about "Count No 'Count," as they called Faulkner then. Two guys were standing around in the tiny post office talking about what a lousy postmaster he was. Came a bucket of water over the transom, from Faulkner, and they were sloshed.

Now I'd like to call Faulkner "Uncle Willy" to change names.

I get so goddamned tired of the name *Faulkner* in this town—
the name used for everything to sell this and that for the Cham-
ber of Commerce; the leeches who leech to him for entire
careers; the local Snopes of lit and art and parasitic industries.
I'm making a thousand to read about him myself, but at least I'm
not using him or his family while I do it. I'll take his magic but
not his money.

End of rant.

I like Uncle Willy better because it soothes the heart for me
and makes me think of the guy and and not just the gasp. And
further because Uncle Willy wrote a story called "Uncle Willy"
that I've read maybe more often than you have lately. Faulkner's
been called *The Squire of Oxford* (James Baldwin); *Marse Bill*
(Turner Cassity, poet); *Mister Bill* (Shelby Foote); *Charlie
Flakner* (Ole Miss Sigma Chi, '84); *Mister Yoohoo Pawtamany*
(Ernest Hemingway).

Turner Cassity said in an interview that Faulkner writes so
much because up there in north Mississippi you can't find anybody to talk to and you try to say everything when you *do* meet a
listener.

But I hold with the Napoleonic complex.

In person Uncle Willy often said nothing at all. And when he
spoke, it was short, eloquent, and courteous. It was only when
he wrote that he tried to own the earth like Napoleon. Faulkner's
favorite novelist, besides himself, was Thomas Wolfe, who tried
to tell everything, literally everything, about his world. He tried
to see every angel on the head of a pin, Thomas Wolfe. I would
guess that Thomas Wolfe is not read so much now as Faulkner
because he never learned to condense all those adjectives and
pentameters to really short literary form. In fact, Uncle Willy
was more the poet.

*As I Lay Dying* is the best novel I ever read. I've read it, I've
taught it, I've read it again. It is so small, so tiny in the hand, and
still, like Beethoven's "Fifth"—which Faulkner told Ben Wasson
he'd like played at his funeral—it is everything and a gem, a tiny
precious stone, a woman can almost, not even needing it any-

more, already too lovely, already moving, tiny, inexhaustible, puny, prevailing, as long as she knew it.

That last of course was a parody of Uncle Willy's writing. He loved the word *puny* all the way through his work. The tiny inexhaustible men and women are the source of what there is to find funny with Uncle Willy.

The little people, slapped around and abused by crassness, cruelty; little people with their dignity like Uncle Willy's; and the little commercial and religious people with no dignity and no worldview at all. And the others—just money in their pockets for some spotted ponies to ride. The best line in "Spotted Horses" is when the Texan (with his constant ginger snaps) is trying to give five dollars back to the poor lady who weaved at night for her money, and Flem Snopes comes out of the fog, wearing his little tiny bowtie he needs to be a clerk in, says, "What's that for?"

Snopes doesn't want to understand anything else except why he's not getting the money. The mean, the person of incredibly narrow scope. Nasty. He can't even make love he's so nasty.

In fact "Spotted Horses" is a very funny story altogether.

Because we'll laugh at the fools all day. Besides sports, weather, and money, we have nothing to laugh at and chatter all day about except the *fools*. The *fools*. Goes back to Shakespeare, the Greeks.

Now I'm going to read "Uncle Willy," a short story of Uncle Willy's.

*Mr. Hannah read a cut version of "Uncle Willy."*

Nobody will find a laugh a minute from Uncle Willy. He conceived of humor, I think, as a large concept that works through whole stories, wherein we laugh at the greed, the injustice, the fools.

At the smallness, like the overdressed Charlie Chaplin who is dragged out of a saloon by a dog while he is simply trying to love a woman. And like Charlie and Uncle Willy and us and all our grand dreams of how life should be, we too get dragged out by the dogs when we're dressed our finest.

This paper is dedicated to Ron Shapiro, who wears a tattoo of

Chaplin on his lower waist, and who has made the often hot, rainy, but usually dullish town of Oxford happy. He has movies every night.

I first saw Chaplin in "The Gold Rush" at Ron's movie house. The little tramp. The little man, the puny, the knocked-about.

Us.

# Lacan and Faulkner:
## A Post-Freudian Analysis of Humor in the Fiction

JAMES M. MELLARD

1

In his explanation of the relationship between the techniques of jokes and those of the dream-work in *Jokes and Their Relation to the Unconscious*,[1] Freud suggests that both operate on similar principles. Dreams are known in their manifest content, he tells us. The manifest content is a "mutilated and altered transcript of certain rational psychical structures which deserve the name of 'latent dream-thoughts'" (160). We understand the latent dream-thoughts, he says, by analyzing the manifest content's parts and following out associative threads, which interweave to lead us to a "tissue of thoughts," which are "perfectly rational" once we have traced out the pattern of associations. "The dream-work is the name for the whole sum of transforming processes which have converted the dream-thoughts into the manifest dream" (160). The dream-work and the formation of jokes coincide in these processes of transformation. The whole is a means of representation, and it functions through three essential techniques in both dreams and jokes. "We found," says Freud, "that the characteristics and effects of jokes are linked with certain forms of expression or technical methods, among which the most striking are condensation, displacement and indirect representation. Processes, however, which lead to the same results—condensation, displacement and indirect representation—have become known to us as peculiarities of the dream-work" (165).

The similarity of jokes to dreams leads Freud to his hypothesis about joke formation: "this is the way in which jokes are formed in the first person: *a preconscious thought is given over for a moment to unconscious revision and the outcome of this is at once grasped by conscious perception*" (166).

We may illustrate Freud's hypothesis by reviewing the analysis he provides of a "joke" from a work of Heinrich Heine. Heine puts his joke "into the mouth of a comic character, Hirsch-Hyacinth, a Hamburg lottery agent, extractor of corns and . . . the valet of the aristocratic Baron Cristoforo Gumpelino (formerly Gumpel)" (140–41). Something of a parvenue, Hirsch-Hyacinth brags that "as true as God shall grant me all good things, Doctor, I sat beside Salomon Rothschild and he treated me quite as his equal—quite famillionairely" (16). The technique here, Freud suggests, "might be described as a 'condensation' accompanied by the formation of a substitute" (19). The composite word—*famillionairely,* combining *familiarly* and *millionaire*—effects the joke, presumably triggering laughter, not just because it compresses two very different ideas into one, but also because it allows the suppressed idea to surface momentarily at the expense of the intended idea. The suppressed "preconscious thought" probably has more to do with the idea of wealth than with familiarity, so it is the fact of Baron Rothschild's millions that undergoes unconscious revision in order to surface to conscious perception in the portmanteau pun, famillionairely. But the pun triggers a joke, in Freud's terms, because it gives a second party—an auditor—a glimpse into the speaker's unconscious. *He* may also share that glimpse, but the joke is at his expense.

Freud's theory of jokes and dreams depends upon a notion expressed in a metaphor of economy, as my language of *expenses, auditors, shares* might suggest. The economic theory is pervasive in Freudian theory in general. According to commentators Laplanche and Pontalis, economy "qualifies everything having to do with the hypothesis that psychical processes consist in the circulation and distribution of an energy (instinctual energy) that can be quantified, i.e. that is capable of increase, decrease and equivalence."[2] In jokes, the various techniques one might enumerate—as Freud does in chapter 2—all involve a saving of psychical energy in some fashion. Most of our psychical energy, says Freud, goes toward repression of sexual and aggressive instincts or drives and the avoidance of the censorship imposed by external and internal obstacles to our desires. In this connection, Freud says that jokes "make possible the satisfaction of an instinct . . . in the face of an obstacle" (101). Thus it is easier to observe the payoff in "tendentious" jokes—jokes that serve a hostile or aggressive purpose—than in more innocent jokes, whose existence the early Freud does admit. "The pleasure in the case of the tendentious joke arises from a purpose being satisfied whose satisfaction would otherwise not have taken place" (117). From the point of view of the audience for the famillionairely remark on which Freud dwells, there is a tendentious objective—to see the braggart upstart insulted or exposed. Thus, the laughter that presumably occurred in Freud's time is at least partially the result of the economy of expenditure of energy permitted by the slip of the tongue. The obstacle to be overcome is essentially social, rather than internal. Good manners would not permit us to insult the braggart directly, but we can readily laugh at the exposure that comes through the verbal compression. But we will also laugh when the "exposure" is of a more innocent nature. This one has made the rounds recently:

> There is the story about the rookie baseball player just signed out of the Arkansas backwoods. A waitress asked him if he wanted a shrimp cocktail before dinner. "No, ma'am," he said. "I don't drink."

Freud's *Jokes and Their Relation to the Unconscious* not only analyzes the techniques and motives of jokes; it is also something of a compendium of jokes, witticisms, and funny stories from literature and popular culture, especially from his own Jewish background. In his attempt to answer all possible critiques of his work, Freud provides innumerable examples of types of jokes in order, ultimately, to show that all basic techniques can be reduced to condensation, displacement, and indirect representation, and that these techniques can be explained in turn through the principle of psychic economy. Freud's study assesses more than twenty different specific joke techniques and provides illustrative examples of them all. Not all the jokes seem very funny to us today, but some—only slightly altered—can still be heard and some show up regularly in media such as television and films. I have heard Mel Brooks do this one of Freud's Jewish jokes:

> Two Jews met in the neighborhood of the bath-house. "Have you taken a bath?" asked one of them. "What?" asked the other in return, "is there one missing?" (*Jokes*, 49)

This joke, for Freud, illustrates the principle of displacement, for the trigger in it "lies in the diversion of the train of thought, the displacement of the psychical emphasis on to a topic other than the opening one" (51). Here, as in the famillionairely remark, the one speaker exposes a thought that resides in him which would be better left concealed. Thus, the joke's economy lies in the opportunity it provides the first speaker—and the audience—to vent a little social aggression. The key to the joke thus lies in the permission it gives for an evasion of the censorship our codes of conduct ordinarily impose on us.

> Achilles—"What preparation would you make for a cross-country flight, Cadet?"
>
> Mercury—"Empty your bladder and fill your petrol tank, Sir."
>
> Achilles—"Carry on, Cadet."[3]

If we turn to Faulkner's fiction, we see immediately that Faulkner used the techniques Freud associates with jokes and dreams in order to vent material that was much more vigorously suppressed by internal and external constraints than nowadays. In *Soldiers' Pay,* for example, Faulkner manages to fuse the techniques of jokes and dreams quite directly through the convention of free association given over to several characters. It is plain enough in this novel that a sexual undercurrent roils beneath the more-or-less decorous surface. We sense it in the implied question of the title: What is to be a soldier's pay? The traditional spoils are honor, wealth, and sexual favor, but the men who return home in this story reap none of these—though they are on the minds of all (except Lieutenant Mahon, who has no mind because of wounds suffered in the war). Much of the humor of the first part of the novel, therefore, arises because of the displacements and condensations of sexual ideas. The rapine and pillaging accomplished by Joe Gilligan and his drunken travelling companion are limited to bottles of whiskey. Pointing to his recumbent pal, Gilligan says to the young Cadet, Julian Lowe:

> "Look at him: ain't he sodden in depravity?"
>
> "Battle of Coonyak," the man on the floor muttered. "Ten men killed. Maybe fifteen. Maybe hundred. Poor children at home saying 'Alice, where art thou?'"
>
> "Yeh, Alice [says Gilligan]. Where in hell are you? That other bottle. What'n'ell have you done with it? Keeping it to swim in when you get home?"
>
> The man on the floor weeping said: "You wrong me as ever man wronged. Accuse me of hiding mortgage on house? Then take this soul and body; take all. Ravish me, big boy." (9)

This is not a great comic passage by any means, but it does illustrate the modes of condensation, displacement, and indirect representation Freud says characterize jokes and dreams. Typically, Freud would suggest that the motives for jokes and dreams are Oedipal; simply stated these are, for the son, to murder the father and to sleep with the mother, but these drives get translated into the more general ones of sexuality and aggressivity. Perhaps more clearly than we want to admit, we can see the Oedipal process at work in Faulkner's transformations and reversals of images. The scene had started with the efforts of one man to light a "sodden cigar," but the man himself then assumes the label "sodden in depravity." Just prior to the quoted passage, Gilligan had mangled an allusion—"Alas, poor Jerks"— that gets transformed into "Alice, where art thou?" In the transformation, the allusive source shifts from *Hamlet* to *Romeo and Juliet,* and the longed-for sexual object has shifted gender, from the Bard's male Romeo to the feminine "Alice."

But that shift seems to fit the psychosexual undercurrent, for if at one moment the lost object seems to be a bottle, at the next the recumbent companion has assumed the role of the imperiled heroine of melodrama. In one more reversal, the "heroine" decides it is better to yield her virtue than to shield it. If there is any humor in the last sentences, then, it comes from the surfacing of the sexual repression. Forget the mortgage: "Ravish me, big boy." If there were any question that the Oedipal theme is central to the more-or-less free verbal associations of Gilligan and his travelling companions, we have only to look at other examples that follow these. The conventional Freudian cathexis of oral drives with the figure of the mother or surrogate surfaces again when Gilligan tries to persuade Cadet Lowe to have a drink:

> "Listen: think of flowers. Think of your poor gray-haired mother hanging on the front gate and sobbing her gray-haired heart out."
> (10)

Later on he placates Cadet Lowe, who wants to resist his mother's desire to have him return home to her immediately:

> "What can equal a mother's love? Except a good drink of whiskey. Where's that bottle? You ain't betrayed a virgin, have you?" (24)

And the Oedipal conflict takes another form in the on-going battle between Gilligan, his companions, and the train's conductor. The conductor is obviously the local manifestation of the authority of the father: "Bless your heart, Captain," Gilligan says to the uniformed gentleman, "your train couldn't be no safer with us if it was your own daughter" (11).


## 2


Jacques Lacan—the French post-Freudian psychoanalyst— offers a way into humor that builds upon the base of Freudian theory, but it is a way that also invokes a more strictly literary technique of analysis, one not interested in the "springs" of humor, but in its manner of expression.[4] According to Lacan, the unconscious is structured like a language, and language—says Lacan, following Ferdinand de Saussure—is constructed along two axes: the paradigmatic and the syntagmatic. The paradigmatic axis is the one along which operate metaphoric substitutions based upon similarity; the syntagmatic is the axis along which form metonymic combinations within a spatial or other context. The function of the paradigm allows us to substitute one word for another when they have similar meanings, sounds, or forms. The function of the syntagm allows for the linking of words so as to form a signifying chain—its role is that of *syntax*. A language thus operates through its ability to select and combine words into larger units of discourse, though every word in a discourse might suffer the substitution of another whose sound, meaning, or associative function is similar. The secret about language that Saussure revealed is that it has no existence outside the system formed by its paradigmatic and syntagmatic features. Language thus exists as a formal structure apart from its referents, the "reality" it is presumed somehow to "imitate."

Lacan has translated the Saussurean "structuralist" description of language into a description of the human unconscious. Just as the content of a language is comprised of signifiers and signifieds, so also is the unconscious a content that can signify itself to consciousness only through signifiers. Lacan represents this relationship as an algorithm in the form of a mathematical "fraction": S/s. But in Lacan's formula, unlike that of Saussure which he modified, the signifier can never cross the bar symbolized by the virgule; it can never apprehend the signified directly. The signifier can approach the signified only through *re*presentation, so there is always distance between the two—as Lacan says, the signified is always sliding beneath or hiding behind the signifier. We want to anchor our meanings, but we can attempt to do so only through tropes, figures, "turns of phrase" such as metaphor and metonymy. With Alice's Humpty

Dumpty, we can say that words mean exactly what we say they mean, but, alas, we can say what words mean only through the use of other words.

Lacan's insistence that the unconscious is structured like a language means that it functions rhetorically when it surfaces into consciousness.[5] The unconscious becomes nothing more— nor less—than a text that manifests itself through the devices of rhetoric. Thus, the unconscious, dreams, jokes, and language are all assimilated to the same tropological system and employ the same devices. For Lacan, these devices are metaphor and metonymy, though other systems of rhetoric such as those of Kenneth Burke and Hayden White posit additional tropes (mainly synecdoche and irony).[6] For literary criticism, the advantage Lacan has over Freud is that these two tropes draw the Freudian concepts of condensation and displacement into alignment with a series of other important concepts of structuralist linguistics, including the notions of the synchronic and diachronic, the paradigmatic and the syntagmatic, and the functions of substitution and combination, as well as similarity and difference. For us, then, Lacan brings Freudian "science" into the metalinguistics of modernist epistemology, but more importantly he transforms psychoanalysis into rhetorical analysis. For me, now, the aim is to consider some of the ways Lacan's rereading of Freud might illuminate Faulkner's use of humor.

In order to illustrate the difference between Freud and Lacan we might look again at the earlier passage from *Soldiers' Pay*. When I examined the twists and turns of language in that passage of drunken free association in Faulkner's first novel, I spoke of condensation and displacement, but for Lacan the terms emphasized would have been metaphor and metonymy. The phrase "Battle of Coonyak" is essentially metaphoric, following the same pattern of condensation as Freud's exemplary *familionairely*: the transformation, which requires no more than the shift of an *o* to an *a* (bottle to battle), almost manages to retain both signifieds, for the multiplying casualities might have resulted from warfare or bacchanalia (one imagines Breughel here). The next turn in that passage was also metaphoric, for if we are to appreciate it at all we have to fill in below the bar the unstated signified—the heroine of melodrama threatened with loss of mortgage or virtue. Lacan would say that the passage has no clear sense until we supply the missing signified: "Metaphor occurs at the precise point at which sense emerges from non-sense."[7] Thus, by way of the metaphoric turns of language, we enter Freud's Oedipal, or, more linguistically, the symbolic dimension of *Soldiers' Pay*. For Lacan, the Oedipal conflict arrives with the Symbolic, of which it is a part.

Perhaps the easiest way to illustrate what Lacan brings to a text's broadly rhetorical dimension is to consider fictional character and plot. Formed of language, they are inevitably involved in both metaphor and metonymy. A character begins, ordinarily, in metaphor by being named; the name becomes the metaphor that stands (word-for-word) for the character. Usually the name is a proper noun, but sometimes it is a metonymy. A function performed (the bartender, the drummer, the bootleg-ger) might provide the "name," or it may be provided by an aspect of the character's appearance or background ("red tie," "New York Jews," "the Texan"). But, whether the original "name" is metaphoric or metonymic, the *process* of characterization is essentially metonymic; it is comprised of a combination of traits displayed over time. We might say that "flat" characters are purely metaphoric, for their entire being is compressed into the name (Dickens abounds in these; so does Thomas Pynchon; in general, Faulkner's tribe of Snopeses illustrates the principle). "Round" characters are metonymic, for their being is not sig-nified in a word *for* word—signifier for signified—relationship, but in a linkage of word *to* word—a string of signifiers connected over space (typographic) or time (narrative).

Humor is often best in Faulkner (as in other authors or perfor-mers) when it grows from character, whether of a metaphoric or a metonymic (flat or round) type. In *Sartoris*,[8] for example, some of the funniest passages occur as a result of an unconscious attack upon the novel's central metaphor: the name "Sartoris."

Miss Jenny Dupre is the agent by which the Sartoris "myth" frequently gets deflated. Perhaps her "carping" is no more than "semi-humorous," as Olga Vickery says,[9] but it is an ironist's antidote to the suicidal madness the name Sartoris conjures. Of Bayard Sartoris's twin brother, Miss Jenny says, "'The war just gave John a good excuse to get himself killed. If it hadn't been that, it would have been some other way that would have been a bother to everybody around'" (31). Of Bayard, who regrets having survived his brother and the war, Miss Jenny tells Narcissa, who has called to see if he has returned after serenading her: "Serenading? Fiddlesticks. What would he want to go serenading for? He couldn't injure himself serenading, unless some one killed him with a flatiron or an alarm clock" (155). Later on, she also tells Narcissa, who has been nursing Bayard as he convalesces from ribs broken in a nearly suicidal carwreck: "'If we could just arrange to have one of his minor bones broken every month or so, just enough to keep him in the house'" (261), she says, they might keep him alive. But they cannot keep young Bayard from killing old Bayard (albeit accidentally), or himself, so the novel ends, having played out the game—and the name— of Sartoris, "a game outmoded and played with pawns shaped too late and to an old dead pattern, and of which the Player Himself is a little wearied" (380).

We can see how the processes of metaphor and metonymy work in the creation of humor in other characterizations. Metonymy functions through the displacement of one signifier toward another within an associative context. In order for a bit of humor in relation to characterization to work, we have to know the context, the metonymic associations enmeshing the character involved. It is often the case that a joke will be pretty good in itself, but it can be made infinitely better by being projected against the background of character. In this respect, much of the best humor of entertainers or comic strips is a result of a deep metonymic contexture of character detail—a long string of signifying elements in the life of, say, Jack Benny, Johnny Carson, or Woody Allen, or Andy Capp, Charlie Brown, or Garfield. The same is often true of characters in fiction. Among the best illustrations of the reliance on contexture of some humor—particularly tendentious or hostile humor—occurs in *The Sound and the Fury*,[10] primarily in the Jason section. Jason Compson is not a nice guy, by any stretch of the imagination, but it is true, I think, that he pinpoints some of the most problematical issues surrounding the Compson family.

Jason is Faulkner's Don Rickles, comic master of the insult. Most of Jason's best lines are insulting to their objects—but, to the detriment of the Compson family's fortunes, they are not necessarily inaccurate. Jason's remark about his brother Quentin builds on our background knowledge of his suicide by drowning: "at Harvard they teach you how to go for a swim at night without knowing how to swim" (243). His remarks about his father also require a background contexture; Father is a well-known philosophical lush, so Jason says of him that "at Sewanee they dont even teach you what water is" (243). And about the two of them, Jason says, "Like I say, if he had to sell something to send Quentin to Harvard we'd all been a damn sight better off if he'd sold that sideboard and bought himself a one-armed strait jacket with part of the money" (245). Jason is resentful that he never had those dubious "university advantages." "I says you might send me to the state University; maybe I'll learn how to stop my clock with a nose spray and then you can send Ben to the Navy I says or to the cavalry anyway, they use geldings in the cavalry" (243). These remarks cannot be funny at all unless we know that Quentin drowned himself, Father drank himself to death, and Benjy has been castrated. Metonymic contexture is almost everything.

Humor of character is a major part of *As I Lay Dying*, too.[11] Much of it comes from the people outside the Bundren family who provide a perspective on them. All the Bundrens—except Addie, perhaps—are objects of the humor of neighbors like Tull. Tull is the Jason Compson of this book. He is especially good on Anse Bundren. Earlier remarks are needed to put Tull's into the requisite metonymic context. Darl, for example, had said of his father: "Pa's feet are badly splayed, his toes cramped and bent and warped, with no toenail at all on his little toes, from working so hard in the wet in homemade shoes when he was a boy. Beside his chair his brogans sit. They look as though they had been hacked with a blunt axe out of pig-iron" (11). Tull's comment builds upon the details Darl has provided: "He puts his shoes on, stomping into them, like he does everything, like he is hoping all the time he really cant do it and can quit trying to. When we go up the hall we hear them clumping on the floor like they was iron shoes" (31). In this same passage, Tull adds characterizing details that crop up later in his remarks about Anse: "He comes toward the door where she [Addie] is, blinking his eyes, kind of looking ahead of hisself before he sees, like he is hoping to find her setting up, in a chair maybe or maybe sweeping, and looks into the door in that surprised way like he looks in and finds her still in bed every time and Dewey Dell still a-fanning her with the fan. He stands there, like he dont aim to move again nor nothing else" (31). Anse's characteristic astonishment and inertia surface again in Tull's observation of the Bundrens at the washed-out bridge site: "Anse was setting there, looking at the bridge where it was swagged down into the river with just the two ends in sight. He was looking at it like he had believed all the time that folks had been lying to him about it being gone, but like he was hoping all the time it really was. Kind of pleased astonishment he looked, setting on the wagon in his Sunday pants, mumbling his mouth. Looking like a uncurried horse dressed up" (117). Tull can roast Anse, but Doc Peabody probably has the best line on him, not to say on Cash and the rest: "'God Almighty,'" he says to Cash, who has let Anse encase his broken leg in cement, "'Why didn't Anse carry you to the nearest sawmill and stick your leg in the saw? That would have cured it. Then you all could have stuck his head into the saw and cured a whole family'" (230).

Just as character develops through tropological enfigurations, plots also develop tropologically. The transformations—or absence of them—that go to make up emplotments are displayed to us through the sense of difference we perceive in our comparison of semantic units (these units can be of almost any size, ranging from brief images to full-scale episodes). Ordinarily, our sense of displacement, transformation, change—in a character or the character's fortunes—will arise from a multitude of explicit or implicit comparative operations. In a novel such as *Absalom, Absalom!*[12] we can see the rise and fall of Thomas Sutpen in a metonymic vignette characterizing him in his full potency, followed by a metaphoric enfiguration that stands in implicit differential relation. The first is his "pistol demonstration," in which he rode "at a canter around a sapling at twenty feet and put both bullets into a playing card fastened to the tree" (33). For years that demonstration of prowess remained in Jefferson's collective mind *as* Thomas Sutpen. The second is the view of him by Quentin Compson. As Quentin describes him in the context of the "affair" with fifteen-year-old Milly Jones, Sutpen is a *"mad impotent old man who . . . must have seen himself as the old wornout cannon which realizes that it can deliver just one more fierce shot and crumble to dust in its own furious blast and recoil"* (181). Most of those allusions and figurative descriptions of Sutpen we see throughout Quentin's and Shreve's characterization of him are differentially related to the earlier characterizations by Rosa and Mr. Compson so that the differences will show clearly the transformations associated with plot structure. Most of these, like Quentin's metaphor of the "old wornout cannon," produce humor, but clearly they "advance" the string of emplotted displacements. In Faulkner, the humor seldom seems unmotivated where characterization and plot are concerned.

3

"Put a beetle in alcohol, and you have a scarab; put a Mississippian in alcohol, and you have a gentleman—"[13]

Since in every meaningful way Lacan is a return to Freud, I want to open up my discussion of the techniques of humor in relation to tropology by taking Lacan back to Freud once

again.[14] In order to show how we can return Lacan to Freud, I
want to look at the function of humor in Faulkner's *Sanctuary* on
a more global basis. What I want to suggest is that the humor
provides us entry to a textual unconscious that seems finally to
be more interesting in Lacanian than Freudian terms. *Sanctuary*
employs the techniques Freud associates with jokes and
dreams—condensation and displacement—as well as, of course,
the tropes of metaphor and metonymy that Lacan says provide
us access to the unconscious in general. The handling of con-
densation/metaphor and displacement/metonymy in the novel
suggests a very problematic textual unconscious revealing an
Eros apparently overwhelmed by Thanatos. But Lacan's idea of
the Phallus and its place in the Symbolic offers a *thematically*
positive solution to this appearance.

Perverse sexuality and murder provide the two most sensational—"horrific," in Faulkner's words (vi)—thanatic elements in
the novel. But Faulkner displaces attention for a brief time away
from these to a sexual element more capable of what Lacan calls
*jouissance* by situating some of the novel's comic scenes at Miss
Reba's—the best little whorehouse in Memphis. Faulkner cannot follow the publishing conventions of the time, however, and
also actually *display* overt sexual activity, whether thanatic or
erotic. By displacing point of view to naive characters who do not
comprehend what the real business activity is at Miss Reba's,
Faulkner creates comic relief that will accentuate the negative
sexuality elsewhere, at the same time he maintains without overt
display a constant cathexis to sexual interests. The humor escapes of course through that cathexis once Fonzo and Virgil
Snopes arrive at Miss Reba's, bringing their normal country
expectations to an abnormal urban environment.

Having gone to Memphis to attend barber's college, Fonzo
and Virgil decide to take a room at Miss Reba's, unaware that it is
a well-known brothel, not a hotel like the Gayoso. Other mis-
construals abound, mainly because of their problems of contexture: they cannot get the right relation of figure to ground.
They first mistake the lattice on the entry of the building as the

door to a "privy," so they are shocked that here the outhouse—or "backhouse"—is in the front, rather than the back. Their sensibilities are really jolted, however, when they see a "plump blonde woman" enter the lattice door in the company of a man. "'Maybe it's her husband,'" Virgil muses (230). But when the man leaves after a time, Fonzo corrects Virgil: "'Caint be her husband. . . . I wouldn't a never left'" (231). Because Miss Reba gives them a room toward the back of the house and then shoves them out during the day, the boys are in and out of the "hotel" for two weeks without ever learning the real nature of the establishment. They are keenly interested, however, in her line of employment, at one point finding a stray female undergarment in the bathroom and therefore concluding she is a seamstress. "'Wish I worked for her,'" Fonzo says to Virgil. "'With all them women in kimonos and such running around.'" "'Wouldn't do you no good,'" Virgil says. "'They're all married. Aint you heard them?'" (234).

Fonzo, the more ardent of the two, has reason to learn after a while what he's been missing in the big city. He discovers brothels. An obliging friend from the barber college takes the boys to one nearby. Afterwards Fonzo says, incredulously, "'And to think I been here two weeks without never knowing about that house'" (235). Virgil suggests, however, that he'd be three dollars richer if they'd never learned: "'Aint nothing worth three dollars you caint tote off with you,'" Virgil philosophizes (236). But since they still don't know about Miss Reba's, the brothers expect to face the madame as if she were their house mother. Fonzo tells her the two have been to a prayer meeting. Eventually, the boys have a family reunion of sorts at the "hotel" when Cousin Clarence Snopes, the state senator, shows up there. Cousin Clarence, mindful of his reputation, would rather continue to keep awareness about Miss Reba's from Fonzo and Virgil; he too takes them to a different house, one with cheaper rates than the three dollars about which tight-fisted Virgil doggedly complains. The place Cousin Clarence takes them to is run by blacks, however, and Virgil's racism runs smack into his frugality. Cousin Clarence's rejoinder is one that surfaces elsewhere in Faulkner's fiction (in *The Reivers*). Slightly modified, it goes like this:

> "Them's [black women,]" Virgil said.
> "'Course they're [black women,]" Clarence said. "But see this?" he waved a banknote in his cousin's face. "This stuff is color-blind." (239).

The last we hear of Fonzo and Virgil occurs at the time of Red's funeral. Miss Reba and the "girls" are feeling piously sentimental, what with a good man gone and women like themselves having to shoulder the blame. At times like these the innocence of youth is a blessing.

> "Children are such a comfort to a body," the thin one said.
> "Yes," Miss Myrtle said. "Is them two nice young fellows still with you, Miss Reba?"
> "Yes," Miss Reba said. "I think I got to get shut of them, though. I aint specially tender-hearted, but after all it aint no use in helping young folks to learn this world's meanness until they have to. I already had to stop the girls running around the house without no clothes on, and they dont like it." (303)

What I want to suggest, however, is not that Faulkner is using the situation of Fonzo and Virgil at Miss Reba's merely to generate a little comic relief. It does that, of course, but mainly this episode illustrates a larger unifying principle about *Sanctuary*, Faulkner's handling of sex and violence in general, and Lacan's conception of the absent signified. The episode of the Snopes boys, taken altogether, is a metaphoric representation of the *metonymic displacement* of the sexuality—if not the violence— that remains hidden behind the signifiers of *Sanctuary*'s text. Furthermore, it serves as a paradigm of the way in which Faulkner virtually always handles sex (and, usually, but not always, the violence). And it is an illustration of the model of both language and the unconscious that Jacques Lacan has proposed. In all three instances—the novel, Faulkner's fiction overall, and Lacan—there is a core of meaning that is constantly *re*-presented

through metaphoric and metonymic condensations and displacements, but that core is not *presented*. It is not named. So what
we are left with in all cases is an absence, a gap, a hole—that
which a deconstructionist such as Hillis Miller would call a *mise
en abyme*, a scene of the abyss. This principle of the absent
signified is illustrated—more interestingly and problemat-
ically—in its thanatic manifestations in two questions: (1) What
does happen to Temple Drake, and (2) how does Popeye "do it"?

There is no humor in the rape of Temple Drake. But once
Temple and Popeye, like Fonzo and Virgil, arrive at Miss Reba's,
there is humor, and it develops in the way in which Faulkner
answers that second question—what is the nature of Popeye's
sexuality? Inevitably, the answer appears in the same devices of
displacement and condensation, metonymy and metaphor, we
would by now expect. Miss Reba claims she knew about the
"funny business" (308) all the while, but has it confirmed by
Minnie only once Temple is confined at the house. Minnie
observes no "signs" (310) of Popeye's sexual activity until "one
morning he come in with Red and took him up there" (310).

> "Yes, sir, Minnie said the two of them would be nekkid as two
> snakes, and Popeye hanging over the foot of the bed without even his
> hat took off, making a kind of whinnying sound." (311–12)

Miss Reba—for all her faults—has nothing if not a conventional
notion of human sexuality. Thus it turns out that her best judg-
mental turn of phrase is directed at Temple's ravisher, at the
same time it *re*-presents once more the nature of Popeye's sexual
behavior:

> "He goes all the way to Pensacola every summer to see his
> mother," Miss Myrtle said. "A man that'll do that cant be all bad."
> "I don't know how bad you like them, then," Miss Reba said. "Me
> trying to run a respectable house, that's been running a shooting-
> gallery for twenty years, and him trying to turn it into a peep-show."
> (307)

Miss Reba's remark here is perhaps the funniest in the book, but
its impact comes precisely from the techniques of metonymic

displacement and metaphoric condensation we have observed elsewhere. There is a double distancing: first, the women don't even consider the possibility that Popeye's having murdered Red—his surrogate "stud," but eventual rival for Temple Drake—might be worse than his sexual peculiarities. Second, the sexual peculiarities themselves are not *named*—they are only represented in a condensed form through Miss Reba's two metaphors from the carnival midway: "shooting gallery" versus "peep show," the one representing "normal" phallic sexuality—recall Sutpen's ancient cannon?—and the other abnormal voyeuristic sexuality. But in fact all these representations—Minnie's reported at second hand and then embroidered by Miss Reba—only have the effect of making us participants at a peep show, too, but we "see" little more than shadows projected on a screen, a sheet, or a bawdy-house wall.

The techniques of displacement and condensation, metonymy and metaphor, are characteristic of Faulkner's answer to the other question: what did happen to Temple? Again, Faulkner steers clear of any "direct" presentation of the rape scene in *Sanctuary*, just as he does virtually every scene of violence (including even Goodwin's immolation). From the outset, the point of view carefully displaces authorial commentary onto the characters, making *Sanctuary* one of Faulkner's most rigorously "objective" novels. Events, moreover, are frequently displaced toward their effects so that in crucial instances we are not ever shown what happens—which is to say again that events are not directly named; and even later reports by characters are radically displaced, given over to metaphor and metonymy—the latter especially. For example, when Popeye shoots the kind-hearted simpleton, Tommy, Faulkner reports to us that Temple hears a "sound no louder than the striking of a match" (121), but she *sees* nothing except wisps of smoke from the pistol in Popeye's hand. Thus Temple has to infer from the surrounding contextual details (as the reader also has to) what has taken place so quickly that even with it in her presence she cannot immediately name it to identify it. A more significant example of displacement is that answering our question about what happened to Temple. We do not have it reported directly to us; instead, Faulkner leads us up to it and then creates a gap in time (the old chapter-break technique). Next we learn of Temple's concern that she continues to bleed, at the same time she worries about being seen by people who know her as she rides through town with Popeye in his car. At this point, we assuredly must infer that at the very least Popeye has assaulted Temple in the usual phallic way; only much later—in a very indirect representation portrayed through metonymically displaced details (corncrib and cornshucks, but not yet that phallically symbolic corncob)—are we permitted to make the inferences that will allow us to reconstruct the causal sequence. And it is only in the chapter on Lee Goodwin's trial (at which Temple perjures herself) that the substitute phallus Popeye had used actually appears and—finally—gets named, though even then its use is assigned to the wrong man.

The question of the phallus that so preoccupies us in *Sanctuary* is precisely the question that Jacques Lacan puts at the center of his post-Freudian analysis. For Lacan, happy to say, the Phallus as a sign constituted in the realm he calls the Symbolic is androgynous.[15] It may be represented in either the breast of the mother or the phallus of the father. What the Phallus—as a proper noun—represents for Lacan is plenitude, ultimate satisfaction. Such plenitude can never be regained once the child leaves the primary world of infantile satieties and enters the secondary realm of language in the transition Lacan calls the "mirror stage." After entry into language, the child's desires are forever to be deferred, displaced, pushed always behind that which would signify the desired other, whether Mother or Father, breast or phallus. In this descent, Lacan's narrative of human development brings us back to the formula— S/s, which represents for Lacan the primal debarring of the signifier from the signified, consciousness from the unconscious, and, alas, our desire for total satisfaction from our attainment of it.

I think it is now legitimate to claim that humor—jokes, wit,

the comic—exists because of this debarment, but, more importantly, art itself exists because of it. Thus, finally, Popeye's horrific efforts in the Imaginary to locate a substitute phallus represent his efforts to discover the Phallus in the Symbolic. I would
argue that he may well be the paradigm for virtually every
important character in *Sanctuary*—and perhaps of all Faulkner's
questing characters throughout the fiction. He could be, as well,
Flannery O'Connor's "Misfit," who when he shoots the grandmother claims, "It's no real pleasure in life." But he is wrong, of
course, and Faulkner with Lacan would agree that there is a
pleasure principle (Lacan calls it *jouissance*) somewhere between our fate and our freedom. Art such as *The Sound and the
Fury, Sanctuary,* and *Absalom, Absalom!* manifests that *jouissance*, and it is manifested, too, Freud and Lacan and Faulkner
would all agree, in our momentary, yet plentiful, accessions to
the domain of humor.

## NOTES

1. Sigmund Freud, *Jokes and Their Relation to the Unconscious,* vol. 8, *The
Standard Edition of the Complete Psychological Works of Sigmund Freud,* trans. James
Strachey (London: Hogarth Press, 1964); references will be included parenthetically in
the text.

2. J. Laplanche and J.-B. Pontalis, *The Language of Psycho-Analysis,* trans. Donald
Nicholson-Smith (New York: Norton, 1973), 127. Essentially a dictionary of terms treated
in a historical context, this book also includes Jacques Lacan's handling of Freudian
language.

3. William Faulkner, *Soldiers' Pay* (New York: Boni & Liveright, 1926), 46; references
will be included parenthetically in the text.

4. The major texts of Jacques Lacan, in English, are *Écrits: A Selection,* trans. Alan
Sheridan (New York: Norton, 1977), *The Four Fundamental Concepts of Psychoanalysis,*
trans. Alan Sheridan (New York: Norton, 1978), and *Speech and Language in Psychoanalysis,* trans., with commentary, Anthony Wilden (Baltimore: The Johns Hopkins
University Press, 1981).

5. Lacan's conception of the unconscious itself, it ought to be pointed out, is
fundamentally different from that of Freud. Freud's unconscious is imagined to "think,"
Lacan's to "speak." Freud's remains rooted in the traditional metaphysics of origin or
presence in which some irreducible cause—a primal scene or trauma—is presumed to
have originated the patient's neurosis or psychosis. Lacan's unconscious is not of this
tradition; instead, it is formed through the play of signifiers, so it remains fluid, indeter-
minant, unanchored. Freud can think of images and words as "signs" that the skilled
analyst might track directly into the unconscious, where the original thought can be
captured. But Lacan regards Freud's signs as nothing but signifiers, as objects capable of
generating "the effects of meaning," but not a meaning totally determined, netted,
locked up. Words for Lacan are "knots of signification," rather than neat building blocks
from which one can erect regular, four-square, totally determinant communication

packages. The "bar" for Freud is that between consciousness and the unconscious, and for him language is a capability of consciousness, of the secondary mental functions only. The "bar" for Lacan, however, is that between the signifier and the signified, for both consciousness and the unconscious are capable of language. Lacan goes so far as to suggest, indeed, that both *are* language, or at least both are spoken *by* language and thus owe their existence *to* language. These differences permit Freud to seek the origins of humor, but permit Lacan to seek only their techniques in the tropes of language. For showing me that I needed to clarify this difference, I wish to thank Charlotte Diggs, a participant of the 1984 Faulkner and Yoknapatawpha Conference.

6. See, for example, Kenneth Burke, "Appendix D: Four Master Tropes," in his *A Grammar of Motives* (Berkeley: University of California Press, 1969), 503–17, and Hayden V. White, *Metahistory* (Baltimore: The Johns Hopkins University Press, 1973) and *Tropics of Discourse* (Baltimore: The Johns Hopkins University Press, 1977). In the interest of clarity, it might be well to provide here a brief definition of the tropes. Metaphor is the original naming operation and identifies one sign with another on the basis of similarity. Metonymy is "name displacement" and identifies one sign with another on the basis of associative context. Road signs on U.S. interstate highways illustrate the two principles: an outline drawing of a truck on an inclined plane or line as a sign in such discourse means watch for descending trucks; the principle behind the message is of likeness, similarity. Images on another sign of a knife, fork, and spoon convey a message of food; the principle here is of associative context—the implements of eating food used to suggest the availability of food. Lacan does not employ the tropes of synecdoche and irony, as Burke and White do. For them, synecdoche is integrative, suggesting the way parts belong to a whole as in concepts of organic unity; irony is dispersive, denying the stability of any sign, message, or meaning since its common definition is to say one thing and to mean another.

7. Quoted in Anika Lemaire, *Jacques Lacan*, trans. David Macey (London: Routledge & Kegan Paul, 1977), 197; *Écrits*, 158. Lemaire's is probably the most thorough "guide" to Lacan's work so far available.

8. William Faulkner, *Sartoris* (New York: Harcourt, Brace, 1929); page references will be included parenthetically in the text.

9. Olga Vickery, *The Novels of William Faulkner* (Baton Rouge: Louisiana State University Press, 1959), 25.

10. William Faulkner, *The Sound and the Fury* [1929] (New York: Vintage Books, 1963); references will be included parenthetically in the text.

11. William Faulkner, *As I Lay Dying* [1930] (New York: Vintage Books, n.d.); references will be included parenthetically in the text.

12. William Faulkner, *Absalom, Absalom!* [1936] (New York: The Modern Library, 1951); references will be included parenthetically in the text.

13. William Faulkner, *Sanctuary* [1931] (New York: The Modern Library, 1959), 29; references will be included parenthetically in the text.

14. See, for example, the essays in Stuart Schneiderman, ed., *Returning to Freud: Clinical Psychoanalysis in the School of Freud* (New Haven: Yale University Press, 1980), and Joseph M. Smith and William Kerrigan, eds., *Interpreting Lacan*, vol. 6, *Psychiatry and the Humanities* (New Haven: Yale University Press, 1983), as well as Lacan's own works, which insist on his rereading of Freud, not his subversion of the master.

15. See Kaja Silverman, *The Subject of Semiotics* (New York: Oxford University Press, 1983), for an excellent discussion of the role of the Phallus in Lacan's "Symbolic" realm. It seems possible to explain Lacan's notion of the Symbolic by saying it is like Freud's Superego, since the Symbolic is the realm of the Law, the "Name-of-the-Father," and similar terms of ultimate authority. But such an identification would be quite misleading. The later Freud sees the Superego as part of the topography of the Consciousness/Unconsciousness. Lacan sees the Symbolic as a function whose place exists in language, not the individual human brain. Moreover, Lacan is very hostile to Ego theory in general.

# "Fix My Hair, Jack": The Dark Side
# of Faulkner's Jokes

## GEORGE GARRETT

My title comes from the final chapter, chapter 31, of *Sanctuary*, the penultimate sequence of scenes just before the final closing down of that story in the set piece of Temple Drake and her father at the Luxembourg Gardens in gray Paris. It is the next to last scene of the next to last sequence in what amounts to an entire sequence of endings set in a row, an ending as final and thorough, wrapped neatly and tied with a bow knot, as anything you can think of offhand. (It is as thorough and as satisfactory an ending as any of the Oz books and shares with them at least the elegant paradox of seeming to invite a sequel to challenge its finality.) My title is the last words in this world, and in this book, of Popeye, as he stands on the scaffold with a rope around his neck waiting to die in payment of and for not any of the divers crimes committed in this story or anything else he may have done or left undone, but for the murder of a policeman in Alabama, a crime of which, to our sure and certain knowledge, he is perfectly innocent.

Here is how Popeye dies. In William Faulkner's words:

> They came for him at six. The minister went with him, his hand under Popeye's elbow, and he stood beneath the scaffold praying, while they adjusted the rope, dragging it over Popeye's sleek, oiled head, breaking his hair loose. His hands were tied, so he began to jerk his head, flipping his hair back each time it fell forward again, while the minister prayed, the others motionless at their posts with bowed heads.
>
> Popeye began to jerk his neck forward in little jerks. "Psssst!" he said, the sound cutting sharp into the drone of the minister's voice;

"pssssst!" The sheriff looked at him; he quit jerking his head and stood rigid, as though he had an egg balanced on his head. "Fix my hair, Jack," he said.

"Sure," the sheriff said. "I'll fix it for you"; springing the trap.[1]

Well, then. A little gallows humor. An ending for Popeye, a moment which is grotesque, grotesquely funny and completely satisfactory in terms of the demands of the narrative and the conventional expectations of the imaginary reader. Popeye surely has to die after all he has done since he first appeared to Horace Benbow, reflected in the clear spring at the root of a beech tree, a man introduced as possessing, in Benbow's way of seeing, "that vicious depthless quality of stamped tin."[2] Popeye is involved from that point on in many kinds of unpleasant and indecent activities, the most formidable, objectionable, and memorable of which (and memorable in the larger sense to people who have never even read the book) is in corncob rape of the archetypal coed—Temple Drake. It was that crime which was to cost Popeye most dearly, which rendered him most liable to the appropriate punishment of hanging by the neck until dead for a crime he did not commit.

Writing about it, making it up and seeing it through its various drafts and versions into print, was something for which the author would have to suffer also. As witness, this brief incident from Blotner's biography. The time is the fall of 1938, seven years and a number of books after the publication of *Sanctuary*:

> It was not all business for Faulkner. Haas pitched horseshoes with him, and Commins took him to see Columbia play Army. At one crucial point in Columbia's last minute game-winning drive, Faulkner leaned over and predicted the next play. When the Columbia quarterback called it, Commins congratulated him.
>
> "From now on you'll always be known as the grandstand quarterback," he said.
>
> "No," Faulkner replied, "I'll always be known as the corncob man."[3]

The truth is that the execution of Popeye, together with the sequence leading up to it, is an extraordinary and virtuoso performance which, continuing up to that gritty, bitter, brutal last moment, ending with the sheriff's brisk one-liner, becomes one of the great fictional hanging scenes in our national literature. It will stand tall and well beside such moments as the execution of Billy Budd, Truman Capote's hanging of Perry and Dick in *In Cold Blood,* and Norman Mailer's celebrated disposal of Gary Gillmore in *The Executioner's Song.* If I digress a moment . . . I find Faulkner's the best achieved and most interesting of the lot. Billy Budd dies completely in character (as, I reckon, all tragic characters have to) as good and as innocent and as simple-minded as he has always been, first to last. Capote and Mailer, each differently, spend a whole book making a kind of case for their criminal protagonists. While not denying their crimes, they work very hard, in text and in subtext, to establish reader engagement and sympathy, long before they bring their people to the edge of the grave. At that edge they then pull out all the conventional rhetorical stops, hoping to move you and me to some kind of pity and terror, and, indeed, succeeding to a considerable extent. Faulkner had a much bigger problem to deal with, and his success is really remarkable. This is a sequence I give to writing students to see how something marvelous, an almost complete turnabout, can be deftly and economically achieved in just a few pages. I justify this brief excursion away from the general topic with the claim that, as elsewhere in many places in the work of William Faulkner, humor of various kinds and forms, several kinds of jokes, then, threaded into the rich texture of complex and often contradictory moods, is an essential part of the whole (and successful) rhetorical effect. Here, as elsewhere, it wouldn't work without the benefit of various kinds of laughter, some of them examples of dark laughter to be sure. We are never far in Faulkner's works from what Jim Cox has called "the incredible laughter that is at the heart of his world." In any case, throughout *Sanctuary* Faulkner, in a fairly unusual gesture for him, made Popeye a strictly consistent, almost fixed character. We get different angles on him which give some sense of change and development, but he, himself, seems to be consistently malevolent and altogether unsympathetic. He is known to us by his actions; but, present even in absence in this story's structure, he is also depicted by the effects, accidental as well as planned, of his actions on others and by the juxtaposition of his acts and many others which are related to him only in the reader's world. That is, on top of everything else, all he has been up to, Popeye also picks up bits and pieces of the sins of others like nettles and beggar lice as we follow the ways Faulkner has chosen for him to walk in through this story. Finally, in exactly the opposite gesture to those of Capote and Mailer, the narrator, from and through several points of view, heaps negative coals upon Popeye's head from first to last or, anyway, almost the last. The steady consistency of this latter strategy works to create a kind of backlash in the reader, not of open sympathy or understanding or any such, but at least a feeling that Popeye, perhaps alone among the crew of characters in *Sanctuary,* is not getting the fully dimensional exploration which the others seem to receive. Then in chapter 31 Faulkner turns things around—not by violating his original presentation of Popeye, but by *adding* two elements: first, a background, horrendous enough and of mixed values, partly composed of terrible suffering and deprivation, partly composed of first acts of wickedness, a background known only to God and the narrator and now, of course, the reader, just as he is caught, tried and convicted for the crime he did not commit. Throughout this last sequence Popeye remains consistent, as tough and arrogant and essentially uncomprehending as ever. But the clever and amazing difference is gained by surrounding him by strangers—District Attorney, Turnkey, his appointed lawyer and his Memphis lawyer, the sheriff, a minister—all of whom find him intriguing and mysterious, all of whom becoming, to one degree and another, sympathetic. This time, just before he dies, we see him as we have not before, and he suddenly gains some stature, grows right before our eyes. So that finally, even when he goes out to the tune of a hard-nosed joke, there is a certain odd nobility about his death. In a Shakespearean sense it is Popeye's most becoming moment of life. And yet he is still the same man who, on the first page, broke up Horace Benbow's enjoyment of his own reflection in a clear spring.

The dark side of Faulkner's jokes, his jests so often played at the expense of our best expectation that we gradually begin to expect them as much or more than anything else, comes from the fact that they are almost always present, even in the most serious works (again in a Shakespearean manner), never more than a paper-thin partition away from the most tragic or poignant or pathetic or simply horrifying scenes and events. If at any moment (sometimes by no more than the purest and simplest and most thoughtless of gestures, like going the wrong way around the town square) the known world can collapse into a bellowing chaos—a chaos composed of murder and mayhem, rape and mutilation, crimes and punishments, a dance of the seven deadly sins and the spectacle of the violation of the deepest taboos of our tribe, just so at any moment, again and again, moments as closely associated as, say, in *Macbeth* the bloody murder of Duncan the King with the drunken Porter's soliloquy, at any of these moments the world, like that clear spring Popeye spat in and shattered, can fall apart helplessly into one kind of laughter or another. The major novels of William Faulkner, whether they *end* as comedy or tragedy, share with *King Lear*, for example, the inextricably mixed patterns of comedy and sorrow. Clearly it was his aim to make us *care* (something which separates him from most writers then and even more writers now), and clearly he figured out very early on that laughter is essential to the deepest kind of caring. The Elizabethans had a proverb that may have some validity—"The maid who laughs is half taken." I'm inclined to believe the proverb applies accurately to the necessary seduction of the imaginary reader.

Since I used one of the final scenes of the final version of *Sanctuary* as my basic example, I'd like to add to it by citing the *beginning* of the original version of the same novel, taken from *Sanctuary: The Original Text*, edited by Noel Polk. The first paragraph or two work much the same way (with some important differences) as the earlier example, from a context of crime and horror to a one-line joke and, in another of Faulkner's habitual gestures, from the contrast of complex style with the simple, from grandiose high style and the vernacular and idiomatic:

> Each time he passed the jail he would look up at the barred window, usually to see a small, pale, patient, tragic blob lying in one of the grimy interstices, or perhaps a blue wisp of tobacco smoke combing raggedly away along the spring sunshine. At first there had been a negro murderer there, who had killed his wife; slashed her throat with a razor so that, her whole head tossing further and further backward from the bloody regurgitation of her bubbling throat, she ran out the cabin door and for six or seven steps up the quiet moonlit lane. He would lean in the window in the evening and sing. After supper a few negroes gathered along the fence below—natty, shoddy suits and sweat-stained overalls shoulder to shoulder—and in chorus with the murderer, they sang spirituals while white people slowed and stopped in the leafed darkness that was almost summer, to listen to those who were sure to die and him who was already dead singing about heaven and being tired; or perhaps in the interval between songs a rich, sourceless voice coming out of the high darkness where the ragged shadow of the heaven-tree which snooded the street lamp at the corner fretted and mourned: "Fo days mo! Den dey ghy stroy de bes ba'ytone singer in nawth Mississippi!"[4]

Speaking of style, though this may seem and, indeed, may well be yet another diversion from the true course, the hard straight ploughed furrow, on my part, I would like to mention a daring and endearing comic device often used by William Faulkner to snatch at more meaning from one event or another and in so doing, among other things, to move us more than usually, to make us care. This device is the seemingly inappropriate use of the high style often to describe the most ordinary things or to deal with events which seem to call for the most direct and transparent prose. Since the high style which Faulkner invented was hypnotically his very own, replete with its own special rhythms and its own rich and repetitive vocabulary, this making fun with that style constitutes almost making fun of it; that is, it constitutes a brave kind of self-parody, one result of which is to make the narrator more sympathetic and the style more acceptable, able to be used grandly precisely because it has also been used humbly and humorously. There are, inevitably, other important effects of the contrast and (sometimes) confusion of styles. For instance, even in parody humble things gain a certain grandeur by being caught and exposed in the net of the grand style. Likewise pompous and important things, captured in the vernacular, are awarded some measure of vital simplicity. Always the two extremes of style inform the spirit of each other. There are so many wonderful examples that you could put together an anthology of them, one of those "exotic flowers from Faulkner's garden," nineteenth-century kind of books. Even so I would like to mention, briefly, a couple or three examples as illustrative of this humorous tendency.

Who can forget the description of a memorable fart which opens book 3, "The Long Summer," of *The Hamlet?* "Sitting in the halted buckboard, Ratliff watched the old fat white horse emerge from Varner's lot and come down the lane beside the picket fence, surrounded and preceded by the rich sonorous organ-tones of its entrails."[5] Could Rabelais have done it any better?

How about this, from *Pylon,* for a man's sudden awareness that, immediately following one amazing sexual experience, in the front cockpit of a flying airplane, he is already triumphantly tumescent again? "It was some blind instinct out of the long swoon while he waited for his backbone's fluid marrow to congeal again that he remembered to roll the aeroplane toward the wing to which the parachute case was attached because the next that he remembered was the belt catching him across the legs as, looking out he saw the parachute floating between him and the ground, and looking down he saw the bereaved, the upthrust, the stalk; the annealed rapacious heartshaped crimson bud."[6] That is the same remarkable organ he had earlier described as "between himself and her wild and frenzied body, the perennially undefeated, the victorious."[7]

For the vernacular style, which is changed and refined by its close proximity to the high style, just as the latter is leavened by association with the former, take the impact of inflation upon Mink Snopes, fresh out of spending thirty-eight years in Parchman and here in the midst of trying to keep track of the thirteen dollars he carried with him as a free man into a strangely altered world. This from *The Mansion:*

> He had given the man at the store one of the dollar bills and the man had given him back change for bread, eleven cents, lunch meat eleven cents, which was twenty-two cents, then the man had taken up the half-dollar for the sodas, which was seventy-two cents, which should have left twenty-eight cents; counting what remained slowly over coin by coin again, then counting the coins he had already set aside to be sure they were right. And still it was only eighteen cents instead of twenty-eight. A dime was gone somewhere. And the lunch meat was just eleven cents, he remembered that because there had been a kind of argument about it. So it was the bread, it would have to be the bread. *It went up another dime right while I was standing there* he thought. *And if bread could jump up ten cents right while I was looking at it, maybe I cant buy a pistol even for the whole thirteen dollars. So I got to stop somewhere and find a job.*[8]

If Mink's reasoning is comic, it is right. And it is no more comic than many of Gavin Stevens's tormented and tortuous musings which are more often likely to be wrong.

Now I would like to shift tone and stance slightly, moving away from the strictly literary to something closely related, but still something else, something which has to do with life in our times, Faulkner's lifetime and ours. These are, to begin with, much more different from each other than we might care to acknowledge. Just as his life proved out to be (I do believe) quite different from what he could possibly have imagined—even he, who was at times painfully, exquisitely prescient, to the sheer edge of prophecy. Keep in mind his sensitivity to the tides and trends of things in this terrible century whose own apt symbol may well be a mountain of human skulls in modern Cambodia, the warehouses of shoes and glasses and false teeth at Auschwitz, or the frozen heads in the freezer of Idi Amin, heads he liked to talk to in the late and lonely hours of the night. Don't forget for a moment the century he saw arrive and lived in; from which Oxford, though quiet and stable, was, clearly, no kind of refuge. Do not forget, either, that it was, *is* precisely his generation which saw more radical changes in the shape and form of things than any other in memory. Ours has merely seen the exploitation of changes which arrived for his generation. A time of arrivals— of the automobile and the airplane, of electricity and modern plumbing, of the radio and motion picture and the television, of the vast and intricate communications network or environment which, however distorted and destabilizing, allows selected events any place to have some impact on any other. An event in Sri Lanka can, for a time at least, impinge upon the peace and quiet of Oxford. For the first time, in his generation, for better and worse, it became possible for anyone in Oxford, Mississippi, (or Truckmire, Georgia, or Kissimmee, Florida, my old home town) to know as much and as easily as anywhere else. It has been a hundred years since people in New York have had the actual ability to know any more than people in Oxford, though they are not among the first to admit this. There are many implications of all this. A single and obvious one is that by turning to consider the world as it was to be found here on his own postage stamp of territory, William Faulkner did so at a time when he was depriving himself of very little and sparing himself of even less except, perhaps, the noise of strangers.

One other bit of background. We have heard, eloquently and provocatively, if briefly, how he was a small man and how that smallness of stature served to shape his vision and a Napoleonic ambition. All of which may well be the case. Who knows? What is undeniable, undebatable, really, is that he was a very small man in a large world of larger men—and women—who was frail and vulnerable, even delicate in flesh as well as spirit, who suffered considerably because of that frailty; but who schooled and taught himself a toughness in a stoic sense, who lived, literally, with his outer and inner wounds without flagging in his work or complaining very much. Had he been larger, stronger, more confidently at ease with himself, his vision (if any other than a private one) might have been uniformly lighter; but I think we can safely agree that a lighter, more moderate vision of reality would have been grotesquely inappropriate to his times and ours and would have betokened not health, but a sort of lobotomized lunacy. It is my best judgment that his styles and forms, and equally his minted currency of dark comedy as the n'er-do-well cousin of stark tragedy, are more aptly suited to this century than the styles and forms of any other writer of his generation.

In any case, in a practical *literary* way, Faulkner imagined that he lived in a world which was sequential, chronological, and mostly progressive. He was fully aware that he was living in a changed and different social world from that of Charles Dickens or of his own great-grandfather. But he did not know, at least at the beginning, that it was also a radically different *literary* situation; that neither writers nor readers nor publishers were the same or doing the same things; that all this had been changed also. Faulkner's failure to perceive or to understand that his literary generation was radically different from the previous generation or two (and the evidence of and for this misunderstanding is overwhelming in the published letters and the biographical studies) is not surprising. It is, indeed, an altogether typical misapprehension fully shared by the finest literary artists, the masters of his own generation and of ours. As far as I can tell, only a few true crazies were undeceived. And these, in their turn, allowed themselves to be deluded by the fundamentally absurd notion that because things were now radically different, there was, therefore, *no* possible connection between now and then. I should add that Faulkner's folly (if that is what it is) appears to be widely embraced by my own generation of writers who, by and large, imagine that they are living in roughly the same literary world which Faulkner knew. Ours is, in fact, so different from that of the earlier generation, his generation, the generation of the masters, that a good case can be made for the idea that what we are doing is not at all the same thing, is almost a different art form. Of course, even if there were no difference between his time and ours, we would still be forever divided from the literary scene and situation faced by William Faulkner by the immutable fact that he who was there is now here. It is he (among others, but perhaps chiefly among them) who has changed things for better and worse for us and for the rest of the world—especially the lately celebrated small band of Latin American authors. If Faulkner was a literary conservative, in the sense that he believed he was living more or less in the same literary world as say Hawthorne and James and Conrad, if he was, as a result, a preserver of literary tradition, he was also, at one and the same time, our most adventurous and successful literary pioneer. There is hardly any place where an American writer can go or would want to go today that William Faulkner hasn't been first. At the same time, as an artist, he didn't stay long in any one place, which means, in fact, that all the literary settling, surveying, exploration, and exploitation remains to be done. To put it another way, if William Faulkner came along now, he would be inhibited, if not prevented, from doing the same kind of literary pioneering he was able to accomplish then. Places which he had not discovered then would surely be labeled terra incognita now. What I mean to say is that our debt to him is much greater than most of us can or will know.

Nevertheless in the thick of his own literary times, William Faulkner gives every sign and clue of being baffled, befuddled, and often almost desperate, trying to survive and perform as an artist. The letters and the Blotner biographies tell a sad professional story. Until after he was awarded the Nobel Prize, there hardly seems to be a day, even part of a day, in which he was free from real practical worries. Not a day of genuine stability or temporary security in which he could count on time to do his work. There were not any fellowships or grants (most of them did not exist then) to help him, to tide him over. Educational institutions, including this one, paid him next to no attention or mind. He had a very hard row to hoe. All of us should keep that in mind. All of the time until the Nobel Prize he was in fact on very thin ice, earning a shamefully meager living by his work and by writing for the movies. And even after the Nobel Prize, he found himself as a man with a better than average income (at last), but having forfeited twenty-five lean years to what might well be called subsistence writing, he had no capital assets to speak of or draw on except Rowan Oak and the farm, both of which proved, at times, to be very expensive assets. When he came to buy a fine house in Charlottesville, he was forced to borrow the down payment from a wealthy dilettante because there was no other way he could make the down payment. Nobel Prize or not, his publisher wasn't in the moneylending business. Not in his case. They put their money where they expected a return in kind. Thus, writers like Irwin Shaw and Philip Roth routinely received advances ten times those of William Faulkner. A so-called serious writer—I am not speaking now of "popular" writers, but of those deemed to be prestigious literary figures—a writer like John Irving has received in advance for one book, even allowing for inflation, more than the entire lifetime earnings from all sources of William Faulkner. You are to understand that his famous agent was not much help at all (though Harold Ober was very helpful and generous to F. Scott Fitzgerald). You need to understand that his publishers gave him contracts which were, in my opinion, less than generous. And they held him strictly to them, their basic premise being that he should, like any other of their authors, earn just what he sold, nothing more and nothing less. Which sounds fine and dandy until and if you choose to consider the inestimable value which his publishers, and chiefly Random House, gained by having him on their list. A good agent or a good lawyer probably could have come up with fairly exact numbers to prove his actual worth to them. And none of that would consider the enormous actual value his work has gained posthumously.

As for honors. Well, they came along all in due time. Some of them, anyway. But they came late, too late to catch up, if not make up, with the times when he was ignored or greatly underrated. It is clear that he was painfully conscious of his status in the literary world, of exactly where he stood. He didn't need Malcolm Cowley to tell him, though he had to put up with Cowley's telling him that, among other things, if he wanted to see the *Viking Portable Library* come to be. Try to understand it—Kurt Vonnegut and John Updike have (separately and equally) both received far more critical attention and support than Faulkner did in his lifetime. James Dickey has many times the number of honorary degrees. Barry Hannah, who spoke here Wednesday night, has already received at least as much favorable critical attention as Faulkner did up until the Nobel Prize. Believe me, it does not make a writer happy or fulfilled to work hard and honestly and as well as he is able to and then receive, in a relative sense, next to nothing, minimal response and reward for his efforts. Believe me, he was not kidding or playing with rhetoric when he described his work in the Nobel Prize Address as "a life's work in the agony and sweat of the human spirit, not for glory and least of all for profit."[9] That is not a modest statement of good intentions. It's a harsh description of reality.

Never forget that at the high tide of his career and creativity, Faulkner lived in a world where J. D. Salinger was widely regarded as clearly his artistic superior.

I mention these little practical matters, often considered too boring or sordid for serious critical consideration, because he had to live with them constantly. Because they had something to do with the way he wrote. He was free, *liberated*, to be an explorer of the form, precisely because it didn't matter much to anybody, beginning with his publisher, what he did. He might as well do what the spirit moved him to do. From this situation, endured, and ultimately prevailed over, came something of his pride, his gravity (which replaced a wild levity of youth), his rare (oh very rare) impeccable integrity as an artist. From it also came a certain professional bitterness. Some fellow writers who were acquainted with him, one way and another, have described him as "bitter." And there is, in his words and deeds, dealing with other writers of all kinds, ample evidence of a kind of bitterness so strong that it might have crippled a lesser artist, a lesser man.

We can thank God that he was strong enough to have it both ways and that his surge to make art, to leave his name and works on the wall, *Faulkner-was-here*, overcame everything else, both reason and passionate disappointment. It is a dark and comic thing, comic at the last because there was a belated happy ending (an ending of just the kind he was so contemptuous of, almost an old-fashioned Hollywood ending) that he persisted, that he lived and wrote the books.

If his professional life was a very hard one (and it was and, for the most part, a good deal more so than that of anyone he knew or knew of), his personal life was hard and disappointing also, full of bitter times and frustrations. The death of his firstborn, Alabama, a death at least partly his own responsibility, was devastating. The death of his brother, Dean, was heartbreaking and terrible too. His health was bad and so were his habits. He felt bad a lot of the time. His marriage was often very difficult, more like a bed of nails than a bed of roses. His love affairs were complicated, difficult also, and usually ended badly . . . for him, at least. None of the women in his life, at least those mentioned in the biography, hasn't, one way or another, profited greatly from her association with him. It is harder to imagine what happy rewards there were for him, beyond the most fleeting, in these matters. Even in these affairs, he seems to have allowed comedy to triumph in the end. It appears in the letters and the biographies that he broke off with each of them, exercising the same formulaic farewell—"Between grief and nothing, I'll take grief." Betting, without any great risk, that his lovers were encountering those words for the first time. Is that a dark joke or not? I think so.

When he was young and had more energy and was still defended by innocence and ignorance, he had a wonderful sense of irrepressible levity. Here he is in a very early interview (1931): "I was born male and single at an early age in Mississippi. I am still alive but not single. I was born of a Negro slave and an alligator, both named Gladys Rock. I had two brothers, one Dr. Walter E. Traprock and the other Eagle Rock, an airplane."[10] All in good

fun. It is a dark irony, if not a dark joke, that Faulkner, who so
cheerfully had fun and games with the press as a young man,
came by the end of his life to view the press as the enemy of
privacy and the American dream, as a deeply destabilizing force.
But he could still joke about it in those days.

Similarly, back in the early days, he had high spirits and
creative energy to burn. There are, for example, the surviving
letters (there were probably more) of Faulkner to Sherwood
Anderson about the mythical Jackson family the two of them
invented. Here I quote from Joseph Blotner's new, one-volume
biography:

> Faulkner wrote Anderson a three-page typed letter about Al Jackson
> and the sheep he raised in the swamp to make their fleece more
> luxuriant, only to find that in time they began to change until they
> resembled beavers and then alligators. The same thing happened to
> Al's son Claude, from herding the creatures in the swamp.[11]

I have seen some of these letters and they are really very funny,
more amusing than simple description can make them.

We gather here in his home town and home place, ironically a
town very slow to recognize its native son's genius, not doing so
at all until the larger world safely did, we gather here to honor
him. And this year the subject has been his rich and various and
inexhaustible humor. There are many kinds and forms of humor
in Faulkner's work, early and late. And there is always a strong
thread of dark, sometimes bitter joking found throughout his
career. No one has called him a comedian in real life, but the odd
thing in the biography is that they all seem to remember funny
things he said or did, almost always straight-faced and deadpan.
I have heard my share of these stories outside of the biography. A
good many of his jokes took planning and preparation. Some of
them are very private, so much so that we may not ever know
about them, beyond guessing. He became a guarded and secret
man. But all the stories from his life serve to confirm the portrait
of a great man whose vision was so open and inclusive that if he
always felt the tears of things, he likewise could hear, as some

hear voices, the sourceless laughter which is at least half the music of this world.

## NOTES

1. *Sanctuary* (New York: Random House, Vintage Books), 307–8.
2. Ibid., 4.
3. Joseph Blotner, *Faulkner: A Biography,* (New York: Random House, 1984), 400.
4. *Sanctuary: The Original Text,* ed. Noel Polk (New York: Random House, 1981), 3.
5. *The Hamlet* (New York: Random House, Vintage Books, 1956), 157.
6. *Pylon* (New York: Random House, 1962), 195–96.
7. Ibid., 195.
8. *The Mansion* (New York: Random House, Vintage Books, 1965), 263.
9. *The Faulkner Reader: Selections from the Works of William Faulkner* (New York: Modern Library, 1971), 3.
10. *Lion in the Garden: Interviews with William Faulkner, 1926–1962,* ed. James B. Meriwether and Michael Millgate (Lincoln: University of Nebraska Press, 1980), 9.
11. Blotner, 134.

# Contributors

**Hans Bungert** is Professor of English and American Literature at the University of Regensburg, Germany, and an officer of the European Association for American Studies. Among his publications are a book on William Faulkner and the tradition of Southern humor and articles on Faulkner, Mark Twain, and G. W. Harris. Currently he is serving as President of the University of Regensburg.

**William Bedford Clark,** Associate Professor of English at Texas A&M University, is the author of numerous articles and books reviews, editor of *Critical Essays on Robert Penn Warren,* and coeditor of *Critical Essays on American Humor.* He is also editor of *The South Central Review: The Journal of the South Central Modern Language Association.*

**William N. Claxon, Jr.,** teaches at the University of South Carolina at Aiken. He received his Ph.D. degree from Indiana University, where he was awarded the William Riley Parker Prize for outstanding teaching by a graduate student. His dissertation, "The Rebel Yell: Masculinity in Twentieth-Century Southern Fiction," concentrates on major male characters in works by William Faulkner, Walker Percy, Reynolds Price, Allen Tate, and Robert Penn Warren.

**James M. Cox,** Avalon Professor at Dartmouth College, has published books on Robert Frost, Edgar Allen Poe, and Mark Twain's humor. He received the E. Harris Harbison Distinguished Teaching Award from the Danforth Foundation and has held fellowships from, among others, the Guggenheim Foundation and the American Council of Learned Societies.

**George Garrett,** Writer in Residence at the University of Virginia, is the author of seven volumes of poetry, five novels, six books of stories, and two plays. He has also written literary

232

criticism, compiled several anthologies, and served on the editorial staffs of *Transatlantic Review, Hollins Critic, Contempora,* and *The Film Journal.* His early study of Faulkner's poetry has for many years been an authoritative source on that subject.

**Barry Hannah** received the William Faulkner Prize for his first novel, *Geronimo Rex,* and the Arnold Gingrich Short Fiction Award for *Airships,* a collection of stories. His other works include the novels *Nightwatchmen, Ray,* and *The Tennis Handsome* and a new collection of stories, *Captain Maximus.* He teaches creative writing at the University of Mississippi.

**Virginia V. Hlavsa** teaches at Queens College in Flushing, New York. Her work on Faulkner includes a dissertation on *Light in August* and two articles, "The Vision of the Advocate in *Absalom, Absalom!*" and "St. John and Frazer in *Light in August:* Biblical Form and Mythic Function."

**Daniel Hoffman** is Poet in Residence and Felix E. Schelling Professor of English at the University of Pennsylvania. His publications include many award-winning volumes of poetry, the latest of which is the epic poem *Brotherly Love,* and numerous critical studies of American writers. His research on Faulkner's use of folklore characters, motifs, and plots was supported through a grant from the Guggenheim Foundation.

**M. Thomas Inge,** Blackwell Professor in the Humanities at Randolph-Macon College, has been a Fulbright lecturer at universities in Spain, Argentina, and the Soviet Union. He is editor or author of over two dozen books on American literature. His studies of Faulkner include *Essays on "Light in August,"* a critical casebook on "A Rose for Emily," and a lengthy entry for the American humorists volume in the *Dictionary of Literary Biography.*

**Thomas L. McHaney** teaches at Georgia State University. He is the author of *William Faulkner's "The Wild Palms": A Study, William Faulkner: A Reference Guide,* and numerous articles about Faulkner and other figures in American literature. He also edited *Faulkner Studies in Japan.*

**James M. Mellard,** Chairman and Professor of English at

Northern Illinois University, has published extensively on modern American literature. His most recent books are *Four Modes: A Rhetoric of Modern Fiction* and *The Exploded Form: The Modernist Novel in America*. Many of his articles have examined the work of Faulkner.

**Patricia R. Schroeder** holds M.A. and Ph.D. degrees from the University of Virginia where she taught as a graduate instructor in 1977–82 and an instructor in 1982–83. She also served as research assistant to Austin E. Quigley, who directed her dissertation on "The Presence of the Past in Modern American Drama." She is Assistant Professor of English at Ursinus College in Pennsylvania.

**Nancy B. Sederberg** received an M.A.T. from Johns Hopkins University and a Ph.D. from the University of South Carolina. Her publications include essays on William Faulkner, Flannery O'Connor, and Eudora Welty and a study of "Antebellum Southern Humor in the *Camden Journal:* 1826–1840." She teaches at Beaufort Technical College.

# Index